Understanding baby loss

Manchester University Press

Understanding baby loss

The sociology of life, death and post-mortem

Kate Reed, Julie Ellis and Elspeth Whitby

MANCHESTER UNIVERSITY PRESS

Published by Manchester University Press
Oxford Road, Manchester M13 9PL

www.manchesteruniversitypress.co.uk

British Library Cataloguing-in-Publication Data
A catalogue record for this book is available from the British Library

ISBN   978 1 5261 6318 9   hardback
ISBN   9 781 5261 9156 4   paperback

First published 2023
Paperback published 2025

EU authorised representative for GPSR:
Easy Access System Europe – Mustamäe tee 50,
10621 Tallinn, Estonia
gpsr.requests@easproject.com

Typeset
by New Best-set Typesetters Ltd

Contents

Acknowledgements

This book is based on a research project funded by the Economic and Social Research Council: '"End of or Start of Life"? Visual Technology and the Transformation of Traditional Post-Mortem' (Ref ES/M010732/1). This project focused on the sensitive issue of baby loss and post-mortem, and won the ESRC Outstanding Societal Impact Prize in 2019. We would like to start, therefore, by thanking the ESRC for funding the original research on which this book is based. The authors would also like to thank all the families and NHS professionals who gave up their time to take part in the research project. Thanks must also be given to the staff of the pathology and radiology departments at Sheffield Children's Hospital, in particular Trudy Donn and Marta Cohen. We would also like to thank bereavement support charities including the Lullaby Trust, Sands, Teardrop and Zephyrs. The key sociological themes articulated in each chapter of this book were illuminated in art form in our project exhibition *Remembering Baby*. We would, therefore, also like to thank visual artist Hugh Turvey HonFRPS, sound artist Justin Wiggan and graphic designer Lee Simmons, who worked with the university research team to curate this exhibition. We are also very grateful to Alison Wright for her excellent PR support and to the many bereaved parents and families who contributed their own beautiful art pieces for the exhibition.

The authors of this book comprise an interdisciplinary team of academics made up of two sociologists (Reed and Ellis) and a clinician (Whitby). Support for the research and book has come from different academic departments at the University of Sheffield. We would like to thank staff in the departments of Sociological Studies, Sheffield Methods Institute and Oncology and Metabolism for supporting the development of the research. More specifically we would like to thank Sarah Neal, Kerry Swain, Maria Teresa Ferazzoli and Janine Wilson for all their help with the project, exhibition and writing from the research, and Kerry Marston Giroux and the bereavement team at Sheffield Teaching Hospitals for their advice and support. We would also like to thank the senior leadership team in the Faculty of Social Sciences at the University of Sheffield, in particular Craig Watkins and John Flint, who have supported every aspect of this research as it has evolved. Kate would also like to thank Claire Alexander at the University of Manchester for her friendship and intellectual guidance.

Finally, the authors would like to thank their families: Leo, Ruby and Max McCann; Dominic, Nick, Sarah, Ann and Lewis Reed; Orla, Ash and Tina Corker; Margaret, John and Anthony Ellis; and Dermott, Maisie and Alice Gleeson. Julie would also like to thank her lifelong friend Helen Moran and 'academic friends' Julia Bishop and Melanie Hall for their insights, encouragement and generous support. This book and the ESRC research project on which it was based have taken us on an incredibly emotional and career-defining journey that could never have been managed without the continuing love and support of our friends and families.

Introduction

I didn't know what to expect, the word 'post-mortem' used to scare me, now it doesn't, as now I know my baby was treated with love, care and respect. (bereaved mother)

Post-mortem examination, also known as an autopsy, is the examination of a dead body to determine the cause of death.[1] It can play an important role in understanding the cause of death of babies and infants (Downe et al., 2012; Lewis et al., 2019). Bereaved parents, however, are often concerned about their baby undergoing a post-mortem examination. They fear the invasive nature of the procedure and worry about who will care for their baby during this clinical process. As the quote above shows, however, once parents are given information about the clinical process, including knowing that their baby will be treated with love, care and respect during the examination, such fears can dissipate. The quote above is taken from the visitor guestbook of a UK-based exhibition *Remembering Baby: Life, Loss and Post-mortem*. The exhibition was based on the findings of a qualitative research project funded by the Economic and Social Research Council (ESRC), which focused on exploring the emergence of minimally invasive post-mortems in perinatal pathology. Drawing on ethnographic data from this research project, this book is our attempt to put into sociological terms what happens when a baby dies.

The book combines an in-depth analysis of clinical and technological aspects of the post-mortem process with detailed understandings of parental and professional feelings, emotions and care practices. It seeks to show that a post-mortem is not just a scientific or clinical examination as often presented in existing academic literature. Rather, we seek to argue that a post-mortem, which straddles the boundaries between life and death, often forms a key part of the bereavement journey and can provide an important source of bereavement support. The book offers a comprehensive and thoughtful account of how parents experience different forms of baby loss, and subsequently make decisions about a post-mortem. It also analyses some of the challenges professionals face when working in this highly sensitive field of medicine. A post-mortem examination can often play a crucial role in establishing cause of death in cases of baby loss and can assist parents with emotional and diagnostic closure. It has, to date, however, remained neglected in existing sociological accounts of reproductive loss. By shedding light on this taboo aspect of healthcare, we seek to offer a valuable contribution to the sociology of emotions, medical sociology, sociology of work, death and dying studies, and science and technology studies (STS).

The rest of this introduction is devoted to providing readers with an overview of key debates in the areas of reproductive loss and post-mortem practice. We begin by outlining existing literature on different types of baby loss, moving on to introduce readers to the deeply sensitive subject of perinatal post-mortem and the hidden and taboo world of the mortuary. We will also outline the theoretical focus of the book and offer background context to the research project on which this book is based. The final section will outline the book's structure, providing a brief synopsis of each chapter.

Conceptualising baby loss

The term 'reproductive loss' is frequently used to refer to cases of early and late miscarriage, termination of pregnancy, stillbirth, perinatal and infant death, as well as maternal death. Feminist scholars have articulated the need to broaden this focus to include other instances in which reproductive futures might have been curtailed. Such cases might include – but are not restricted to – infertility, assisted reproduction, involuntary sterilisation of women with intellectual disabilities, and fertility loss after cancer treatment (Earle and Letherby, 2007; Letherby, 2012; Dyer et al., 2012; Tilley et al., 2012). In all these cases women and their partners experience significant loss as their hopes and imagined futures of having a family are severely constrained. While noting the importance of including this broad range of experiences under the rubric of reproductive loss, this book focuses specifically on the issue of perinatal post-mortem. Our analysis will be restricted, therefore, to a focus on miscarriage and late pregnancy loss, termination of pregnancy, stillbirth, Sudden Infant Death Syndrome and various forms of neonatal death. Rather than describe these different forms of loss as either pregnancy or reproductive loss, however, we will use the term 'baby loss'. This is because parents in our study referred to their loss as baby loss, regardless of when the death occurred.

There are significant differences both within and across different categories of baby loss. For example, in the UK, stillbirth refers to instances where a baby dies after twenty-four completed weeks of pregnancy.[2] Parental experiences can therefore be very diverse: the pregnancy might reach full term and the baby might die during labour, or a mother might be induced because her baby has died during pregnancy. Pregnancy loss that occurs before twenty-four completed weeks of pregnancy is termed miscarriage or late fetal loss.[3] While other countries adopt similar forms of categorisation, the timing around how a baby's death is classified can and does vary. For example, in the USA, if pregnancy loss occurs before twenty weeks it is considered miscarriage. If by contrast the death occurs after twenty weeks, it is considered a stillbirth (CDC, 2020).

While definitions around miscarriage and stillbirth vary cross-nationally, there is a globally agreed definition of what constitutes neonatal death. According to the World Health Organization, neonatal death refers to 'deaths occurring during the first four weeks after birth' (WHO, 2006: 1). Neonatal death may occur for very diverse reasons – for example, it can be caused by congenital abnormality or be the result of obstetric complications before or after birth (WHO, 2006). An apparently healthy baby may also die suddenly and unexpectedly after birth. If such a death occurs in the first twelve months of life, it is referred to as Sudden Infant Death Syndrome (SIDS); after that period it is classified as Sudden Unexplained Death in Childhood (SUDC) (Lullaby Trust, 2022). In this book we explore parental and professional experiences of these different forms of loss, and their relationships to the post-mortem process.

Termination of pregnancy (TOP) due to the diagnosis of fetal anomaly is not something that is usually considered in the context of debates on baby loss. According to Pitt et al. (2016), the politicised and polarising nature of international debate around pregnancy termination means that the voices of women who experience late termination for fetal anomaly often remain unheard. The anti-abortion movement and the disability rights critique of prenatal diagnosis and subsequent pregnancy termination decisions are two elements of this debate (Hubbard, 1997; Shakespeare, 1999). Much existing literature on TOP has focused on first and second trimester screening and diagnostic testing for chromosomal anomalies such as Down's Syndrome (Rapp, 2000). Less is known, however, about women's experiences when severe anomalies are found in late pregnancy, when termination procedures may also include the controversial practice of feticide (Graham et al., 2008).[4] As Pitt et al. (2016) argue, women who go through TOP due to the identification of severe fetal anomaly often experience an acute embodied transition from live pregnancy to pregnancy loss. Parents and professionals in our study also talked about TOP for fetal anomaly as a form of loss. Where appropriate, therefore, we have sought to include these experiences in our analysis of baby loss.

In considering diverse forms of loss, our intentions are not to conflate them. Rather, we acknowledge that there is significant diversity not just across but also within these categories. Our approach in this book, therefore, focuses on analysing and detailing parental and professional experience in relation to specific individual, social and cultural contexts. In doing so we also recognise that there are different routes both in and out of the post-mortem process depending on the type of loss experience (from miscarriage to SIDS). This is something we will outline in more detail in the next section.

Sensivity and sadness: introducing perinatal post-mortem

Perinatal post-mortem (or autopsy) refers to clinical examinations conducted when death has occurred as a result of miscarriage, termination of pregnancy, stillbirth, neonatal and late neonatal death, and infant deaths up to one year. In the UK there are currently two types of post-mortem – a coronial post-mortem and a hospital post-mortem. A coroner might choose to order a post-mortem examination if a death is perceived to be sudden, violent or unexplained (such as in the case of Sudden Infant Death Syndrome – SIDS). Hospital post-mortems might be requested by doctors to find out cause of death. Sometimes, relatives might also request a post-mortem. It is important to note, however, that hospital post-mortems cannot take place without the consent of relatives (NHS, 2022). The human tissue act of 2004[5] requires that consent be obtained (usually from the next of kin) for autopsies not conducted for medico-legal reasons (Burton and Underwood, 2007). Similar approaches to autopsy have been adopted across Europe and the USA, although there are variations (Svendsen and Hill, 1987). In the USA, for example, laws pertaining to authorisation for autopsy often vary between states (Connolly et al., 2016).

Full post-mortem remains the clinical gold standard in the UK and includes dissection, blood, fluid and tissue sampling, as well as other tests as deemed appropriate. Minimally invasive post-mortem (MIA) is an emerging type of procedure, often involving external review, placental examination and ancillary tests that form part of the formal autopsy process, combined with magnetic resonance imaging (MRI) or computer tomography (CT) scan. This type of post-mortem is an option that is not yet available universally across the UK. It tends to be offered as a second-line option, if relatives do not wish to consent to a full post-mortem (Whitby, 2009) for religious or other reasons (Watts, 2010; Sebire and Taylor, 2012).

Post-mortem examination can be an extremely valuable source of information about cause of death across the life course. It can play a key role in the advancement of scientific knowledge, clinical governance and medical education (Burton and Underwood, 2007). Information provided by autopsy can also benefit family members seeking closure after the loss of a loved one (Rankin et al., 2002). Medical research shows, however, that the level of consent for perinatal post-mortems is decreasing (Lewis et al., 2019; Stock et al., 2010). Research has identified a number of reasons why parents do not want to consent to a post-mortem for their baby. According to Rankin et al. (2002), for example, parents express concern over the invasive nature of the examination. This is especially the case in the UK context in the aftermath of the organ retention scandal of 1999, when it was discovered that bodily organs and tissues of babies and children were being used by some hospitals for purposes other than autopsy (Sheach Leith, 2007). The availability of minimally invasive techniques may improve post-mortem take-up in these cases (Ben-Sasi et al., 2013; Kang et al., 2014; Lewis et al., 2017). Religious beliefs may also affect post-mortem decision-making in a range of ways including, for example, concerns that the post-mortem process will delay burial arrangements (Rankin et al., 2002; Breeze et al., 2012; Heazell et al., 2012; Downe et al., 2012; Ben-Sasi et al., 2013; Kang et al., 2014; Lewis et al., 2017, 2019).

Interaction with professionals can significantly influence parental decision-making on post-mortem examinations (Lewis et al., 2019). Not all health professionals are aware of the benefits of post-mortem examination, for example, and they therefore do not always offer it to parents as an option (Okah, 2002; Rose et al., 2006). Professionals might also lack the appropriate training to take informed consent (Stolman et al., 1994; Rose et al., 2006; Downe et al., 2012), or worry about upsetting familes by starting a conversation about a post-mortem (Stolman et al., 1994; Rose et al., 2006). In this book we seek to unpack these tensions and challenges in more detail, exploring some of the reasons why parents might refuse a post-mortem, but go on to articulate feelings of regret later. We also examine the role that technology can play in this process by exploring the emerging use of MRI as part of MIA. Our analysis of parental experience of post-mortem, however, is not restricted to a focus on the examination itself, but is situated within the wider context of 'life' and 'loss', 'grief' and 'memorialisation'. This is because a post-mortem does not occur as an isolated clinical event, but is, rather, an important part of parental and professional experience of the wider baby loss journey. As well as examining parental experiences of post-mortems, however, we will also examine some of the challenges faced by professionals working in this challenging field of medicine. In doing so we seek to shed light on the social and clinical context in which post-mortem practice takes place, focusing in particular on the mortuary.

The mortuary: hidden worlds, taboo work

Sociologists have often focused on how death and its associated experiences have become increasingly institutionalised, professionalised and privatised. Mellor and Shilling, for example, argue that traditional ideologies – such as religion – which once helped to manage the social, symbolic and existential threats posed by death, have become 'increasingly precarious and problematic in the conditions of high modernity' (1993: 411). Dying can consequently be a profoundly lonely experience, one hidden away from public view and social consciousness (Elias, 1985). Furthermore, death reveals the body's ultimate vulnerability, thus undermining the self-securing body work that modern individuals are increasingly expected to engage in (Shilling, 2003). This might perhaps explain the increase of particular institutional practices around death that involve the sequestration of the body (Lawton, 2000). It is unsurprising, for example, that autopsy – and in particular corpse dissection – takes place behind closed doors in the hidden world of the mortuary, or that the mortuary itself is often viewed as a place of mystery and is associated with sadness, grief or repulsion (Brysiewicz, 2007).

The fact that a post-mortem takes place primarily in the hidden space of the mortuary, combined with its association with dead bodies, has meant that sociologists have often explored this form of work through the lens of dirty or tainted work (Ashforth and Kreiner, 1999). In recent research, however, there has been an attempt to move away from this focus on taint to highlight a more progressive vision of the post-mortem examination and the work surrounding it (Woodthorpe and Komaromy, 2013). Such a view is keen to show how a post-mortem can provide relatives with important diagnostic and emotional closure (Gassaway, 2007; Reed and Ellis, 2019, 2020). This more enlightened portrayal of the post-mortem reflects the increasing visibility of such work in contemporary popular culture. For example, post-mortem practice is now widely represented in television dramas as highly skilled, professional work (Reed and Ellis, 2020).[6]

The number of qualitative studies on post-mortem practice and the mortuary has increased in recent years (Horsley, 2008, 2012). Few of these, however, have been conducted in the UK context (Woodthorpe and Komaromy, 2013). Such studies also tend to focus their analysis on particular professions, notably pathology and the different sub-specialisms within it, for example anatomical (Horsley, 2012) or forensic pathology (Timmermans, 2006). Other key professional groups such as mortuary technicians (APTs) have, until recently, been neglected in research (Woodthorpe and Komaromy, 2013).

Certain sub-specialties within pathology have been overlooked too, for example perinatal post-mortem (Sheach Leith, 2007; Reed and Ellis, 2020), along with certain aspects of professional practice. Research has tended to emphasise, for example, the scientific rather than emotional aspects of post-mortem work (Timmermans, 2006; Brysiewicz, 2007). In this book we seek to explore the hidden world of perinatal post-mortem, highlighting the ways in which this is not only highly skilled medical work but also a deeply emotional, caring and sensory form of work. In advancing this argument we will also seek to show how post-mortem practice not only transcends professional boundaries but also hospital spaces (Reed and Ellis, 2019, 2020).

Having introduced the reader to the hidden and taboo area of the post-mortem, we now want to move on to outline the conceptual and methodological approach taken in the research on which this book is based. This will also frame and advance the book's overall argument.

Theorising the sociological senses

The practice of post-mortem examination has long been associated with a tacit use of the five senses to determine cause of death (e.g., the smell of the body, the taste of urine, the touch of skin) (Van den Tweel and Taylor, 2013). Even in contemporary society, trained sensory perceptions such as sight, smell and touch are integral components of diagnosis during autopsy (Horsley, 2012). However, the use of the senses is not just restricted to medical practice; they are also important tools for practising the craft of sociology. This is because, as Vannini et al. (2012) argue, human senses and sensations are also a social matter because *humans sense as well as make sense.* Our senses can be sites of human agency, as well as a locus of social control (Vannini et al., 2012). To explore and fully understand the sensitive and sensory area of perinatal post-mortem, therefore, this book will be informed by a sensory sociological approach, an approach that incorporates both theory and method.

The use and role of the senses has become increasingly important in social research. Qualitative researchers, for example, have shown how ethnographic research is itself an embodied and sensory experience, highlighting the importance of taking in sights, sounds, smells and feel during fieldwork (Pink, 2008; Davies, 2011; Rhys-Taylor, 2013). Sociologists have also highlighted the importance of using particular senses in order to effectively and reflexively study various social phenomena. Back, for example, draws our attention to the importance of sociological listening. According to him, listening is tied to the art of description, involving 'patience, accuracy and critical judgement' (Back, 2007: 21). This requires the listener to challenge their 'preconceptions and position' while simultaneously engaging carefully with 'what is being said and heard' (Back, 2007: 23). It also means sometimes engaging in difficult and challenging dialogue.

The value of employing an ethnographic 'eye' when studying various social phenomena is also something that has been emphasised by sociologists (Turco and Zuckerman, 2017). According to Crow, for example, Goffman had a rare 'eye' for detailed and sharp ethnographic observation that enabled him to 'penetrate the veil of secrecy' pervading everyday social practices (Crow, 2005: 106–7; Back, 2015). Other sociologists have argued that we can use our senses to develop a deeper and more reflexive approach to research. In his work on social suffering, for example, Bourdieu advocates the use of 'a sociological "feel" or "eye"' to develop what he refers to as a 'reflex reflexivity'. This is a process whereby the researcher reflects not only on the impact of their own personal biography on research, but also on the effects of the wider social structure within which the research takes place (Bourdieu, 1999: 608).

In this book we seek to use our sociological senses to try to 'make sense' of the sensitive and traumatic arena of baby loss and post-mortem examination. As with Goffman, we attempt to use a sharp ethnographic eye for detail in order to lift the veil on the taboo world of the post-mortem, to uncover a range of hidden experiences and practices (Crow, 2005). In doing so we aim to explore the ways in which certain practices surrounding post-mortem examination can enable us to reconceptualise 'life' beyond the old boundaries of 'death' (Braidotti, 2013). Drawing on Bourdieu (1999) we also aim to use our sociological 'eye' to situate our analysis of post-mortem practice not just in a particular clinical setting, but also within the wider social, cultural and political context. The challenging subject matter of this book also demands that we engage in critical sociological listening (Back, 2007). For example, the importance of being *listened* to and *heard* was crucial for our research participants, who often felt that other people didn't want to listen to their experiences because they were simply too distressing to bear. This book will also act as a plea for sociologists, therefore, to open their ears and engage in dialogue on difficult and challenging issues (Back, 2007).

Finally, we want to develop and use our sociological sense of *feeling*. Our use and meaning of the word *feeling* here is twofold. First, we aim to use emotion to *feel* our way along the complex and difficult journey of post-mortem with parents and professionals. Kleinman and Copp (1993) argued that feelings can be effectively used as analytic tools in the research process. We draw on the notion of *Gefühl* (feeling) in this context to deepen our *Verstehen* (understanding) (Weber, 1968). *Feeling* sociologically, we argue, can enrich our ability for empathy, enabling us to achieve the 'highest standard of understandability' during data collection (Turco and Zuckerman, 2017: 1280). Secondly, *feel* in this context will also be used to refer to *touch*. As we will show in the next section, material objects formed a central part of our ethnography. The importance of touch was also central to the care practices that we observed in the mortuary. As several authors have argued, the use of different senses combined with feelings often helps us to better understand social situations (Telle, 2002; Brenneis, 2005). By employing our sociological senses (seeing, listening and feeling) in this way we hope to be able to offer a sensitive account of the sensory arena of baby loss and post-mortem examination.

The study

The study on which this book is based focused on exploring the emerging role of MRI in perinatal post-mortem. The study was funded by the Economic and Social Research Council and ethical approval was received from the Health Research Authority, UK. The project had two aims: first, to understand how parents and families who have experienced baby loss feel about, and experience, the (MRI) post-mortem process, and secondly, to explore the impact of this new technological application on professional practice and relationships between professionals from different fields. Our exploration of the role of MRI in post-mortem practice was situated within the wider post-mortem landscape. The study therefore included a focus on parents' and professionals' experiences of different types of post-mortems including minimally invasive (MIA), coronial and hospital. We also sought to explore the experiences of those who have declined a post-mortem examination. In order to understand parents' decision-making process and general experience of post-mortems, we situated our exploration within their journey of life, loss, bereavement and memorialisation.

Professional participants

The study was based primarily in a mortuary connected to a histopathology department at a teaching hospital in the north of England.[7] Access to National Health Service (NHS) staff and facilities was navigated via an NHS collaborator. Our approach to research was also informed by an advisory board which included members from different stakeholder groups (for example, various NHS staff and representatives from bereavement support charities such as Sands and the Lullaby Trust). In order to fully explore professional experience across both life and death, we recruited participants from a wide range of occupational groups including midwives, pathologists, coroners, obstetricians, neonatologists, anatomical pathology technicians (APTs), police officers, medical illustrators, nurses, hospital chaplains and bereavement support officers. We recruited 27 participants in total. The study included ten male and seventeen female respondents of a range of ages. These included people in various posts, in low-paid roles (assistant bereavement support officers) as well as those in senior status positions (clinical heads of department). Professionals varied in the amount of experience they had in their roles, from six months to thirty-five years. We used go-along ethnography to conduct our fieldwork with professionals. Go-along is a hybrid method involving interviewing and participant observation with research participants in their own environments (Reed and Ellis, 2019, 2020). This flexible approach enabled us to build an understanding of the complex and sensitive nature of the post-mortem process. Once we had built up an understanding of the different hospital processes through fieldwork with professionals, we began to collect data with parents.

Parent participants

We conducted twenty-two in-depth interviews with bereaved parents. Culturally and historically, pregnancy and childbirth has been the province of women (Meerabeau, 1991; Rapp, 2000). While men's roles in pregnancy and childbirth have expanded considerably over the past few decades (Reed, 2012), women's embodied knowledge of the fetus still provides them with a tactile awareness and sense of knowing the fetus that men cannot share (Sandelowski, 1994: 233–4). As others have argued, such embodied gender differences can influence mothers' and fathers' experience of baby loss (Murphy, 2012). Our study was focused primarily on exploring women's experiences of loss; where possible, however, we did seek to gain the views and experiences of fathers. Overall, six men were interviewed as part of the research. Four interviews were conducted jointly with both parents attending, the rest were individual. One female participant found it too difficult to talk about her experiences of loss and so chose to provide us with a written statement instead. Gender was not the specific focus of this study. Gender differences in the experience of baby loss did emerge, however, during data collection and will, therefore, be considered where appropriate throughout the book.

While our study focused specifically on parental experience of loss, we did include one set of grandparents at their request. Parents were recruited through bereavement charities, local online forums and hospital consent forms. We acknowledge the significant diversity in parental experiences of loss as highlighted in existing literature (Earle et al., 2012). Due to our focus on post-mortem examination, however, our analysis was confined to cases of baby loss where a post-mortem was offered (for example, in instances of late miscarriage, termination of pregnancy, stillbirth, SIDS and other forms of neonatal death) or ordered by the coroner. Twelve parents in our study had lost their babies through SIDS, four from stillbirth and two through late miscarriage. One respondent had terminated two pregnancies due to severe fetal anomalies identified during pregnancy, and two parents had experienced neonatal death.

Respondents' ages ranged from 28 to 68. Along with differences in age and experiences of loss, different socio-economic groupings were also represented in the study. Respondents included women and men from a range of occupations (from hairdressers to school-teachers), the unemployed and those currently not looking for employment. Although existing studies have highlighted differences in religion and attitude to post-mortem examination, there has been a relative paucity of research on the experiences of black and minority ethnic women. What research does exist has shown that black and minority ethnic women are less likely to be asked by professionals for post-mortem consent (Henderson and Redshaw, 2017). All participants in our study identified as British but chose not to disclose information about ethnicity. Unfortunately, we are unable, therefore, to make any specific comments about the effects of this issue on decisions around post-mortem consent. Only four participants identified as being specifically religious (either Muslim or Anglican) (Reed et al., 2021).

Data collection and analysis

The fieldwork was conducted over a period of eighteen months by Reed and Ellis, both sociologists. Ethical approval was sought prior to conducting the research, securing further approvals as the project progressed in order to extend recruitment and allow for in-depth ethnographic work in the mortuary. We employed our sociological senses throughout fieldwork, paying close attention to what we saw, heard and felt. During professional interviews, observations and tours we invited staff to tell us about their work practices, sometimes as they were actively engaged in these practices. We observed minimally invasive post-mortems in the mortuary, attending to the role and movement of objects in post-mortem practice. We often followed professional respondents as they went about their day-to-day work practices in different locations. By adopting this flexible and mobile approach, we were able to appreciate the ways in which different aspects of post-mortem work occur in different locations (Reed and Ellis, 2019).

Miller (2010) draws our attention to the centrality of material objects in both shaping and being shaped by everyday practice. Objects are part of everyday practice and, as will be explored in this book, also help to create a 'sense' of place. It was imperative during our go-alongs, therefore, that we paid attention to the role of material objects in professional practice. We employed our sociological senses (in particular, sight and touch) during go-alongs, paying close attention to the role and movement of different forms of materiality – from baby sleepsuits to biological tissue samples – in the mortuary and beyond. Similarly, during our interviews with parents, we wanted to understand their experiences through the wider lens of bereavement and loss. We encouraged parent participants, therefore, to bring objects such as photos, baby clothes and memory boxes to the interviews. These objects enabled the research team to explore the parents' journey from pregnancy through to loss. Where appropriate, we asked parents about their experience of the mortuary and bereavement suite as hospital spaces. However, due to the extremely sensitive nature of the study, we interviewed parents in their homes or in public places as appropriate (Reed and Ellis, 2019, 2020). To preserve the anonymity of the professionals and parents who took part in the study, we have selected appropriate pseudonyms to use in outputs and publications arising from the research. Other details such as hospital locations and the names of family members discussed by participants in their interviews (including deceased babies) have been anonymised so that individuals cannot be identified.

Social researchers have often highlighted the importance of taking a reflexive approach to research on death and dying. In particular they point to the emotional labour involved in undertaking research that deals primarily with issues of mortality. To deal with the sensitive nature of this project, we engaged in a number of reflexive self-care practices during fieldwork. These included allowing time between interviews and debriefing where necessary (Borgstrom and Ellis, 2017). We digitally recorded the interviews, and in order to build ethnographic context, we also took brief notes during the observations and interviews, turning these into fuller accounts afterwards (Walford, 2009). Once we started generating a body of fieldnotes and interview transcripts, we began to analyse the data, drawing on a thematic approach. We sought to categorise, summarise and reconstitute data in order to identify emerging themes and concepts (Braun and Clarke, 2006). This was an iterative process, which took place throughout data collection. Using verbatim interview quotes and fieldnotes based on data collected during this project, we seek, in this book, to document parental and professional experiences of life, loss and post-mortem examination.

The structure of this book

This book is split into seven substantive chapters, beginning in Chapter 1 with a focus on trauma. Trauma and suffering are part of the fabric of everyday social life, and, as such, have become an increasing concern in contemporary sociology (Bourdieu, 1999; Wilkinson, 2005; Alexander, 2012; Benzer and Reed, 2019). Drawing on data from our study, this chapter explores the deeply traumatic nature of baby loss. Parents often articulated an acute sense of shock at their unexpected loss, and a fear of what they might witness when they miscarried or delivered their baby. Other parents spoke about clutching at straws as they experienced agonising days of watching and waiting while their baby fought for life in intensive care. Regardless of the type of loss experienced, many parents articulated an acute sense of trauma at being discharged from hospital with no baby to hold in their arms. Reflecting on emerging themes in the sociological literature on trauma (Bourdieu, 1999; Alexander, 2012), the chapter concludes by focusing on the ways in which trauma around baby loss can be experienced as both an individual psychological event as well as a collective experience.

Women's rights to make decisions over their reproductive health have been central to feminist debates over several decades (Markens et al., 2003; Reed, 2012). As Rose (2001) has argued, biological life is now firmly entrenched in the domain of decision and choice. When a serious fetal anomaly is diagnosed in late pregnancy, women are often expected to make choices over whether or not to terminate. Parents and professionals are also faced with difficult decisions around when to resuscitate babies or end neonatal life support. In the event of losing a baby, parents are also suddenly faced with making a range of difficult decisions, including whether to consent to a post-mortem. Chapter 2 focuses on exploring the difficult and often urgent decisions parents must make after they lose a baby, and seeks to extend existing sociological thinking on reproductive choice and decision-making (Press and Browner, 1997; Kerr, 2004).

Chapter 3 focuses directly on the post-mortem examination, centring its analysis on the development of minimally invasive autopsy using magnetic resonance imaging. MRI is often perceived to be the 'gold standard' in healthcare (Joyce, 2006). Its use in autopsy, however, signals the emergence of a new application of the technology (Fligner and Dighe, 2011). Drawing on data from the study, this chapter explores parents' and professionals' feelings towards post-mortem MRI. For parents, MRI can be used to plan a less medicalised birth/ death. It offers important information about why their baby died. The MRI image validates their baby's existence, offering parents an important sense of closure. While post-mortems using MRI had not been available to a number of parents in this study, most expressed an interest in this becoming more accessible in the future. This was a view readily shared by professionals, especially when parents did not wish to consent to a full post-mortem. The chapter concludes by focusing on this novel technological application, exploring the extent to which MRI can enable us to reconceptualise 'life' beyond the old boundaries of 'death' (Braidotti, 2013).

Emotion, a key area of interest in contemporary sociology, forms the central focus of Chapter 4. This chapter offers a sociological analysis of emotion in relation to baby loss and post-mortem practice. It focuses on examining parental experiences of emotion or *being* emotional as well as exploring emotion work in different types of professional practice. While parental and professional data form the central focus of the chapter, we also provide a sociological exploration of the emotional nature of *doing* research in this area. Throughout the chapter we explore the acute trauma and sadness of both experiencing and witnessing baby loss and post-mortem examination. The chapter also seeks to uncover some of the more life-affirming emotions often experienced in this context – for example, articulations of parental and professional pride – which often remain hidden from view (Reed and Ellis, 2019). The chapter concludes by reflecting on the ways in which the articulation and management of emotions is contingent on the social relations and structures surrounding them (Barbalet, 1998; Bericat, 2016).

Chapter 5 focuses on the hidden care work that takes place in the mortuary. The concept of 'care' has been used by sociologists to explore a range of issues (for example, nurture, treatment, protection, containment) in various settings – from children's homes to residential care for older people (Oakley, 1974; Thomas, 1993). Care is often the central focus of sociological research on palliative or end-of-life 'care' (James, 1992). In contrast, ethnographies of post-mortem examination tend to focus on the scientific rather than emotional or care work involved (Timmermans, 2006; Brysiewicz, 2007). Drawing on data from the study, we explore the various care practices enacted by different types of health professionals (such as bathing, dressing and talking to babies) that take place in the mortuary. These practices, although hidden from the view of the public and other clinical staff, were often crucial to parental and professional experience of the post-mortem process. By uncovering some of these hidden care practices the chapter seeks to extend existing sociological literature in this field.

Memory-making has often been central to research on reproductive loss. For example, research on baby loss has focused on exploring the role of ultrasound images, footprints, photos and gift-giving as part of the creation and maintenance of fetal personhood and memorialisation (Layne, 2000; Garattini, 2007). Attention has been given in wider studies on death and dying to the intersection of material culture and place (Prendergast et al., 2006), and more recently to the emergence of less traditional commemorative practices (Cann, 2014). Chapter 6 explores memory-making as a dynamic social process that occurs across time and place. As our findings show, it often begins in the hospital, where parents are given a memory box which they then fill with a range of different items over time. Professionals also prepare for and engage in a range of memory-making activities with parents, in the hospital but also in different settings such as memorial services. The chapter concludes by reflecting on the social and relational aspects of memory production, and on the broader material turn in sociology, where it is argued that material objects both shape but are also shaped by everyday practice (Miller, 2010).

The penultimate chapter seeks to bring together literature from the sociology of the family and intimacy with the interdisciplinary field of death and dying studies to explore perinatal loss through a relational lens. It does this to examine the role of relationships across the journey of reproductive loss. The chapter begins by exploring the impact of baby loss and grief on intimate relationships and wider family members (for example, grandparents, aunts and uncles). It also explores the ways in which parental experiences of a post-mortem are deeply informed by biological connections and social relationships. While most of the chapter focuses specifically on the impact of baby loss on family relationships, it also seeks to examine the role that friends, work colleagues and health professionals can play. This is because, as Towers (2019) argues, bereavement is embedded in all social relationships. The chapter concludes by highlighting the socially embedded nature of baby loss, reinforcing the centrality of social relations across the entire baby loss journey.

In the concluding chapter, we aim to draw together some of the significant conceptual, substantive and methodological themes that have emerged throughout the book, reflecting on their wider significance for existing debates in medical sociology, STS, death and dying studies, and research methods. We begin by examining the complex relationship between life and death, analysing and reflecting on parental coping strategies after loss. The chapter also considers the relationship between gender and reproduction, shedding light on the implications of our research findings for wider sociological debates on gender and masculinity. Existing conceptualisations of post-mortem practice tend to focus only on the clinical aspects of the examination. We aim to use this conclusion to lobby for the development of a more enlightened approach to post-mortems, one that acknowledges the centrality of care and emotion. This chapter examines the sensory and sensitive nature of the research on which this book is based, offering suggestions for how researchers can successfully navigate emotions in research. As is shown throughout the book, while baby loss happens to individual mothers and fathers, both parental and professional experience of this loss are profoundly shaped and mediated by the social. The conclusion draws to a close, therefore, by reflecting on the classic sociological relationship between the individual and society.

Notes

1 For further information, see https://www.nhs.uk/conditions/post-mortem (accessed March 2022).
2 For further information, see https://www.nhs.uk/conditions/stillbirth/ (accessed June 2023).

3 For further information, see https.//www.nhs.uk/conditions/miscarriage/ (accessed June 2023).

4 When undertaking a termination of pregnancy for fetal anomaly, the intention is that the fetus should not survive the TOP. In the UK context, feticide refers to the clinical practice undertaken by an obstetrician prior to birth to ensure that the fetus does not survive the birth. The Royal College of Obstetrics and Gynæcology currently recommends feticide for terminations over 21+6 weeks (RCOG, 2010).

5 The Human Tissue Act was passed in England and Wales in 2004, https://www.legislation.gov.uk/ukpga/2004/30/contents. The Human Tissue Act (Scotland) was passed in 2006, https://www.legislation.gov.uk/asp/2006/4/contents.

6 For example, the UK BBC television crime drama *Silent Witness* or US-based crime series such as *Crime Scene Investigation*.

7 Histopathology is the study of diseased tissue, including its examination under the microscope.

Chapter 1

Trauma

> It had happened. You'd gone in [to hospital]. The baby had died. You'd delivered this baby and as far as they were concerned it was a matter of getting you on your feet and getting you home. That was the situation at the time but you're in terrible shock. You don't think you are but you are. In fact you don't even know what shock is until something like that comes and then it's disbelief, then it's anger, then it's grief and that's the last thing really but that didn't happen straightaway. (Dawn 59; baby son Alex died at twenty-nine weeks in utero thirty-three years before our interview)

The term trauma has a long history of use in medicine and surgery (Meštrović, 1985). In classical medical usage, 'trauma' tends to refer to a blow to the tissues of the body (or more recently, the mind) resulting in an injury or 'some other disturbance' (Erikson, 1991: 455). According to Hirschberger (2018: 6), although the common use of the term often refers to relatively mundane affects (for example, being traumatised by a visit to the dentist), the psychological definition of trauma includes encounters with death, or extreme death anxiety, as a key component (Galea et al., 2003; Smelser, 2004). As Thompson and Walsh (2010) argue, much of the literature on trauma focuses on its psychological impact. For example, literature that explores the trauma of pregnancy loss tends to focus on various psychological impacts, particularly post-traumatic stress disorder (PTSD) (Murphy et al., 2014). Thompson and Walsh (2010) argue, however, that it is important to consider the sociological dimensions of trauma, not least because social divisions (based on class, gender, race and ethnicity) shape people's life experiences, including how trauma is both experienced and responded to. Alexander further argues that the idea of trauma is something widely experienced and intuitively understood. Such 'rootedness is the life world', according to him, 'is the soil that nourishes every social scientific concept' (2012: 7).

The death of a baby is an immensely shocking and traumatic experience (Berry et al., 2022). This chapter seeks, therefore, to offer a sociological exploration of the deeply traumatic nature of baby loss, focusing on the initial event itself (for example, the moment a mother went into premature labour, or when parents discovered that their baby had stopped breathing) and its immediate aftermath. As the quote above from Dawn, one of the mothers in our study, shows, parents often articulated an acute sense of shock and trauma at their unexpected loss. For some parents this occurred when they woke up in the morning to find their baby had died at home suddenly in its sleep; for others it occurred when they went into labour prematurely, or when their baby was stillborn at full term. Focusing particularly on the initial traumatic event and immediate aftermath, the chapter aims to explore the various sites, sounds and visions of trauma as experienced and witnessed by parents and their families. Part of the chapter has a focus on parents' experiences of PTSD, and engages with some of the psychological literature in this field. The primary aim of this chapter, however, is to explore the ways in which the trauma experienced by parents – both during and after baby loss – is also socially framed and mediated. We seek to show how the experience of baby loss appears to threaten parents' sense of ontological security, their identity and place in the social world. While it is an individually lived experience, it is also collectively mediated and *felt* (Erikson, 1991).

Developing a sociological approach to trauma

Over the past decade there has been a growth in sociological literature that seeks to explore experiences of social suffering (Kleinman et al., 1997; Bourdieu, 1999; Das, 2000, 2001; Wilkinson, 2004, 2005). Such literature focuses on 'a wide range of spectacular and ordinary occasions when human dignity is violated and people come to some manner of grief and harm' (Wilkinson, 2004: 114). Sociology has, however, been strangely silent about trauma, with most academic work in this area coming from the discipline of psychology. In their work on trauma and social work practice, Thompson and Walsh (2010) have sought to advocate a psychosocial approach that aims to incorporate both psychological and sociological components into its analysis. By contrast, Alexander has sought to develop a more explicitly sociological approach to understanding trauma. He argues that existing approaches to trauma tend to be underpinned either by enlightenment thinking or by psychology, which often view traumatic events as naturally occurring episodes that shatter an individual or collective sense of well-being. For Alexander, thinking sociologically about trauma requires us to take a reflexive approach, recognising that 'trauma is not something naturally existing; it is something constructed by society' (2012: 7).

Sociologists who have written about trauma tend to focus on the distinction between individual and collective trauma. Trauma at the individual level often refers to a blow to the psyche that can shatter our view of ourselves and our position in the social world (Erikson, 1976; Janoff-Bulman, 1992). According to Thompson and Walsh, it is an existential injury insofar as it can damage or even destroy our sense of self and how we fit into the wider world. Trauma poses a threat to our ontological security because it undermines our sense of self and identity, leaving us feeling insecure (Thompson and Walsh, 2010: 379). According to Erikson (1991), by contrast, collective trauma refers to the psychological reactions to a traumatic event that affect the fabric of social life and bring into question the very nature of humankind. As Hirshberger argues, individual and collective memory of trauma is different. Collective memory persists beyond the lives of individual survivors of events, and 'is remembered by group members that may be far removed from the traumatic events in time and space' (Hirschberger, 2018: 1).

Sociologists writing on trauma have often focused on individual and collective experiences of trauma as distinct analytical categories. Erikson, however, usefully helps us to move our thinking on trauma beyond this sociological dualism. Trauma, according to Erikson, is often understood as a lonely experience that sets an individual apart from 'the everyday moods and understandings that govern social life' (1991: 471). Paradoxically, however, he argues that the drifting away from society is accompanied by revised views of the world that in their turn become the very basis for communality (1991: 471). He argues that, at times, otherwise unconnected individuals who share a traumatic experience can seek one another out and form a sense of communality on that basis. This often involves a common language, a kinship among those who have come to see themselves as different (Erikson, 1991: 461).

In this chapter we draw on this emerging body of sociological literature to explore trauma after baby loss as experienced by parents and families. The chapter aims to move away from lay understandings that frame trauma as if it were something naturally occurring and preordained. Drawing on Thompson and Walsh's (2010) psychosocial approach, we will show how trauma can inflict a massive injury to parents' sense of self, posing a threat to their identity and feelings of ontological security. Our main aim, however, is to explore the ways in which trauma is framed and mediated by the social (for example, social context, gender roles, social relations etc.) (Alexander, 2012). Through this process we seek to advance a dialectical approach to individual and collective experiences of trauma. As we will show, while parents experienced trauma on an individual basis, they often grieved collectively, thus reinforcing the deeply social experience of trauma in this context (Erikson, 1991). Note that some of the quotations used in this chapter on trauma offer graphic illustrations of death, and might, therefore, be upsetting for some readers. We feel it is important, however, to tell our research participants' stories as they articulated them to us.

Initial shocks: examining locations of trauma

We begin by examining the importance of place and location as initial sites of parents' trauma. We take Pollack's (2003: 798) twofold definition of place as a physical location as well as something that is created through human interaction. Sites of trauma become invested with meaning through the intersection of these two aspects. Parents in our study experienced their loss at different points during their pregnancy, the neonatal period and beyond. They also experienced their loss in different locations, such as at home, in hospital, in parks and when on holiday. The loss sometimes occurred when they were alone and at other times when they were with other people. These physical and interactive sites framed their initial experiences of shock and trauma.

Some parents lost their baby in hospital, both shockingly and unexpectedly. Fran lost her baby boy Lee in hospital, just before she was due to be discharged after giving birth. His death occurred just over five years before our interview when he was only three days old. She described her terror:

> Yeah. Lee was born by emergency caesarean. I was forty-two weeks and was induced. I was kept in the hospital because something wasn't quite right. Not with me, but with Lee. And there'd been several things over the course ... after he was born that there was nothing that anyone could put their finger on. The morning that we were due to come home Lee stopped breathing and it was absolutely terrifying. Obviously went through resuscitation and died just before seven o'clock in the morning. Oh, it was absolutely traumatic, to be quite honest.

The hospital was often a site of trauma for parents, with health professionals becoming key participants and witnesses in the unfolding trauma. Some parents, however, were out in public with friends and family members when their baby died suddenly. Bev lost her baby boy George at two weeks old nineteen years before our study, when she was at a friend's house with her toddler son. She had vivid memories of the acute trauma she felt when her baby suddenly stopped breathing:

> We got there [to her friend's house], sat down, everybody else was there [Bev's friends and their children], the nearly two-year-olds were all running around, and I got him [baby George] out of the... He started to cry, got him out of the car seat to feed him and I was breastfeeding. And I started to feed him, so he cried. And then he stopped crying, and then I looked and there was some blood coming out of his nose. And I knew immediately really that he'd stopped breathing and then he was dead.

Most mothers in the study who lost their baby during the neonatal period were with the baby when they died. There were, however, two families in the study whose babies died suddenly while in the care of other people (not family members). Parents, in these cases, had to receive the traumatic news that their baby had died from someone else rather than bearing witness to the initial traumatic event themselves. Georgia lost her baby boy Charlie one year prior to our interview. He died aged six months while in the care of childminders. The quote below expresses the shock and trauma that

Georgia felt when she received the call from the childminders informing her that her baby had died.

> And I was just at work. It was about eleven o'clock, and I got a
> phone call. It was the childminders. It's a husband and wife team
> that do it, and it was Ron, and he said that Charlie had died on the
> phone, and he said the ambulance are here and they're working on
> him. He said, but I can't leave Anne. I said, no, Ron, you need to go
> with him, he can't go on his own, he can't go with no one with him.
> And then I could hear the ambulance leave on the phone. I then rang
> Chris [her husband], because he was actually at home, because at the
> time he was off sick with stress and anxiety, and he'd started a job
> in Shaport for a few weeks but it wasn't right for him, so he was off
> work. So I rang him and said he needed to go round to the childminders,
> that they're saying that Charlie's died, you need to get there.

Most of the parents in the study had custody of their baby when
they died. There was, however, one mother, Rosie, whose baby
Camilla suddenly died aged four months while in foster care, just
over a year prior to our interview. Because her baby did not live
with her, Rosie did not find out straight away that she had died.
She was only made aware of baby Camilla's death after the event,
when a police officer arrived at her house unannounced to give her
the news. The quote below shows how shocked Rosie was and how
she could not believe what she was being told.

> He said, I've got some very bad news, it's little Camilla, I'm afraid
> she's passed away. I think that's how he said it. And it's like, you
> sit there, and you're like, it's like, has that actually just gone in my
> ears? Did I hear right? And I think I just looked at him. And of
> course, my husband was in the other room, the DI wasn't expecting
> him to be there, obviously he overheard what he was saying, so he
> came straight into the kitchen, as well. And so it was like, it was
> about quarter past eleven at night, and so by that time they said, we
> couldn't go to the hospital, which really annoyed me. It was strange.
> A surreal experience. It didn't really register for a few minutes. Quite
> a weird one.

All the parents in our study remembered and talked about the
initial location where their loss was felt or triggered. Place, particularly
the place where their baby had died, was imprinted in their minds
as a site of trauma, informing their understanding and feelings about
what had happened. While physical location was important, however,

what was also crucial to parents' initial experience of trauma were their interactions with others – with partners, friends, police etc. This reinforces the ways in which meaning can be ascribed to trauma through the intersection of social and physical space (Pollack, 2003). The roles that different individuals played in shaping these initial experiences of trauma, however, warrant further exploration. We move on in the next section, therefore, to explore the role of key witnesses in the unfolding trauma.

Fathers and children: participants and witnesses of trauma

According to Oliver, the verb 'to witness' has a double meaning. It can refer to someone providing an '*eyewitness* testimony based on firsthand knowledge, on the one hand, and *bearing* witness to something beyond recognition that can't be seen on the other' (Oliver, 2015: 483). Witnessing, according to Oliver, has 'both the juridical connotations of seeing with one's own eyes and the religious connotations of testifying to that which cannot be seen' (2015: 483). In our study, mothers were almost always centrally involved in the initial trauma, either physically through miscarrying or giving birth, or when caring for their baby while on maternity leave. They were direct participants, but also *bore* witness to the terrible trauma of watching their baby dying. Fathers (and sometimes children), on the other hand, played a different role. While some fathers were not present during the initial traumatic event, others were first-hand witnesses, as we will explore in this section.

Several fathers in the study were not with their partners when they experienced miscarriage, went into premature labour, or when babies died during the weeks and months following birth. Male participants in the study were often at work when the event happened and often articulated what it felt like to receive 'the call' from their partners or other relatives informing them that something was wrong. Ricky's partner Esther went into labour at twenty-four weeks and six days gestation. Ricky described the moment when he received the call from his father-in-law Ben while he was at work, informing him that Esther had gone into premature labour:

> I got a phone call about twenty to ten, roughly about that time saying that she'd gone into premature labour and they'd obviously give her

everything to slow her down, that kind of occurring really quick. So that were a massive... My first question were what's going to happen to Esther first, but then what does this mean. And obviously Ben were in shock as well, my father-in-law...

While some fathers were not physically present when the initial trauma occurred, others bore witness to their babies being stillborn or dying prematurely. As well as witnessing horrific scenes, men also often appeared to try to shield their partners from what was going on. Wayne's baby Flo, for example, died while his partner Sherene was in labour. The baby was subsequently declared stillborn. Clinicians performed a test on Flo after she had been born that was physically traumatic. Wayne describes the terror of witnessing this directly as a father:

> And then they asked for permission to take a heart sample there and then [from baby Flo], which I reluctantly gave but asked them not to do in front of Sherene, but they just did it anyway. So she saw that. There was a lot of blood. So from my perspective, Sherene didn't really see this because she was at the other end of things, so to speak, but it was really, really traumatic for me because there was blood everywhere, all over the floor, and I was stepping in and stuff.

While some fathers witnessed the trauma of a stillbirth and subsequent invasive testing, others were privy to their baby undergoing cardiopulmonary resuscitation (CPR). Resuscitation of infants can be an intensely physical procedure which can be very traumatic to witness. Family presence when a relative is undergoing CPR remains a topic of debate (Maxton, 2008). Studies on adult resuscitation have shown that most family members benefit from the opportunity to be present (Back and Rooke, 1994), with reports of parents of paediatric patients also expressing a desire to be present (Dingeman et al., 2007; McGahey-Oakland et al., 2007). Watching their baby undergoing CPR, however, was described by parents in our study (particularly fathers) as a brutal experience. This was outlined by Nathan, who could not bear to witness the attempted resuscitation of his baby daughter Aria:

> And we were shown our way into the hospital, and there was a private room, we were put in there. And then a doctor came in, and just explained what they were doing, what they'd tried. Said that they were doing everything they could, but she [baby Aria] wasn't responding.

And we had to be ready for what might inevitably happen. And then said, it's your daughter, you can go in, there is a lot of people working on her, there's a lot of activity, it's going to look very violent. And in we went, and I walked in the room, and that was the last time I saw her alive, and I just turned around and walked out, 'cause it's the most horrific thing you can ever see. I've done first aid training, I've done resuscitation of dummies and all that sort of thing, but until you actually see someone going through that, and I've been at first aid where they say, it's very violent, you'll hear ribs cracking and everything, and all that horrible stuff, but you're trying to save someone's life, but then you see it on an eleven week old, and what's more, your eleven week old, and it's just terrible. It's one of the things that every now and then comes back to you. So, I turned around and walked out again, I couldn't see all that.

While both mothers and fathers often bore witness to their child undergoing CPR, in cases of SIDS the baby's siblings (mostly young children) were also sometimes present. Children in these situations were not only deeply traumatised by seeing their parents in severe distress, but also by witnessing their parents or health professionals performing CPR on their younger brother or sister. For example, Sam's baby Aurora died just over three and a half years prior to our study, suddenly and unexpectedly aged seven weeks. When Sam gave birth to Aurora she already had two children by a previous partner and one other child with her current partner. Sam described the general trauma her children experienced when CPR was being performed on their sister and discusses the trauma that one child (Arthur) felt in particular:

Yeah, poor Arthur came in here and saw Tom [baby's father] working on her doing the CPR. Yeah, I don't know, there's a lot of ... they were quite scared to go upstairs on their own the day immediately after. They get a bit funny now, they like someone to walk up the stairs with them at night, they like all the lights to be on and little things.

Experiences of the initial traumatic event were clearly different for mothers and fathers. Mothers' experiences were often embodied and almost always central, because they were the ones giving birth or who were physically present when their baby died. Fathers, on the other hand, were sometimes participants in the trauma (through administering CPR), but were mostly witnesses to the event. Men often acted as an eyewitness, providing testimonies during interviews on what happened. They also bore witness to something unspeakable occurring to one of their children (Oliver, 2015). While research on perinatal loss has begun to explore the impact of baby loss on sibling experience (Bornemisza et al., 2021), this is something that requires much greater consideration. We will explore this issue further in Chapter 7. In the next section, we move on to explore the role of the senses in parents' initial experiences of trauma.

The role of the senses: 'seeing', 'touching' and 'hearing' trauma

The senses, as we seek to show in this section – particularly *sight*, *touch* and *hearing* – play a key role in framing parental experiences of trauma. Although parents sometimes have mixed feelings about the possibility of viewing and holding their deceased baby, recent research on stillbirth has shown the importance of parents at least being offered this opportunity, because it can help them to process their grief (Üstündağ-Budak et al., 2015). Research has also emphasised the importance of preparing parents for what they might *see* when they give birth, particularly in the context of second trimester loss (Smith et al., 2020). Parents in our study sometimes had conflicting feelings about seeing and holding their baby once it had died, and did not always feel well prepared for what they might witness. For example, several respondents lost their babies between sixteen and eighteen weeks' gestation. In these cases, mothers did not always feel prepared for what their baby might look like. Amy, for example, miscarried her baby girl Clementine at sixteen weeks. Despite being worried about what she would see when she gave birth, and whether the fetus would look like a baby, she still wanted to see her child:

> So they got her [Clementine] out, I was in shock, I was on another… I was not myself really, because I were just, like, I want to see her, I want to see her, well I didn't know it was a her then, so it was, I want to see it, I want to see it, can I look at it? And that Esmeralda [the nurse] were, like, yes, we'll show it to you soon, yes, like, and then they put her in a little … what are they, like, a sick tray thing?

Babies who had died suddenly in the weeks and months following birth had to undergo a coronal post-mortem examination. Parents were invited to spend time with their baby both before and after the post-mortem. Parents often described their fears about seeing and holding their dead baby in the mortuary, especially after the post-mortem examination had taken place. This was articulated by Bev, who was worried about viewing her son George in the mortuary.

> But anyway, he [police officer] then took us to the hospital to... I think it was called Violette Villa at the time, and we saw George. And I was scared stiff about seeing him. They talked to us about... You did always get the feeling that they were very caring, they were lovely and that he would look a bit different but basically the same. And he had a white knitted hat on.

Parents were also worried about touching their dead baby. Ivy's baby Brian died suddenly at four and a half months over thirty-seven years before our interview. She talked about the undertaker bringing the baby home so that they could spend time with him before the funeral. Brian had been kept in the fridge in the mortuary to preserve his body. Ivy was shocked by how cold he felt and by the fragility of his tiny body:

> But when the undertaker brought Brian home, obviously he was cold, frozen I would ... we presumed, he looked beautiful other than the temperature of him. But then the funeral director said to me don't pick him up because his head might fall off. So that was pretty shocking because he just looked like normal.

Some parents in the study felt pressure to hold their baby even when they found the prospect traumatic. This pressure came not from health professionals but from other family members. Penny's baby boy Dustin died suddenly aged six months, seven years before our study. She described the pressure she felt from her mother to hold her baby and articulated how traumatic and shocking it was because he was so cold:

> My parents were away, and I rang them and they came up [...] to the hospital. All my sisters came. I've got three sisters. Awful. They [the clinicians] gave me a bit of diazepam because I was totally out of it, and they said, do you want to hold him, and I didn't want to, but my mum made me. She just said you'll regret it. Oh god, he was hideous. He was all cold. It was just hideous [crying]. Oh, it was just awful.

Parents' traumas were not only mediated by sight and touch but also by sound. Anna lost her baby Lily at twenty-three weeks over three years before our interview. Many hospitals in the UK now have special soundproofed rooms for parents to spend time with their babies after they suffer a late pregnancy loss or give birth to a stillborn baby. There was no such special room afforded to Anna when she lost her baby. She was placed in a normal hospital room where she could hear women giving birth to live, healthy, full-term babies. These sounds were extremely traumatic for her, as the quote below indicates.

> I'm in a hospital room, I can hear babies crying next door. It was a private room, but you could hear babies through the walls, screaming, 'cause I'm next to where they take them after delivery, whatever they're called, I don't know […] So I can hear them all crying, and I'm thinking, what the … are you joking? Like, I want to get out of here as quickly as possible, I just need to not be here, and as I say, we had the funeral pretty quickly after that.

Parents' experiences of trauma in our study were strongly mediated by the senses – particularly sight, touch and sound. As Vannini et al. (2012) argue, human senses and sensations are not just biological and physical experiences but also a social matter. This was certainly the case for parents in our study, as these sensory experiences, although physically manifested, were also strongly shaped by the presence and influence of other people. In exploring the senses in this section, we have highlighted some of the fear parents articulate over seeing and holding their baby. Parents in our study also talked about their sadness and shock at leaving hospital with empty arms after losing a baby. We explore this and other immediate aftershocks in the next section.

Aftershocks and empty arms

'Aftershock' is a term commonly used by geologists to refer to smaller earthquakes that follow the main event. We use aftershock here to refer to the physical and emotional shocks that parents encountered after the immediate event of their loss. Leaving the hospital without a baby, despite having given birth, was one of the initial aftershocks felt by parents. Parents who had lost babies though late pregnancy loss or stillbirth often went into hospital full of hope and expectation that they would be giving birth to a live/healthy baby, only to find themselves at the centre of tragedy. Wayne, for example, talked about the hope parents feel when they are getting ready for their baby's birth. As a pregnancy progresses and the baby appears 'healthy', parents often buy items for their baby (for example, a cot, pushchair, clothes etc.). As the following quote from Wayne illustrates, it is then a deep and cruel shock for parents when things go wrong during labour.

> We had all the room set up, everything was ready, the family were ready, we'd rang them on the way in and everyone was expecting a baby. You come out and the sun's shining, it was spring, everything looks nice, everything's prepped for your life being ... taking on a new chapter, and then you're in this horrible situation.

The experience of the trauma of leaving hospital empty-handed without a healthy baby is commonly expressed by baby loss sufferers. It is something that is symbolised by the name of pregnancy loss support charities such as Aching Arms. One of our participants, Dawn, whose baby Alex died in utero at twenty-nine weeks' gestation, described the ways in which this left her feeling a sense of shock and disbelief:

> Shock, I think you... I'm not quite sure you realise you're in so much shock. You've gone in expecting a baby. You come out with empty arms and disbelief. I think you just cannot believe... I mean, you want to cry. I suppose some women do. I couldn't cry. I had no idea. I didn't know where I was or what I was doing, as such, and I think part of me was trying to keep a brave face for everybody else who came in the room and in fact I should not have done that. I should have allowed my grief to come to the surface. It did eventually. Not straightaway but it did eventually and when it did then I began to be very ... quite unwell at home. I was quite poorly but it didn't happen straightaway, and I think it's shock. I don't think I'd ever had such a shock in all my life.

While most parents (mothers in particular) felt their baby's physical absence immediately and acutely, some mothers were also faced with the physical and emotional side effects of giving birth. As Smith et al. (2020) show, women who go through premature labour often experience postnatal physical symptoms, such as bleeding, breast milk coming in and hormonal swings. Many of the women in Smith et al.'s study who gave birth prematurely between twenty and twenty-three weeks were unprepared for these physical legacies of birth. This was also the case for some of our mothers. Ricky, for example, described the physical manifestation of shock that his partner Esther experienced when she gave birth to their son, Oliver, prematurely at twenty-five weeks. He described the ways in which Esther's body wasn't prepared for labour and childbirth:

> She were on every pain killer to just relieve ... because as well because it were happening at such a premature stage of her pregnancy she obviously were having to adapt her body a lot earlier than what it were ready [...] so that itself caused a lot more distress and she were in shock, so it were like ... she obviously [...] never unprepared to deliver a baby, but she were a lot more ... we just didn't know what to do. We were just like well, we're not ready for this. We were literally about two or three weeks away from having us birthing class things weren't we?

While the literally embodied nature of pregnancy (Murphy, 2012) meant that women often had to deal with the physical side effects of giving birth, the shock of losing a baby could lead to a range of unpleasant side effects for both parents. Some participants were warned by professionals about these potential side effects of shock. Olivia's baby boy Ian died suddenly at home when he was six weeks old, just nine months prior to our interview. She lived in a region of the UK with access to a SIDS rapid response team. This meant that a group of professionals (nurses, midwives and police officers) went to visit the parents at home in the aftermath of the death. As her account shows, the team tried to warn Olivia about some of the physical side effects of shock:

> So we had two members of that team [multi-agency response team] come and visit us at eleven o'clock that morning. They gave us some leaflets and information around bereavement, how to talk to children about death because, of course, we had my ... my son at the time who was two and a half years old. They also told us things around how your body's gone into shock and it's not unusual to be sick and have diarrhoea and have memory lapses and not know what you're doing and all sorts of wonderful things.

We have focused on the immediate aftershock of losing a baby in this section. In doing so we have begun to highlight some of the physical manifestations of trauma that parents experience. Research has consistently shown that acute trauma exposure can lead to negative physical health consequences – from gastrointestinal upsets to problems with the immune system (D'Andrea et al., 2011). Trauma can also have a range of devastating psychological consequences, including anxiety, depression and PTSD (D'Andrea et al., 2011). We will pick up on this in more detail in the next section by exploring the impact of trauma on participants' health and well-being, focusing specifically on PTSD.

Pregnancy loss and post-traumatic stress disorder (PTSD)

The psychological impact of infant loss, and in particular PTSD, have become the subject of much baby loss literature on trauma. In the UK, to qualify as having experienced a traumatic event an individual must meet two sets of criteria as outlined in the *DSM-IV*.[1] A person must have either witnessed or directly experienced an event that involves actual or threatened death or injury to the self or others (criterion A1; APA, 1994: 467). They must also have had an emotional response which 'involved intense fear, helplessness, or horror' (criterion A2; APA, 1994: 467; Bedard-Gilligan and Zoellner, 2008). Infant death meets the current criteria for PSTD as outlined in *DSM-IV* criteria A1 and A2. In their systematic review of the literature on stillbirth, Heazell et al. (2016) showed that the most frequently reported experiences of parents after stillbirth were negative psychological effects including high rates of depressive symptoms, anxiety, PTSD, suicidal ideation, panic and phobias. Research in this area has tended to highlight a strongly gendered dimension to these experiences. Fathers are more likely to experience loneliness, anger, guilt and helplessness (Badenhorst et al., 2006), whereas mothers are significantly more likely to experience anxiety and depression than their male partners (Bennett et al., 2008; Murphy et al., 2014). In this section we focus on exploring parental experiences of PTSD, highlighting the seemingly gendered nature of this experience.

While both mothers and fathers talked about feeling depressed after losing their baby, only female participants mentioned being diagnosed with PTSD. Fran, for example, lost her baby boy Lee over five years before our study. He was only three days old when he died unexpectedly in hospital. She articulated how she was diagnosed with PTSD, and how she still has flashbacks to the traumatic event, even now:

> Yeah. I was diagnosed with post-traumatic stress disorder and still to this day can suffer from flashbacks. Find it very difficult to be in a hospital environment. Can't really do that very easily. If the girls [her living children] are ill it tips me over a bit because... Yeah, definitely. For both of us.

Another respondent, Anna, was treated for PTSD. She recalled in detail her experience of loss, the trauma of the event, the flashbacks, the inability to stop thinking about her baby and what happened. She also highlighted the need for further research on this issue.

> And actually I've been treated for post-traumatic stress disorder, in the light of everything that happened. That is something that people need to research into, because the amount of parents who are being treated for grief, and loss, when actually they are suffering from post-traumatic stress because the horrific nature of what they're going through, and they are directly involved in that, leads people into this heightened state of trauma where they can't move on from that, and the flashbacks and the reliving it over and over and over again, was just re-traumatising you all the time, you were constantly being re-traumatised every time you thought about it. And there isn't a day that you don't think about it.

Our data appeared to reinforce the gendered nature of a PTSD diagnosis, already highlighted by the literature. While many female respondents discussed suffering from depression or being diagnosed with PTSD, none of the male participants did. However, their female partners often suspected that men were suffering just as much as they were, but that their suffering was often in silence. Anna felt this was the case with her partner, Mark, who had to watch from the sidelines as she gave birth to their baby prematurely. She told us: 'it wouldn't surprise me if he isn't suffering from post-traumatic stress, because actually he witnessed it all'.

The gendered nature of the psychological impact of baby loss trauma was also reinforced in other ways by participants. For example, men would sometimes comment on the state of their partners' mental health. This can be seen in the account below from Rosie, who discussed the ways in which her partner Liam monitored her mental health:

> Yeah, he gets it. He said I'm not depressed, so that's a good thing. He said, I've got traces of post-traumatic stress dotted around, because I do tend to let, like certain things will set me off, or I'll be out, and I can't do the crowds and noises, and I just want to get home. Yeah, there's little parts that point to that, but some things don't. So, like he said, get the court stuff out of the way, which is obviously done now, and then focus on me really, or me and my husband. And start to heal, is one of the way of putting it.

This gendered element to PTSD is not only reinforced by the baby loss and PTSD literature but by the wider mental health literature. As studies often show, women are more likely to self-report mental health problems and suffer psychological distress (Tedstone Doherty and Kartalova-O'Doherty, 2010). Research has also tended to show that while women are more likely to experience depression, men are more likely to report alcohol problems (Kessler et al., 1994). There is, however, also gender bias and stereotyping evident in the diagnosis and treatment of mental health problems, with research showing that women are often more likely to be diagnosed with depression and subsequently to be prescribed medication (Stoppe et al., 1999; Simoni-Wastila, 2000). As Tedstone Doherty and Kartalova-O'Doherty (2010) argue, this can limit the interpretation of gender differences in mental health. It is hard to know how much such gender bias was prevalent in the actual diagnosis of PTSD among respondents in our study. The influence of gender on the experience of, and response to, baby loss will be explored in more detail in later chapters. In the following section, however, we explore the impact of baby loss trauma on respondents' self-identity.

Individual trauma: survival and change

As noted earlier, trauma experienced at an individual level is a blow to the psyche that can inflict a massive injury on a person's sense of self. It can change the way we see ourselves and our place in the social world, posing a threat to our identity and feelings of ontological security (Erikson, 1976; Janoff-Bulman, 1992; Thompson and Walsh, 2010). The traumatic event of baby loss, as research has started to show, can affect mothers' approach to life and death, self-esteem and their own sense of identity (Heazell et al., 2016). Parents in our study, particularly mothers, talked about how their experience of baby loss had changed them permanently. Bev talked about how the grief and shock comes in stages but also about how the experience has changed her as a person.

> It's changed me totally, really. Well, I don't know really where to begin. I think that when you have a certain unexpected death, I mean the shock element is massive and you just go through, well, the grief… It's like layers and layers upon layers if you like. And I remember in that first year definitely there were times where I'd suddenly feel oh, I've come through some massive stage.

Many parents, particularly mothers, said that the experience of losing a baby made them change their outlook on life completely. As a result they have sought to reprioritise what is important in their lives. Dawn, for example, who lost her son Alex over thirty-three years before our study, discussed the ways in which the experience changed her. She also highlighted the gendered nature of this suffering and the ways in which she feels that men often suffer their grief in silence:

> It changes you a little bit. I think it changes you. You don't always know it has for a long time and suddenly the things you thought were important in your life aren't, you know, you think this is important and this has got to be done and you must have this house and you must do … and it's not important at all [laugh]. When you lose a child nothing's important in your life. I found that out. I felt that. I'd never really looked at it that way but, yes, it does change you a little bit and I think dads sometimes can get left out, can't they? I think dads can get left behind a little bit because the focus is on the mum, the grieving mum, the poorly mum and he's suffering every bit. Oh, sure he's not gone through the physical pain and the problems but he's suffering. Everything you're feeling he's suffering just as much I'm sure. They do get overlooked a little bit and because they're expected to be the strong, the rock, the support but who's supporting [them].

A traumatic event is seen as something exceptional, something that marks an individual out as different (Erikson, 1991; Alexander,

2012). As Layne (2012) argues, regardless of how common pregnancy loss is in society, it tends to be experienced by individuals as an extraordinary event. The experience of losing a baby is clearly an extreme and atypical experience. As demonstrated by our respondents, however, while the pain and trauma of losing a baby never goes away, it does just become the 'new normal' – part of their everyday routine. Anna, who lost baby Lily three years before our interview, articulated this:

> You think you're going to feel, the kind of sorrow that you feel at the start, and the kind of overwhelming sadness, you think that's going to last forever. And it doesn't. It doesn't last forever. What it does is just become a new normal [...] a different threshold for pain, and a different outlook on life.

The trauma of losing a baby clearly affected parents' sense of identity, who they were and their place in the social world (Thompson and Walsh, 2010). Several participants in the study discussed the ways in which losing a child is the worst thing that could happen to anyone, because it challenges the normal order of things. Some women did raise the issue of gender differences again. Women often felt that their male partners had been changed by the experience of baby loss but that they had suffered in silence. This is something that we will continue to explore throughout this book. While baby loss strongly impacted on parents' sense of self-identity, however, parents were seldom alone in their grief. The final substantive section of this chapter therefore moves on to explore collective experiences of trauma and grief.

Collective trauma, grief and support

As Erikson argues, trauma is often understood as a lonely and isolated experience because those who experience it 'so often drift away from the everyday moods and understandings that govern social life'. However, he also argues that, paradoxically, such drifting away is accompanied by 'revised views of the world' that can become the new basis for communality (Erikson, 1991: 471). While respondents tended to discuss their own personal sense of trauma and shock, their grief was also often collectively felt. Feelings of collective trauma and grief often began in the hospital with professionals and family members. Health professionals who were with parents when they lost their baby during pregnancy or birth often shared in parents' shock and grief. It was not unusual, for example, for health professionals to cry with parents when their baby died. This is something that parents often found hugely comforting, as Anna articulates: 'the midwife that delivered her [baby Lily], and I think this is nice, people would say it's unprofessional, I think it was nice, she just stood and cried. Because it was so shocking.'

One of the things that parents often found particularly challenging after their baby had died was telling friends and members of their wider community about their loss. During her interview, for example, Olivia commented on how hard it was going to her neighbour's house to tell her that her baby Ian had died. She could see the trauma that this news inflicted on her neighbour, who wasn't sure how to respond:

> In terms of how people deal with us there is an element of, and I really appreciate this, isn't it terrifying to be faced with a bereaved parent? It's such a shocking and awful thing. I remember going next door and telling my next-door neighbour and I knocked on the door and told her what happened I just remember seeing her shaking and her voice was trembling and I completely get that overwhelming, oh, my goodness [small laugh] what on earth do I say to this woman who has just told me that her baby's died? So I've actually had a very … I've tried to put people at ease, [be] upfront and tell people what I want and what I need.

While it was often hard for parents to inform members of their wider family and community, it was also difficult for them to inform work colleagues. Some parents, however, found comfort in colleagues knowing what had happened and sharing in their grief with them. Anna, for example, informed her line manager, who then read Anna's text message out to other work colleagues, who were very distressed to hear the news. Sharing the news in this way, and knowing that work colleagues felt upset, helped Anna to feel less alone in her grief:

> And I sent this text message to my closest friends, to some members of my family, and to my manager, 'cause I thought, if I just send her

that now, I then won't have to have any more conversations about it, and I don't want to talk about it. And she said, and I received that, and I went onto the floor, 'cause we have an open plan office, she said, I went onto the floor, and she said, I didn't know what else to say, so I just read out your text message, and she said and everybody was visibly upset, and she said there were certain members of staff that had to leave because they were just so upset. And it was so, they're the kind of things we want to know, because as horrible as that sounds, it does make you less alone in your grief, if other people grieve with you. Although at the time you can't take anybody else's grief on, at least you know that it means something to somebody.

Erikson (1991) has argued that individuals who may not be connected to one another, but who share a traumatic experience, can seek one another out and form a commonality on that basis. Sharing in a traumatic experience can involve the creation of a common language, a kinship among those who have come to see themselves as different. This was certainly the case for participants in our study, who often found comfort through connecting with others who had experienced the loss of a baby. Some participants sought collective support through organised UK-based baby loss charities such as Sands or the Lullaby Trust. Knowing that other people have gone through baby loss and found a way to survive was a huge source of comfort to parents. This was articulated by Olivia:

> I'm of the opinion that your child has died, you should take every piece of help anybody will possibly offer you and give it a go. I actually think I probably don't need it but that while there's still a huge amount of change going on in my life, getting through the first anniversaries, getting through a subsequent pregnancy, that it's helpful. What I find the most helpful is meeting other people that have been through this, so Sands, the Lullaby Trust. I've also been lucky enough through other connections to meet various other people.

Although baby loss occurs to individual mothers, fathers and couples, as our data shows it is also an experience that is collectively and communally felt – with professionals, family members, neighbours and work colleagues. For many participants, survival of trauma was also contingent on reaching out and connecting with others who had been through similar experiences. This, we argue, suggests the need to acknowledge the dialectical relationship between the individual and society in our framing of trauma and baby loss. We will expand on this further in this chapter's conclusion.

Conclusion

This chapter has centred its analysis on respondents' experiences of trauma, focusing on the initial traumatic event itself and the immediate aftermath. Research on trauma, as articulated in the introduction, has tended to be driven by medicine and more recently by psychology. While recognising the psychological and physiological impact that the loss of a baby can, and does, have on parents, we have sought to emphasise the ways in which trauma is also mediated by the social. The geographical site where parents experienced their trauma, along with their interaction with others present 'on scene', clearly framed their initial experiences of baby loss. The embodied and sensory nature of parents' experience – what they could see, feel and hear during the initial trauma – was also deeply influenced by social relationships. It is important to recognise, therefore, the ways in which the psychological and physical (both geographical and physiological) intersects with 'the social' to frame parental experience of trauma.

Parents' experiences of trauma in this context also appeared to be informed by gender. In our study, mothers were almost always with their baby when it died – either literally through giving birth, or because the baby was in their care. By contrast, men were often physically absent. While men did sometimes act as direct participants, for example by giving their baby CPR, their main role was to act as an eyewitness to the unfolding trauma, providing testimonials about what had occurred. They did, however, also bear witness to an unspeakable loss. Men's roles here could, therefore, be reflective of what Robinson and Hockey (2011) have referred to as masculinity in transition, as they were both active fathers and partners, while also sometimes reverting to more traditional masculine roles of breadwinner and protector (Reed, 2012). Furthermore, while gender could influence parents' direct experience of trauma, it also seemed to feed into their experiences of PTSD. Women were more likely both to discuss and to be diagnosed with PTSD, something often highlighted by the broader literature on mental health (Murphy et al., 2014).

When bringing a social perspective to the area of trauma, one of the things that sociologists have sought to do is examine the differences between individual and collective experiences. Much of the sociological literature so far has tended to be focused on examining experiences of collective trauma (for example, the Holocaust or the Vietnam War) (Alexander, 2012). When dealing with parental experiences of baby loss, however, we have sought to put forward a dialectical approach. Parents in our study experienced baby loss trauma as individuals – as mothers and fathers. Trauma, in this way, often threatens parents' sense of identity and their place in the social world – their sense of ontological security (Thompson and Walsh, 2010). However, while baby loss trauma is experienced on an individual basis, it is also collectively felt. By this we mean that others – health professionals, family members, neighbours, co-workers – all share in the experience of loss. When trying to deal with their individual grief, parents also often reached out to others. Not only did this bring about new forms of community, but it was also often used as a strategy by parents for long-term survival.

Finally, sociologists writing about various aspects of social life (from popular culture to work) often highlight the ways in which mundane everyday activities can become exceptional (Highmore, 2002; Robinson, 2008, 2015). Similarly, experiences and activities that might be framed as spectacular and extreme can become part of normal everyday life (Granter et al., 2015). Trauma is often used in a colloquial sense to refer to the response to participating in relatively mundane activities (for example, being traumatised by taking an examination at school) (Hirschberger, 2018). To say that an individual, or group of people, have experienced trauma, however, tends to refer to them being privy to an event (or sequence of events) that is exceptional and distressing, often an encounter with or witnessing of death (Galea et al., 2003; Smelser, 2004; Alexander, 2012). For parents in our study, the trauma experienced through baby loss was extreme and catastrophic; it was not, however, a one-off exceptional event. This trauma became a 'new normal' for parents, part of the fabric of everyday social life. We will return to this juxtaposition of the everyday and the extreme in other chapters. In the next chapter, however, we will focus on decision-making.

Note

1 The *Diagnostic and Statistical Manual of Mental Disorders* (*DSM*) is the classificatory system and diagnostic tool published by the American Psychiatric Association. It is used to identify and diagnose mental disorders.

Chapter 2

Decisions

Decision-making is a central part of our everyday social lives – from deciding what clothes to wear to bigger decisions around careers and sexual partnerships. According to Schwarz (2018), decision-making may be based on formal calculation, informal lengthy deliberation or may be totally spontaneous. Regardless of how decisions are made, however, they are always framed within the context of choice. Choice, as Schwarz goes on to argue, is widely experienced as a pervasive aspect of human life, particularly in contemporary Western society. As Giddens argues, 'in post-traditional contexts, we have no choice but to choose how to be and how to act' (1994: 54). While choice is seen by many as a positive attribute of contemporary society, sociologists have often taken a more critical view, highlighting the ways in which the decisions individuals make are not necessarily based on free choice, but are rather informed and constrained by wider social structures (Bauman, 2007; Hughes, 2010; Nettleton, 2021). As Schwarz (2018: 849) argues, sociologists, therefore are often interested in uncovering hidden determinants of choice.

In contemporary society, biological life, as Rose (2001) has argued, is firmly entrenched in the domain of decision and choice. This is something that has been particularly debated in the area of women's reproductive health (Reed, 2012). Women's rights to make decisions over their reproductive health have been central to feminist debates for several decades (Markens et al., 2003). As new reproductive technologies emerged and developed during the late 1970s and 1980s, some feminists warned of the patriarchal desire to control reproduction encapsulated in these developments (Corea, 1985). The notion of reproductive choice and autonomy became central, therefore, to much subsequent feminist work on reproduction (Petchesky, 1984). While highlighting the importance of choice, however, feminist authors have also questioned women's ability to make free and autonomous decisions. Earle and Letherby (2007), for example, argue that reproductive control is merely an illusion and that reproductive experiences must be understood within the context of contemporary social and medical discourses which influence the choices and control that woman have.

This chapter explores the issue of choice in life and death decision-making around reproductive loss. Drawing on data from the study, the chapter focuses on three key aspects of life and death decision-making: parent decision-making during *life* focusing on late termination of pregnancy after the diagnosis of severe fetal anomaly, professional decision-making about when to attempt to *restart life* through the resuscitation of pre-term infants or when to *end life* by turning off neonatal life support. The chapter mainly centres its analysis on *after-death* decision-making, focusing on the post-mortem. By exploring the complex and often urgent nature of parental and professional decision-making during reproductive loss, this chapter seeks to extend existing feminist debates on reproductive choice and decision-making (Press and Browner, 1997; Kerr, 2004) and contribute to wider sociological debates on the social constraints of choice.

Start- and end-of-life decision-making

The termination of pregnancy (TOP) due to the diagnosis of fetal anomaly is not something that is usually considered in the context of debates on baby loss. According to Pitt et al. (2016), the politicised and polarising nature of international critiques of pregnancy termination means that the voices of women who experience late termination for fetal anomaly often remain unheard. The anti-abortion movement and the disability rights critique of prenatal diagnosis and subsequent pregnancy termination decisions are two elements of this debate (Hubbard, 1997; Shakespeare, 1999). Much existing literature on TOP has focused on first and second trimester screening and diagnostic testing for chromosomal anomalies such as Down's Syndrome (Rapp, 2000). Feminist scholars have tended to question the notion of choice in this context, arguing that although it appears as though women are offered the choice to have screening and testing, on receipt of a positive diagnosis abortion is often presented as the normal course of action (Rothman, 1986). Less is known, however, about choice and decision-making when severe anomalies are found in late pregnancy, when women are almost at term and when termination procedures may also include the controversial practice of feticide (Graham et al., 2008). In such instances, as Pitt et al. (2016) argue, women often experience an acute embodied transition from live pregnancy to pregnancy loss.

While some parents are faced with making difficult decisions around termination, professionals (in consultation with parents) often face the heart-breaking decision of when to attempt resuscitation or turn off neonatal life support. Decisions around withholding or withdrawing life-sustaining treatments in the perinatal context are usually made in obstetric wards or neonatal Intensive Care Units (NICUs). Decisions are made by professionals based on their judgements about what is in the best interests of the child and their future quality of life (McHaffie et al., 1999). Facilitating decision-making and implementing decisions about life-sustaining treatments is a core part of clinical practice for doctors working in intensive care (Manalo, 2013). The decision about how and when to discontinue treatment can be controversial and complex, often posing significant ethical challenges to healthcare professionals (Soltani Gerdfaramarzi and Bazmi, 2020). Conflict can often occur between families and clinical teams in such situations over issues relating to pain management and decisions over treatment (Way et al., 2002).

As well as being faced with decisions around whether/when to restart or end life, parents must also make a number of decisions after their baby has died, from naming their baby to post-mortem consent. While a post-mortem can play an important role in understanding the cause of death of babies and infants (Downe et al., 2012; Lewis et al., 2019), research continues to show that the incidence of consent for post-mortems is decreasing (Stock et al., 2010; Lewis et al., 2019). Parents often feel overwhelmed with information after their baby has died and can fear the invasive nature of the examination. Decision-making around post-mortems, therefore, remains a difficult topic for both professionals and parents (Heazell et al., 2012; Reed et al., 2021). In the following sections we focus on exploring start- and end-of-life decision-making around these three areas – termination of pregnancy, end-of-life support and post-mortem examination. Drawing on data from the study, the chapter explores the ways in which parents are offered a choice 'officially' in each area – for example, the choice of whether to terminate a pregnancy, end life support or opt for a post-mortem. As we will show, however, parents and professionals seldom experience this as *real* choice. This is because, in many cases, none of the options would ultimately alter the outcome of reproductive loss (Toerien et al., 2018).

'Choice' and 'loss': fetal anomalies and the late termination of pregnancy

According to Pitt et al. (2016), women terminating pregnancy due to severe fetal anomaly often experience a transition from being a pregnant woman to being a woman dealing with loss. Due to the sensitive and politically charged nature of debates over termination, however, these experiences are often absent from wider discussions on reproductive loss. Existing literature has tended to draw attention to the traumatic nature of decision-making in this context. Research has often highlighted the importance of offering women choice over how and where termination takes place – in gynaecology or labour wards (Fisher and Lafarge, 2015). Furthermore, if termination takes place after a certain gestation period (twenty-one weeks plus six days in the UK), feticide may be used to ensure that the baby is not born alive, often causing additional trauma (Graham et al., 2008; Pitt et al., 2016).[1] This section focuses on exploring professional and parental experience of TOP due to severe fetal anomalies. Through this process we aim to highlight the complex and deeply traumatic nature of decision-making around this issue. We will problematise the notion of choice in this context, while articulating the need to analyse experiences of TOP through the lens of loss (Pitt et al., 2016). In doing so we acknowledge that our data on the actual experience of TOP is limited, and therefore make these claims very tentatively.

One specialist consultant gynaecology nurse, Jackie, took part in our study. Her role mostly involved dealing with early pregnancy loss. Jackie usefully outlined the differences between early and late stage termination. She also distinguished between termination for social reasons and termination due to the identification of fetal anomaly. She highlights the importance of treating women going through late termination as labouring women:

> We only offer surgical terminations up to thirteen weeks [in this anonymised clinic]. So, all our women, whether they'd want to be pregnant or don't want to be pregnant would be having it done medically from thirteen weeks upwards. But socially we only do them up to eighteen weeks [...] It's rare that we would get anybody that's twenty weeks [in the gynaecology clinic] in any case for fetal abnormality. They more than likely would want to go to the labour ward. And they often do want to, because they want to be treated like a labouring woman, as opposed to a woman that's having a termination.

Obstetricians are often the professionals who support women in their decision-making around second and third trimester termination due to fetal anomaly. Gina, an obstetrician, talked about the difficulties women face when making decisions about termination of pregnancy in this context. She felt that in these instances TOP should be treated as a form of loss and that women going through this experience should be offered comparable support to those experiencing other forms of perinatal loss. This would include, for example, the opportunity to participate in memory-making activities:

> I've got a couple of ladies coming in to terminate their pregnancy, well one to terminate their pregnancy and one who's actually coming today, she was planning to terminate but she's actually miscarried, you know the heartbeat's gone and she will be offered that sort of thing because it's very much a wanted pregnancy it's just she's having to make a decision, you know, they're having to make decisions that are very difficult for them. And then they may also as well, some of them decide to have things like there are sort of, you can get footprints made of the baby, you know, in like a clay, that sort of stuff and quite a lot of them will sometimes then if they've got that print have it made into like a little necklet or, so there's lots of mementos and things that are available and they are encouraged as well, well not encouraged but asked whether there's anything that they want to put with the baby, you know, so some of them will have, some of these babies remember will have siblings and the siblings may want something to go with the baby.

Only one parent in our study, Yasmine, had undergone TOP due to the identification of severe fetal anomalies at around seventeen weeks' gestation. Yasmine discussed how difficult the decision to terminate had been, because at seventeen weeks the baby felt very real to both her and her partner. Feticide was not used in this instance because the fetus was under twenty-one weeks' gestation. Yasmine had developed a deep bond with her baby. Her main concern was that she did not want her baby to suffer:

> And he [the obstetrician] gave us the information we needed then, as I say, for the decisions in terms of, you know, the fact that then we could decide either to terminate the pregnancy or not [...] Questions coming up, of course, was, you know, if you do decide to have a termination, it was going to be a proper delivery, and then what happens, would there be any chance of the baby being born alive. And it was going to die ... then he would say ... you know, so he let us know that it would die during delivery. And then we wanted to know whether there was a likelihood of it suffering any pain during that process, you know, all those sorts of things [...] And all that information was provided carefully and very ... you know, so that you knew what the best decision for your child would be, essentially. Because by then it was very much our child.

While obstetricians supported parents around TOP decision-making, after termination parents often turned to other professionals such as hospital chaplains for emotional and spiritual support. Chaplains frequently provided parents with an invaluable source of aftercare and support. If requested, they would conduct a ceremony for parents to mark the birth and death of their baby. This was articulated by a Church of England chaplain, Frank, who explained that 'it's often when a decision's been made and a termination has happened, and then we're called to do some sort of ceremony because the parents want to mark what's happened. So I think actually around the point of decision-making we're not always involved.'

Receiving neutral and non-judgemental support from hospital chaplains was important for some parents, particularly those who had a strong religious faith. Maryam, a Muslim chaplain, commented that parents from the Muslim community often felt unable to talk about their decisions with religious leaders in their own community and therefore sought religious solace from the chaplain in the hospital.

She stated that their role as hospital chaplains is to support families, not to make judgements about any decisions they might have made to terminate a pregnancy:

> They [parents] won't go to the community leaders with it because it's that oh well I'm gonna be judged. For me every time I see a patient we're not here to judge that's not our job wherever you'd seen us. Nobody whether it's within the hospital or out of the hospital, nobody … who are we, you know, and I'm always having that conversation with patients just putting them at ease and then they'll open up and speak to you.

For several decades feminists have problematised the notion of choice in the context of prenatal screening and diagnosis (Press and Browner, 1997; Markens et al., 2003; Earle and Letherby, 2007; Reed, 2012). We acknowledge that we have limited data on the actual experience of TOP and therefore must be cautious regarding any claims we make on this issue. Our data does indicate, however, that decision-making in the context of TOP for fetal anomaly is often difficult and traumatic, and that choice in such contexts is often illusory (Earle and Letherby, 2007). Continuing with a focus on decision-making, we move on in the next section to explore decisions relating to resuscitation and neonatal life support.

Deciding when to restart or end life

When a baby is born prematurely, health professionals are often faced with difficult decisions about when and whether to attempt resuscitation (Reed et al., 2020). Similarly, when a baby is in neonatal intensive care and on mechanical life support, professionals, in consultation with parents, must make difficult decisions around when to withhold/withdraw life support (McHaffie et al., 1999). This section focuses on exploring some of the difficulties and grey areas around decision-making in this life and death context, further problematising the notion of choice.

The issue of when and whether to resuscitate a fetus or baby is often problematic for emergency health workers such as paramedics, as they are often first on scene in cases of miscarriage, late fetal loss, SIDS and SUDI, and are required to make rapid decisions about whether and when to resuscitate (Reed et al., 2020). Similarly, when a baby is born prematurely in hospital, health professionals (such as midwives, neonatologists, paediatricians etc.) must make difficult decisions about when to resuscitate. Although continued improvements in neonatal and obstetric care in the UK have led to an increase in survival rates among premature babies, complex decision-making over when and whether to resuscitate cannot be reduced to basic rules (Mahase, 2019). In our study Wendy, a senior midwife, talked about some of the challenges regarding resuscitation practice for extremely premature babies born under twenty-seven weeks' gestation:[2]

> I think there's a grey area around twenty-three-week babies, twenty-two-week babies and if parents ask for resuscitation obviously you get the paediatricians to come and see them and they will counsel them and say at twenty-two weeks your baby … it's cruelty to do this to your baby almost. At twenty-three weeks it's a bit different because obviously people read about these miracles of twenty-three week babies. So I've known paediatricians come and just very gently go through the whole process of resuscitation, and they've sat down and they said if your baby shows any promising signs we will do the best we can. And occasionally they'll go just not through the motions, that sounds like they're not trying, but they will show parents that they are there, and they are trying…

While decision-making relating to resuscitation was often very challenging for professionals, so too was decision-making around when to withdraw treatment and effectively end life. In the hospital context, consultant obstetricians, neonatologists or paediatricians tended to take responsibility for breaking bad news to parents and for making difficult end-of-life decisions. In these complex situations, it was the senior doctors – the consultants – who tended to be most involved with the parents. This was articulated by consultant neonatologist Brian, who explained that 'most of the initial conversations are directed through the consultant. So breaking bad news, breaking good news, making end-of-life decisions. Making … getting parents involved in treatment choices is pretty much led by the consultants.'

Religious-cultural backgrounds often profoundly influence decision-making around death (Manalo, 2013). While senior doctors took responsibility for making difficult life and death decisions, therefore, hospital chaplains also often played an important support role for parents during this time, as Frank's account below shows:

> Yes, so certainly around at what point might life support be switched off, both with adults and with babies. We may be called in to help someone talk through that and what a Christian, for me, perspective might be on that and obviously my colleagues of other faiths would have that from other faith perspectives.

According to Cortezzo and Meyer (2020), when goals have transitioned to end-of-life care, parents' main concern is that their child will not experience pain and physical suffering. They hope for a peaceful death with minimal discomfort for their child. When it comes to moving from active treatment to palliative care, professionals in our study often talked about the need to be honest with parents about what might happen, and about their baby's chances of survival. Tammy, a trainee paediatrician, stated that there is never a right time to talk to parents about this issue, but that it is important to raise the possibility with parents from the beginning:

> Very often, the question is when do we talk about palliative care? And I'm one of those people who say right at the beginning, there is never a right time, but this family needs to know that there will come a point where it is the right thing to do, you don't wait for things to be so poorly where everyone is upset, mostly the family, and you walk in and say, now is the time to pull out, because that's never been part of your thought process, because there's thought processes to treat and fight and keep going, but with any condition, with anything in life, there is that choice and, again, palliation is not active withdrawal, palliation is keeping comfortable and saying, this is enough in terms of what we're doing for them.

Tammy went on to discuss how difficult it is to make the decision to withdraw or end life support. She was keen to show that health professionals would only reach this end point when all treatment options had been exhausted. She also emphasised the fact that, although the consultant would be the one to take overall responsibility for decisions made, nevertheless end-of-life decision-making is always something that is discussed and agreed by the whole clinical team:

> That decision is never taken lightly, it's a very hard decision and if a medical team has reached that point, we have given it everything, more than everything, you know you start pushing limits for every

single aspect of treatment, if we have reached that point, there has already been millions of discussions, you know, between the senior most people around, between the nursing team, between everyone possible, before even that subject is approached to a family.

According to Way et al. (2002), families may believe they are causing the patient's death by agreeing to withdraw life support. In such instances, relatives can feel less burdened by guilt if clinicians strongly recommend that life support be withdrawn rather than asking the family to make the decision. In our study, Tammy felt strongly that parents should not be put in the terrible position of feeling that they must make the decision over whether and when to withdraw or end life support. She problematises the very notion of choice in this context:

> I think the way we are phrasing it, families feel they have to make the call and I think that's awful for a family and I often sit down with them later and say, please realise that if we have come and spoken to you, we think we have reached that point a long time ago and it's not a decision that we're asking you to make, it's just that we realistically think there is no way forward and that's us, as doctors, you know, they feel that it is a choice, but it isn't, it's a funny thing isn't it? If you're so sick and you've been so sick that we have done so much for them, what is the choice then?

In their study on choice in a neurology outpatient clinic in the UK, Toerien et al. (2018) found that patients were offered formal choice in that they could try different treatment options. In their study, however, choice did not exist in a substantive sense because often no option was presented to patients that would make a real difference to their health outcomes. Similar issues were raised around end-of-life decision-making in our study. As Tammy's quote shows, while it might appear that parents are being given agency and choice over when to turn off life support for their baby, there really is no choice at all. By the time this stage has been reached, health professionals will have exhausted all other clinical options. The lack of real agency in choice highlighted in this particular clinical context reinforces broader sociological arguments about the ways in which individual choice is often constrained by a range of different factors (Bauman, 2007; Hughes, 2010; Schwarz, 2018). This is something we will consider further in the conclusion to this chapter.

In the next section, however, we move on to explore after-death decision-making.

After death: post-mortem decision-making

Once their baby has died parents are often faced with making several different decisions in a short space of time, from what to name their baby, through to decisions over memory-making and funeral planning. We will focus on the issue of memory-making and funeral planning in more depth in Chapter 6. In this chapter, however, we focus specifically on one of the key clinical decisions that parents must face once a baby has died, the decision over whether to consent to a post-mortem examination for their baby. A hospital post-mortem by consent was not an option for 57% of parents in our study. These parents had been through the coronial post-mortem process due to their baby's unexpected death. Out of those parents who could give consent, 44% agreed and 56% refused. The issue of disagreement between parents about whether to have the examination or not did not arise for our participants – though in England and Wales there is currently an absence of clear guidance for professionals about what should happen in this instance. It is usually the case that if a mother wants a post-mortem, then her wishes take precedence, as the results may help her in the management of any future pregnancies. It is less clear what should happen if the father wants the examination and the mother does not (Sands, 2017). Parents in our study identified several reasons for not consenting to a post-mortem. These included information (too little or too much), lack of encouragement, wider cultural representations of post-mortems, protective parenting, fear of the invasive nature of the examination, emotional trauma, and having no further questions about the death. As we will explore in this section, parental choice over post-mortems is not something that is made freely, but is strongly mediated and constrained by cultural, social and clinical factors.

Multiple decisions, information and time

After their baby's death parents tended to be overcome with shock and grief. At this time, however, they are often presented with a huge amount of information and asked to make decisions on a range of difficult issues. When faced with such a large volume of information, parents in our study often found it hard to prioritise. The decision over whether to consent to a post-mortem often seemed to get lost during this process. This was articulated by Anna, who lost her baby Lily at twenty-three weeks and declined a post-mortem examination:

> They give you a lot of information, when we first went in, and it was, you're going to have this baby now, they sort of give you all this information about decisions you'll have to make, and they bundle it in with everything. So, they bundle it in with topics like, holding your baby, naming your baby, saying goodbye to your baby, funeral for your baby, post-mortem for your baby. Like, everything's grouped in together. So you suddenly, you have to prioritise in your head, about which bits are important.

Parents often felt that a post-mortem did not seem as important as other decisions they had to make after their baby had died (such as funeral arrangements). This was articulated by Charlotte, who declined a post-mortem examination for her baby boy Leo, who was stillborn at term:

> Yeah, because it's like where are we going to bury him, I don't even know how we are going to pay for a funeral, I've never done a funeral, I mean, Leo was the first person that I know that died. I've got all sets of grandparents, I'm so lucky in that I've got to this age before anyone's died and then as if it was him, and I had no experience of anyone dying, especially in the job that I used to work in, I feel like I spent a lot of time around death and grief and grieving relatives and things like that but I didn't really understand it, I don't think you do until it happens close to home. So I feel like there were a lot bigger things at play rather than a post-mortem, because I did think it would be really down to me. Well, I assumed originally that it was going to be like a coroner job, and then when there was like have a think whether you want to or not, and it was all, oh, I don't know, I don't know.

Being presented with so much information as well as being asked to make multiple decisions after their baby has died clearly impacts parents' ability to make free and informed decisions about a post-mortem. Conversations about the post-mortem get lost in the broader context of decisions that need to be made about other issues. As other studies have shown, receiving the right kind of information at an appropriate time from trained professionals is crucial to improving future consent rates for post-mortems (Rose et al., 2006; Stock et al., 2010; Downe et al., 2012). In the following section we move on to explore some of the other factors that influence parental decision-making over post-mortems, beginning with the fact that parents often feel that their baby has suffered enough.

Reasons for non-consent

Research has consistently shown that parents are often reluctant to consent to a post-mortem for their baby due to fears over the invasive nature of the procedure (Rankin et al., 2002). Parents in our study articulated similar concerns, often refusing consent because they felt that their baby had suffered enough. Parents wanted to preserve their baby's personhood during that interstitial phase between life and death, in the mortuary, and before a funeral had taken place, and did not, therefore, want to put them through any further testing. This was articulated by Una, whose baby boy was born stillborn at twenty weeks: 'We requested not to have a post-mortem because his tiny body had been through enough and we knew it wouldn't tell us anything we didn't know about why he died.'

Parents were not only reluctant to consent to a post-mortem due to their fears over what the examination entailed, but were also worried about the length of time that their baby would be away from them during the examination. Not all parents in our study had access to hospitals with specialist perinatal pathology staff and appropriate paediatric facilities. In these cases, babies might be sent to other hospitals in a different location for post-mortem examination. This could extend the time that a baby would be away from their parents. Parents often could not bear their baby being away from them for any length of time, as Anna told us: 'I wouldn't have even given them her [baby Lily], because I wouldn't have wanted her away from me for that long. [You have] to put your life on hold, just waiting and waiting and waiting.'

Existing research has shown how parental and professional interaction can have a huge impact on parent decision-making about post-mortems. As Lewis et al. (2019: 1249) argue, parents often look to professionals for guidance and require a conversation about the post-mortem that is both 'open' and 'honest'. In our study professionals often played a big part in influencing parents' decision-making over post-mortems. Esther and Ricky lost their baby Oliver one year prior to our interview. He was born prematurely and died at twenty-five weeks. They decided not to consent to a post-mortem. This was partly because they felt that they had received enough information about his cause of death, but also because they felt that Oliver had been through enough during his short life. Esther and Ricky both felt that their decision to decline a post-mortem was strongly supported by the neonatologist who was looking after their baby. This is articulated by Esther in the quote below:

> And he [the doctor] was saying we don't want to put you through it, we don't want to put him through it but we might not have a choice. And then the coroner came back and said no, we don't need a post-mortem. But it wasn't just the one reason, it was, also he's pre-term, it was also his respiratory distress. But we just didn't want it for him. We know why he's died.

The findings of several studies have shown that not all health professionals are aware of the benefits of post-mortem examination and therefore don't always offer it to parents as an option (Okah, 2002; Rose et al., 2006). While lack of formal training in taking consent is an issue highlighted by some studies (Stolman et al., 1994; Rose et al., 2006; Downe et al., 2012), other research shows that professionals often worry about upsetting familes by starting a conversation about a post-mortem (Stolman et al., 1994; Rose et al., 2006). Some parents in our study felt that professionals had strongly deterred them from consenting to a post-mortem because they – the professionals – did not feel that it would provide parents with answers. Anna, for example, felt that she had been encouraged by professionals not to have a post-mortem.

> And as the days went on, and we hadn't had her, you have more time to think about things. And I can't remember if they revisited it or not. I think they probably did, and I only say this, 'cause I don't want to be unfair to them, but we did have a conversation after that, about a post-mortem, because they'd said that there really wasn't a lot of point. It was going to take six weeks, and you probably wouldn't get any answers. And I remember thinking, it sounds like her opinion, this, but it was an opinion that I valued, and it was the matron at the time.

In support of the findings of other studies, therefore, our research shows that multiple factors influenced parent decision-making over post-mortem consent – from problems with the timing and amount of information given to parents through to the influence of professionals. These are issues that need further attention if consent rates are to improve in the future (Rose et al., 2006; Stock et al., 2010; Downe et al., 2012). What was striking in our study, however, was the number of parents who regretted not consenting to a post-mortem, which is something we explore in the next section.

Experiencing regret

In their study on autopsy after stillbirth, Holste et al. (2011) found that parents were generally satisfied with their decision to agree or disagree to autopsy. Data from our study on perinatal post-mortem suggests that parents who did not consent to a post-mortem examination could regret it. Anna, for example, articulated feelings of regret at not having consented to a post-mortem. When Anna gave birth to Lily prematurely at twenty-three weeks, health professionals speculated that this was due to her having an incompetent cervix.[3] When Anna had her six-week medical check-up after her loss, however, the doctor felt that they could not be sure about this diagnosis because no post-mortem had taken place. This led Anna to regret her decision not to give her consent for a post-mortem. She felt that professionals should have been more honest about the benefits of the examination at the time of her loss:

> If I'd have known, if there'd been something genetically wrong with her, then I would know for future pregnancies, because if there's something genetically wrong, and this is definitely going to happen again, and there's no way of preventing it, I could kind of do with knowing that now, not when I have to go through this again […] So yeah, I do wish that, in some ways, I'd had a post-mortem. I still don't think I would have liked the idea of her not being here for six weeks, and I may have still chosen not to have one, based on that, but I think they should have been more honest about the benefits of it, because they were so negative about it, I was like, well why would anyone choose to have one?

Not consenting to a post-mortem had a significant impact on several parents in our study, who, like Anna, regretted not consenting but also felt as though they had not been encouraged to consent by the professionals. This was expressed by Charlotte:

> And also I wish we had been encouraged to have a post-mortem, that is something that doesn't make sense to me, why I didn't do it, why we didn't do it, why they [the health professionals] didn't encourage it … the consultant came in and said have you thought about a post-mortem, we were like, we don't know, and he was like, well, it's basically just like cot death only he didn't make it to his cot [stillborn], and it's just going to prolong things, and they probably won't find anything anyway…

While some parents who had not consented to a post-mortem regretted their decision, those parents whose babies did go through a post-mortem (either coronial or consented) appeared not to regret this and often found the process beneficial. More specifically, the post-mortem appeared to assist parents with emotional and diagnostic closure, as well as with future pregnancy planning (Reed et al., 2021). This was articulated by Wayne, whose baby daughter Flo died during labour. Both he and his partner had consented to a hospital post-mortem:

> But, of course, finding out what's happened is really important in thinking about your future family. So, you know, is there something genetic or is there something medical that we might be avoiding in the future. So the post-mortem … the desire to find out why, that was the main reason, you know, is there something that we can do to avoid this happening again, essentially […] Yeah, don't regret it, don't regret the post-mortem at all. Never really think about the post-mortem. I don't think about the post-mortem. Yeah, the only thing that occasionally … obviously, think about her sometimes, think about what could have been sometimes. I mean, it was … yeah, that's it.

While some parents did not consent to a post-mortem, several articulated feelings of regret later. As we will go on to explore in subsequent chapters, parents who did consent, or who had undergone coronial post-mortem, tended to feel some relief that their baby had been through a post-mortem, even if the examination did not always provide them with clear-cut answers. Furthermore, what we have started to show in this section is the way in which parents' ability to make free and informed choices about post-mortem examination is often mediated by their interaction with professionals. Parents often feel that professionals discourage them from consenting. We will move on in the final substantive section of the chapter, therefore, to shed light on the role of professionals in the consent process.

Difficult conversations and the process of consent

As argued in the previous section, parental interaction with professionals can have a huge impact on parent decision-making on post-mortem examination (Lewis et al., 2019). As part of our research, through interviews and go-along tours, we invited professionals to tell us about the post-mortem process and about how they approached the issue of consent. Professionals began by telling us about the changes in consent processes in the aftermath of the organ retention scandal of 1999, when it was discovered that body organs and tissues of babies and children were used by some UK hospitals for purposes other than autopsy (Sheach Leith, 2007). Informed consent was subsequently placed at the centre of the UK's Human Tissue Act of 2004 (2006 in Scotland), and has remained an extremely emotive and contested issue ever since, particularly in the context of paediatric post-mortems. One of the consultant obstetricians we interviewed as part of our study – Ethan – talked about the ways in which post-mortem consent has now become more formal:

> It's certainly more formal, because of the issue they had in Bristol and Liverpool with bits of bodies going missing, so I think, since then, the process is a lot more formalised. In the past, when I was trainee, you would just document in the notes that post-mortem has been agreed to. I can't recall patients signing a consent form, not off the top of my head, whereas now, there is a very detailed form that they need to go through.

At the time our research, only doctors could take consent (outside the pathology suite) in the two different NHS foundation trusts where the study took place. Professionals felt that this policy related to clinicians having overall legal and medical responsibility. Midwives, however, were often the ones who initiated a conversation with parents about post-mortem consent. They spoke about this as being a difficult conversation to introduce and something that had to be dealt with on a case-by-case basis. This was articulated by senior midwife Wendy:

> So you judge it on how much time you've got basically, because you're usually aware of whether... I mean obviously if a woman is ill then you know you've got a little bit of time on your hands, and you're not going to start talking to her if she's really poorly by then saying oh, and about the post-mortem. So you try and be as sensitive about it as you possibly can. But I will often just say there's certain decisions you need to make about your baby, things like funerals and whether you want any further investigations.

Dave, a consultant neonatologist with thirty years of clinical experience, talked about the difficulties of being open with parents about what the examination entails, because people's perceptions of autopsy are often based on what they see on TV. According to guidelines from the Human Tissue Authority, professionals involved in taking consent for perinatal post-mortem should have observed a post-mortem examination prior to taking consent (HTA Code B:19).[4] Dave emphasised the importance of this policy:

> I think they have seen mortuaries of adults possibly having a post-mortem but in terms of the babies I don't think they ever think about a baby on one of those slabs or if they do it'll be a bit of a nightmare and yet we're trying to describe to them what needs to be done because we have to. You can't or the guidance is that you shouldn't be asking the consent for a post-mortem unless you've been to one yourself. So you do have to know exactly what goes on.

Regardless of who took consent, however, the process was still extremely sensitive and difficult for professionals. Carmen, an anatomical pathology technician (APT) and the mortuary manager, stated that she always gave parents detailed information about the examination before attempting consent. She felt it was crucial to be as honest as possible with family members, especially after the organ retention scandal. She also highlighted the importance of finding an appropriate quiet space in which to take consent:

> When we do consent it's just really finding a nice relaxed area to do it so we like to do it here in the conservatory because it's just a little bit nicer, and we'll just obviously go through... I always talk about the post-mortem before I actually go through the form, so I'll explain

about the incision and it's a really difficult position to be in but I think it's always best that you be honest.

Our data shows diversity in how professionals approached the issue of post-mortem consent. Paediatric pathologists, for example, tended to argue strongly that all parents should at least be offered the opportunity of a post-mortem as a basic right. Other specialists made a judgement call on whether to offer it based on individual parent circumstances. Some doctors did acknowledge that a form of medical paternalism was often in operation during the consent process, as articulated by consultant neonatologist Brian, who explained: 'I'm well aware that our overall post-mortem rate is probably well below what it could be or should be [...] We're probably paternalistic, in terms of making decisions about whether they should have one or not.'

Offering choice and taking informed consent is supposed to protect the rights of patients and militate against medical paternalism. In practice, however, as the quote from Brian suggests, consent is often mediated through an unequal doctor and patient relationship (Corrigan, 2003), whereby health professionals make judgement calls over patient decision-making (Reed et al., 2021). While medical paternalism appeared to play a strong role in parental decision-making in some contexts, in other cases professionals felt that they just didn't try hard enough to encourage parental consent for post-mortem examination. This was articulated by Wendy, the senior midwife:

It'll be obstetricians that do it. So sometimes if that person, that obstetrician, consultant particularly knows that lady, for whatever reason, they've seen them lots and they knew this was going to happen, then they will come back whether they're on duty... Well, whether they're on the labour ward rota or not. And they might say well, I'll do this, it's fine, don't worry about it. But other times it's literally a case of can you please just come and talk to this lady about post-mortems, because she wants to go home and she needs a chat. But you can sometimes ask and I sometimes wonder if that's the right thing to do or not. We'll say to people do you think you will have a post-mortem? And if they say no, rather than say go into it in depth and say well, can we get someone to come and chat to you about that, we'll say okay, that's fine then. And then you'll just go doesn't want post-mortem. So you'll not go down that line any more. You'll not pursue it.

Decision-making around post-mortem examination and taking and giving consent is therefore difficult for both bereaved parents and professionals. For those parents whose babies do not need to undergo a coronial post-mortem, the examination should be presented and offered as a choice. As shown in these last few sections, however, this is clearly not always the case. Parents' ability to choose to consent to a post-mortem is clearly not free but is mediated by a range of factors, including their interactions with professionals. Bias around professionals' own perceptions of post-mortem examination can impact on whether they offer parents a choice and on the kinds of information they impart. This can lead, in some cases, to medical paternalism, whereby doctors use their clinical judgement to make decisions on parents' behalf (Reed et al., 2021). We will move on in the conclusion of this chapter to reflect on the issue of choice more fully.

Conclusion

Choice is viewed as a fundamental and distinguishing feature of contemporary social life. It is supposedly at the heart of neoliberal health and welfare policies which proffer patient centred/shared decision-making in healthcare (Nettleton, 2021). As sociologists have often sought to show, however, choice 'is not an innocent term' (Brown and Webster, 2004: 62) but is something that 'is circumscribed and is invariably compromised by prevailing social norms and values, as well as people's social, economic and cultural resources' (Nettleton, 2021: 130). In this chapter we have sought to highlight the ways in which choice in start- and end-of-life decision-making is socially and culturally mediated and informed by the medical setting in which it takes place. For example, while parents might be offered the choice to terminate a pregnancy or opt to consent to a post-mortem for their baby, such choice is often strongly circumscribed by a medical division of labour and by medical paternalism. Choice in all three contexts, therefore, is often illusory either because it is strongly mediated by social and cultural context, or simply because none of the options that might be offered have any bearing on outcome (Earle and Letherby, 2007; Toerien et al., 2018; Nettleton, 2021).

As highlighted in this chapter, decision-making around late termination of pregnancy due to the identification of severe fetal anomalies is difficult and traumatic for parents. Our data on the actual experience of TOP is quite limited and therefore we are cautious regarding any claims we make on this issue. While women might be offered the formal choice to terminate a pregnancy in this context, such choice might not always be substantively felt by women (Toerien et al., 2018). In such cases babies are often very poorly and may not survive labour; some women even miscarry their baby before termination takes place. Women often feel strongly bonded with their baby during the second and third trimester of pregnancy and frequently experience termination as an embodied sense of loss. Due to the sensitive and politically charged nature of debates over termination, however, these experiences are often absent from wider discussions on reproductive loss (Pitt et al., 2016). As well as exploring late termination of pregnancy due to fetal anomalies within existing feminist debates on choice and prenatal diagnosis (Press and Browner, 1997; Markens et al., 2003; Earle and Letherby, 2007; Reed, 2012), we argue that these experiences should also be explored as a form of reproductive loss.

When a baby is born prematurely, health professionals are often faced with difficult decisions about when and whether to attempt resuscitation (Reed et al., 2020). Similarly, when a baby is in neonatal intensive care and on mechanical life support, professionals, in consultation with parents, must make difficult decisions around when to end life support (McHaffie et al., 1999). In this chapter, we have sought to highlight some of the difficulties and grey areas around professional decision-making over resuscitation and withholding/withdrawing neonatal life support, again problematising the very notion of choice. In the case of ending life support, for example, professionals will often consult with parents over the final decision, despite there often being no other options left. Choice in this instance, therefore, can feel like an illusion (Earle and Letherby, 2007), because no option is being offered that could change the ultimate outcome of death (Toerien et al., 2018). In our study, professionals such as Tammy the paediatric trainee questioned whether attempting to offer choice in such contexts is appropriate because it can make parents feel responsible for their own child's death. Our data suggests the need, therefore, for sociologists to further consider the implications of choice in circumstances where the long-term costs for those responsible for making them are substantial.

Post-mortem decision-making after a baby has died is another area that is challenging for both bereaved parents and professionals. In support of the findings of other studies, our research shows that multiple factors tended to influence parental decision-making over post-mortem consent – from problems with the timing and amount of information given to them through to the influence of professionals. Parental interaction with professionals could also have a huge impact on parental decision-making on post-mortems (Lewis et al., 2019). Several parents in our study either hadn't been offered a post-mortem or felt discouraged by professionals from consenting. Informed consent aims to protect the rights of patients and militate against medical paternalism. As our data shows, however, in practice consent is often mediated through an unequal doctor/patient relationship (Corrigan, 2003; Reed et al., 2021), whereby health professionals make judgement calls over patient decision-making. This not only appears to reinforce the existence of asymmetrical relationship between doctors and parents but also indicates that a strong medical paternalism is at work in this context (Reed et al., 2016). This is something we will return to in other parts of this book. In the next chapter we move on to explore the role of post-mortem examination more fully, highlighting in particular the importance of minimally invasive autopsy.

Notes

1 For full discussion of when and how this is used, see RCOG, 2010.
2 For further information on resuscitation guidelines, see 'Perinatal management of extreme preterm birth before 27 weeks of gestation: A British Association of Perinatal Medicine (BAPM) Framework for Practice' (2019), https://www.bapm.org/ (accessed January 2022).
3 An incompetent or weakened cervix can, in some cases, be identified as a cause of miscarriage. In such cases the muscles of the cervix (the neck of the womb) may appear weaker than usual, causing the cervix to open too early during pregnancy. See https://www.nhs.uk/conditions/miscarriage/ (accessed January 2019).
4 See https://www.hta.gov.uk/guidance-professionals/regulated-sectors/post-mortem/post-mortem-model-consent-forms/sands (accessed August 2022).

Chapter 3

Technology

The use of dissection in autopsy can be traced back to ancient Greece, with the first recorded dissection of the human body occurring around 335–290 BCE (Van den Tweel and Taylor, 2013). 'Seeing' has always been central to this core practice of pathology. According to Prior, one witnesses two orders of dissection: the physical dissection of the flesh and bone and the theoretical/conceptual dissection that has long preceded the former. Both rest on observation: 'The centrality of seeing is embodied in the very terms necropsy – to look at the dead, and autopsy – to see with one's own eyes' (Prior, 1987: 362). The advent of microscopy during the nineteenth century extended the ability to 'look' further into the body, shifting the unit of analysis from bodies and organs to cells. Today a range of techniques and technologies are used in combination to aid dissection and determine cause of death. Visual technologies have become central to this process; for example, the microscope is essential for biopsy and X-rays for examining problems with the skeleton. Despite technological advances in this area, until recently dissection has continued to be revered as the prime technique used to establish cause of death (Prior, 1987). However, with the emerging application of a new generation of visual technologies such as magnetic resonance imaging (MRI), this long-established practice looks set to be transformed.

MRI is currently viewed as the 'gold standard' in healthcare, the epitome of what is possible in medical visualisation (Joyce, 2006). However, its use in autopsy signals the emergence of a new application of the technology. Most commonly associated with identifying problems in the fetal or infant brain, clinicians argue that it can now be used to identify problems with most organs in the body except the heart (Griffiths et al., 2005; Whitby et al., 2006). Its use in life (fetal MRI) and after death (termination and neonatal death) can inform conventional autopsy (Fligner and Dighe, 2011). However, growing evidence suggests that it not only assists pathologists in autopsy, but may obviate the need for dissection or at least minimise the focus on it (Brookes and Hagmann, 2006). Early clinical work in this area also highlights its importance when parents do not wish to consent to an invasive autopsy for religious or other reasons (Watts, 2010; Sebire and Taylor, 2012). Deaths of infants and children are regarded as worthy of maximum investigative resources post-mortem (Prior, 1987). However, it is extremely stressful for parents to be asked for invasive autopsy authorisation (Laing, 2004). MRI stands poised to provide parents with more information on their child's death without the need for invasive dissection, and with an important image that may assist them in the process of memorialisation and grief. The emphasis on MRI use in this context is set to play a key role in both parental experience and clinical practice.

Important sociological questions are raised about the potential of this technology to change both professional practice and parental experience of loss. However, to date there has been limited work in this area. For example, existing research on technologies of death and dying tends to focus on the impact of ventilation and resuscitation technologies in enactments of death (Timmermans, 1998; Hadders, 2009). Similarly, while various studies have focused on the role of ultrasound technology in pregnancy and pregnancy loss (Draper, 2002; Keane, 2009), very little is known about MRI use in this context (Reed, 2013). Drawing on accounts from both parents and professionals, the chapter explores some of the benefits and challenges to the development of minimally invasive autopsy (MIA), assessing its future potential. In doing so we analyse the ways in which this novel technological application has the potential to challenge the boundaries between 'life' and 'death' (Howarth, 2000; Braidotti, 2013).

Visualising life and death

The use of imaging technology in different clinical settings has been well documented by medical sociologists. As Blaxter (2009) argues, a common theme in the sociology of medicine has been to explore the ways in which visual technologies – from X-rays to computer tomography (CT) or magnetic resonance imaging – privilege the image over the body and its experience. The development of such technologies has come to define professional expertise, leading to an expansion of medical control (Conrad, 1979). Visual technologies are often viewed as central to the medical gaze, a form of monitoring and disciplining the body (Foucault, 1975). According to Prasad (2005), MRI technology allows for the production of the body, facilitating an almost unlimited extension of the medical gaze. Some sociologists and STS scholars have sought to challenge this view, highlighting the utility of technology for both professionals and patients (Berg and Mol, 1998). More recently sociologists have sought to show that patients are not passive recipients as often portrayed, but are, rather, active participants in the production of medical images (Radstake, 2007; Wood, 2016). While sociologists have paid significant attention to the role of imaging technology in life, limited attention has been paid, so far, to its role in death, particularly in post-mortem examinations.

Visual technology – ultrasound in particular – has come to occupy a particularly significant position in healthcare at the very start of life, during pregnancy. According to Zechmeister (2001: 392), the significance of ultrasound in obstetrics can be regarded as threefold: on a clinical level it provides information and evidence; on a second level it is linked with surveillance; and on a third it is a tool created for a new myth – the fetus as image. Ultrasound use in pregnancy provides important clinical information and helps parents to create a sense of fetal personhood (Reed, 2012). Images produced through ultrasound can also form an important part of memorialisation practices and the maintenance of personhood in cases of baby loss (Layne, 2000; Garattini, 2007). When it comes to post-mortems, however, imaging technology is used to establish cause of death while minimising bodily invasion. One of the key reasons identified in existing literature as to why parents do not wish to consent to a post-mortem for their baby relates to their fears over its invasive nature and their baby's bodily wholeness after the examination (Rankin et al., 2002; Sheach Leith, 2007). In this chapter we explore the ways in which MIA using MRI can help to preserve a baby's body wholeness in that interstitial space between life and death, thus reinforcing a sense of fetal personhood.

This chapter takes a *technology-in-practice* approach to explore the emerging role of post-mortem MRI. This means that we seek to explore the role of MRI post-mortem in its social and cultural context, acknowledging the complex web of material, social and political relationships and networks that inform its use (Timmermans and Berg, 2003). As sociologists have often highlighted, MRI is a complex technology that cannot be reduced to the straightforward production and use of an image (Joyce, 2006; Reed et al., 2016). We will therefore not just focus on the actual scan, numbers and other measures that describe the body and its functions, but also the final stage of translation – the reports and records into which these are distilled (Blaxter, 2009). As we will show, parents were often very positive about MRI, mostly because they did not wish their baby to undergo an invasive examination. While professionals still see full post-mortem examination as the gold standard, they were also generally positive about the increasing use of MIA, with many feeling that it will become further incorporated into pathology in the future. The chapter concludes, therefore, by arguing that although increasingly important, the use of MRI post-mortem (as elsewhere) is only one part of a much broader diagnostic jigsaw (Prasad, 2005; Reed et al., 2016). Note that some of the quotations used in this chapter on post-mortem examinations offer graphic illustrations of the process. and might, therefore, be upsetting for some readers. We feel it is important, however, to tell our research participants' stories as they articulated them to us.

Fetal MRI: a technology at the intersection of life and death

Although the focus of this chapter is on post-mortem MRI, we will begin by introducing the reader to fetal MRI. This is because MRI use during pregnancy can often be used to inform a post-mortem examination. In the UK pregnant women are offered an ultrasound scan at around twelve weeks to ascertain the viability and gestational age of the fetus. They are also offered a second scan at twenty weeks to identify a range of potential medical problems (Pilnick, 2002; Reed, 2012). Despite advances in screening in recent years, not all abnormalities can be diagnosed using ultrasound. In these cases, a further form of examination of the fetus may be desirable (Jokhi and Whitby, 2010). MRI is now starting to be offered in several fetal medicine centres across the UK to back up routine ultrasound screening or provide further information. The initial focus of fetal MRI was on the central nervous system. However, techniques have recently evolved so that further evaluation of other organ systems, the anatomy of the umbilical cord, assessment of the placenta as well as assessment of maternal structures have all become feasible and clinically useful (Whitby and Wright, 2015). Fetal MRI is a technology that is used across both the start and end of life. It can inform parental decision-making during pregnancy regarding termination and help professionals plan for labour and surgery post-delivery (for example, in cases of tumours or diaphragmatic hernia). It can also be used to inform post-mortem in various ways, as will be explored in this section.

Professionals often found that women who had undergone a fetal MRI to help diagnose problems during pregnancy were often more receptive to their baby undergoing an MRI scan as part of a post-mortem. In these instances, professionals tended to feel that this was because women understood the images produced by MRI, having been through the process before, as Gina, an obstetrician, articulated:

> I think that's where some of these women if they don't want a post-mortem afterwards, if they've had an MRI antenatally they're quite happy for the baby to go and have an MRI, do you know what I mean, because they sort of I think understand the process, the images, do you see what I mean?

Fetal MRI can also play an important role when parents have consented to a full post-mortem. For example, after a post-mortem examination has taken place the results are often cross-checked against the original fetal MRI results to assist clinicians in the confirmation of a diagnosis. Gina went on to outline this process:

> If they've [pregnant women] got a fetal abnormality and they have an MRI as part of the work up and then perhaps they either have a stillbirth or they decide not to continue, they decide to terminate their pregnancy, I will then also get the post-mortem report you see, and so [...] I'll often feedback (to the radiologist) and say the post-mortem confirmed the MRI findings.

Furthermore, the results of the fetal MRI can be useful in some cases where parents have declined a post-mortem examination. In the absence of a post-mortem, they can help to establish cause of death or provide parents and professionals with further information. Sometimes professionals felt that fetal MRI could lessen the need for a post-mortem examination because the cause of death had already been clearly identified during pregnancy. This can be seen in the account below from Ethan, an obstetrician:

> Well, some people choose not to [consent to post-mortem], it's as simple as that really and I have to say I agree with them for certain problems, if they've had an antenatal MRI scan and that says, the baby's brain is deformed and it's got a large spina bifida, I don't think you're going to add very much with post-mortem and some people just have an aversion to baby being dissected really, so I don't push it. I think there are some circumstances where we just don't know where the information would be important, so you know if you have an antenatal loss that is unexpected, then I would be more encouraging to have a post-mortem in that situation, in case you pick something up that we've not identified.

The role of MRI post-mortem, therefore, begins in 'life' during pregnancy through the use of fetal MRI. It can be used to inform parents' life and death decision-making and guide and confirm a post-mortem diagnosis. It is therefore a technology that crosses the boundaries between early life and death. As we have begun to indicate in this section, however, technologies such as MRI often do not produce answers by themselves, but are part of a broader assemblage of materials used to form diagnosis (Prasad, 2005; Latimer, 2013; Reed et al., 2016). This is something we will return to throughout this chapter. In the following section we move on to focus specifically on the role of MRI in death by examining the development of minimally invasive autopsy using MRI.

Post-mortem MRI: the emergence of minimally invasive autopsy

Minimally invasive autopsy (MIA) is an emerging type of post-mortem, often involving external review, placental examination and ancillary tests that form part of the formal autopsy process. These tests are then combined with MRI or a CT scan. According to Thayyil et al. (2013), MIA using MRI can have an accuracy level comparable to that of conventional autopsy for detecting cause of death or major pathological abnormality in fetuses, newborns and infants. It may, however, be less accurate in older children (Thayyil et al., 2013). While imaging techniques are often used as part of a full post-mortem in hospitals, validating MRI as an alternative to conventional autopsy has only recently been explored (Addison et al., 2014). Most clinicians agree that conventional autopsy is still the gold standard in perinatal post-mortem (Addison et al., 2014; Lewis et al., 2018). MIA, however, is a viable alternative to traditional autopsy when a full post-mortem is refused by parents for religious or other reasons (Hyde et al., 2020). Our study was based in an area of the UK which ran a clinical MIA service. Professional respondents involved in the pioneering development of this service all felt that it was time to move forward with MIA as a second line option. This was articulated by Ava, a very senior pathologist, in our study:

> So I think that now is the right time for that to progress [...] Because of course it cannot only be post-mortem MRI, it has to be post-mortem MRI with minimal invasion. The minimal invasion of the body to take blood samples, to take skin samples, to do genetic analysis, to take maybe a biopsy of an organ that looks abnormal on the MRI. So the post-mortem MRI with minimal invasion will be much more accepted by the families. What we have to make sure is that the quality is the same, at least the same if not better.

According to Whitby et al. (2006), post-mortem MRI imaging can provide similar information to autopsy for gross pathology of most organ systems. It often provides more information in cases of central nervous system abnormalities but is less accurate for cardiac abnormalities. It is particularly useful for providing information about the brain. A trainee paediatric pathologist, Ruth, informed us that there are physiological challenges involved in performing an autopsy on a fetus, especially when it involves examining the brain. In these cases, MRI was often particularly useful. She elaborated on this:

> So, MRI looks better at soft tissues, and will give you a better vision of the brain, really, or construction of the brain. Because a lot of times, when we do brains in babies, and especially pre-term babies, they're incredibly soft, so taking them out can be difficult, if the tissue's autolysed, then the structure is probably gone if it's autolysed[1] [...] So, it's difficult to see the structure in some babies, or I find it very difficult, doing my training, anyway.

While all the professionals we interviewed saw the emerging use of MIA as a positive move, professionals involved in taking post-mortem consent all identified a full post-mortem as the continued gold standard.[2] These professionals endorsed the view that MIA should only be offered as a second line option, as emphasised by Carmen, an APT:

> Well our understanding is that when they [professionals] go and speak to the families they'll always say a full post-mortem is the gold standard because any other you're not going to get the full range of test results or results that you would like from a post-mortem; and if they refuse, they don't want an incision, then you'll say well, you know, we could go down the route of we'll do just a limited one, we'll just look at the head, or we'll just look at the heart, and if they still refuse then we'll say we could look at an MRI post-mortem, which is non-invasive but would mean obviously taking a tissue sample for carrier type.[3]

Imaging technologies such as MRI can be used as an adjunct to a full post-mortem or as part of an alternative form of post-mortem. According to Addison et al. (2014), to be considered as a useful adjunct, MRI should be able to detect abnormalities that are difficult to identify during a full post-mortem. For example, an MRI scan of the brain as a routine adjunct to perinatal autopsy may provide important information, especially – as the quote from Ruth shows – when the fetal brain is autolysed (Addison et al., 2014). Professionals in our study most often spoke about the use of MIA using MRI as an alternative to a full post-mortem. Some professionals did, however, also refer to the role of MRI as adjunct to guide the full examination. Its role in this context was outlined by Carmen:

> I sometimes see the images especially if it's a bleed on the brain then you can actually, they're usually really good and they'll say, oh look, we've found this, and so at least you know what you're looking for if you have to do a post-mortem after, because sometimes we do an MRI and then we do a full post-mortem as well.

It is clear from the accounts of professionals in our study that MRI use post-mortem is an emerging technology in practice (Timmermans and Berg, 2003), as it is gradually being used in different ways to help identify or confirm cause of death. In keeping with the findings of other studies, most professionals in our study were positive about the use of MRI as both an adjunct to and alternative to a post-mortem, although it was also clear from professional accounts that MIA using MRI should only be offered as a second line option when parents decline a full post-mortem. Professionals did, however, identify various organisational challenges to MRI use in this context, which we go on to explore in the next section.

Organisational challenges to post-mortem MRI

Existing studies on MIA have raised various implementation challenges that need to be considered before the technology is implemented as a clinical service in hospitals. According to Lewis et al. (2018), for example, consideration must be given to the skills and training require-ments for pathologists and radiologists who would be responsible for running such a service. There also needs to be appropriate access to scanning equipment and required computational infrastructure. An MIA service is based on teamworking between different medical specialties (particularly pathology and radiology), thus requiring the development of a cooperative environment (O'Donnell and Woodford, 2008) and a multidisciplinary approach to interpret results. Other issues such as cost implications, equity of access and acceptance from health professionals and hospital managers must also be factored into implementation plans (Lewis et al., 2018). MIA was already a service in the hospital trust where our study was set. There was a very strong collaborative relationship between pathology and radiology across the study sites, and all our data emphasised the importance of taking a multidisciplinary approach. Professionals in the study talked, however, about a range of organisational challenges that they faced when using MRI tech-nology post-mortem. We explore some of these challenges in this section.

MRI is most often used to scan the living and is frequently already operating at maximum capacity. Carmen identified access to the scanner for a post-mortem as the main challenge that professionals currently face in relation to MIA. As she states: 'I think the only challenges I can see at the moment really is finding enough capacity on the MRI scanner.' In our study, participants also identified sig-nificant logistical challenges to using MRI scanners as part of MIA. This was related to the need to move babies between different hospital sites for scanning. The Primrose Villa mortuary was in a designated children's wing.[4] By contrast, the maternity unit was in a separate hospital. It is considered best practice that dead bodies should be moved between different geographical sites by a registered professional (for example, porters if movement is within a single hospital, or a funeral director if it involves movement between different hospitals). This often made it logistically difficult to arrange post-mortem MRI, as highlighted by a neonatologist, Brian:

> So the one case I did last year, it was a Muslim family, who ... they'd agreed on additional testing, so they'd had muscle biopsies and skin biopsy when the baby was still alive. The baby was too sick to have a neonatal MRI, but they were quite happy to consider a post-mortem MRI. But it was just so frustrating to say ... to find the bereavement service saying, I'm not sure we can send the baby over to Newman's Hospital today, we can't get a porter, I'm not sure if we could get a taxi. And it was thinking, well, what's the point of doing it, if you're just ... if that's what's stopping us facilitating it?

Moving babies around even one hospital site could be challenging (although hospital staff were able to do this themselves). Babies that were going for an MRI scan needed to be moved from the mortuary to the radiology suite. Our study took place in a children's wing of a busy teaching hospital. It was not deemed appropriate for children attending hospital with their families to see dead babies being moved along hospital corridors. Certain props were therefore used while moving babies around. Babies were often swaddled in blankets and moved around in a stroller as if they were alive. This was articulated by Carmen:

> We've got a pram that we can put the baby in which is fine and over the years I've never ever been stopped once, you know, because we always make it really discreet and that and it's nice, and even the families that we've spoken to say, oh, it's quite nice, they always say, oh, you take them round in a pram, oh, that's really nice. But it's really the logistics of when there is not a lot of staff just getting in and out of the department that's all.

There were also other associated challenges. While staff in the mortuary were used to handling dead bodies, staff in other parts of the hospital were not. For example, some radiographers did not want to handle dead bodies (especially babies). This meant that radiology staff had to be warned when a post-mortem case was being sent across to them from the mortuary. This was articulated by Carmen:

> Well we always pre-warn them [radiographers] so we always phone them first and make an appointment and so the baby goes round there and then obviously some don't mind and some do. So they try and work it out between them who is happy to do it. Occasionally if they haven't got any staff that are happy to handle your child or your baby, and I wouldn't really expect them to, so I always ask them are you okay or would you like me to do it, because we've all been passed to be able to go in the MRI suite. So there is occasions when I take the baby and put it actually on the MRI and then I sit and wait while they do it and then take the baby off and bring it back.

The logistics of taking babies for a post-mortem MRI could therefore be fraught with difficulties – both emotional and organisational. Ava, a very senior paediatric pathologist, stated that in order to make the service more efficient, they needed an MRI scanner in the mortuary. However, Ava noted that there were significant financial challenges related to this:

> The problem is, first we need to get an MRI in the mortuary, so that is a challenge, and it's a financial challenge, I don't know how we're going to make it, we have these expectations, so at the moment we have this place in the mortuary and hopefully we will do something else, to get the MRI. I think that to cover that, we are working very closely and very well with radiology, so this has to be a partnership. And the good thing is that because we are not the [United] States, that you are run only by money, we are run by money, but at the end we don't have this kind of private income and competition, that we can work together with other departments, as we are with radiology, so I think that is great.

Although most professionals were supportive of the development and use of MRI post-mortem, therefore, various organisational challenges hindered the process. Most of these challenges were related to the logistics of moving babies around the hospital (and between sites) for scanning because this activity required specific personnel. The Human Tissue Authority provides guidance for best practice on transportation. A licence is also required to store dead bodies (even just before and after a scan in a specific locations).[5] Records of the dates and times of the movement of dead bodies must be kept, along with records of the personnel involved. Even when dead babies are being moved around a single hospital space for scanning, they still need to be moved in a way that is discreet. This relates partly to what sociologists have highlighted as the increasingly institutionalised, professionalised and privatised approach to death, resulting in the sequestration of the dead body (Mellor and Shilling, 1993; Lawton, 2000). It also reinforces the notion of 'death work' as work that is often 'hidden' from public view (Reed and Ellis, 2020). Placing an MRI scanner in the mortuary was identified by professionals as the main way to overcome some of these logistical challenges and cultural taboos, although there are huge cost implications.

Having explored professional views of post-mortem MRI, we move on in the next section to explore parents' fears over the invasive nature of a full post-mortem examination, further examining the value of MRI in this context.

'We don't want our babies dissecting': the fear of bodily invasion

Existing research has identified a number of reasons why parents often do not wish to consent to a post-mortem examination. One of the key factors highlighted by these studies is parental concern over the invasive nature of the procedure. According to Rankin et al. (2002), parents often feel that their baby has suffered enough. They don't want them to be cut up and are worried about their baby's appearance after the examination. Sociological research has also shown how, in light of the organ retention scandal, parents often raise concerns about the preservation of their baby's body wholeness (Sheach Leith, 2007). These issues are strongly reinforced by our parent data. Parents often based their understanding of a full post-mortem examination on gruesome representations of autopsy in crime-related television dramas. They did not want their baby to undergo such a brutal examination. This was articulated by Amy, who declined a full post-mortem but did consent to an MIA: 'I just thought a post-mortem is where they chop you up, take your organs out, weigh them, you know, like what you see on crime programmes, that's what I had in my mind.' Moreover, in the aftermath of their loss parents continued to speak of their baby in the present tense, often feeling that a post-mortem examination would be akin to putting their baby through invasive medical procedures while they were still alive (Reed et al., 2021). They often spoke of not wanting their baby 'messing with' – as Anna explained: 'we don't want our babies dissecting, and we don't want them messing about with, unless it's absolutely necessary'.

A hospital post-mortem was not an option for twelve parents in our sample. These parents went through the coronial post-mortem process due to their baby's unexpected death. Although they did not make an active choice about the post-mortem, they still articulated concerns about their baby undergoing such an invasive medical procedure. This was articulated by Mike, whose baby Mia died suddenly aged two weeks:

> Yeah. You don't know whether anything you do or say can help or not, but what have you got to lose? [Laughs] That's how I felt about it. But it was still upsetting, the PM thing. It's normal for it to be. She'd been through enough. You don't want people cutting her up.

Research has indicated that in cases where parents were fearful about the invasive nature of a post-mortem examination, the availability of minimally invasive techniques could improve rates of consent (Ben-Sasi et al., 2013; Kang et al., 2014; Lewis et al., 2017, 2019). In our study, professionals tended to feel that parents found an MIA using MRI more acceptable because it was far less invasive to their baby's body. This was indicated by Gina, an obstetrician:

> There are some women who don't want their baby to have any … to be messed with is how they describe it to me […] I don't want my baby messing with, but then in that circumstance will accept a post-mortem MRI because of the fact that it's not interfering, it's no cuts on the baby, they're not taking any tissue from the baby.

Some professionals in the study expressed the view that the increase in MIAs in recent years (for both children and adults) had been driven significantly by the activism of families who did not want their loved ones to undergo an invasive procedure. This was articulated by a coroner, Vincent:

> I think we've been gently pushed towards it [MIA], I think rightly enough, don't take the wrong view, we've been gently pushed towards it by the fact that people do not want us cutting up the body of their

loved ones and lots of people are very relieved when we say, well we do a scan first, or, hey, we've done a scan and we've found the cause of death.

While parents often did not want their baby to be interfered with, there are a number of other reasons why they might be unwilling to consent. For example, religion can affect parental decision-making in a range of ways including, for example, concern that the post-mortem process will delay burial arrangements (Rankin et al., 2002; Breeze et al., 2012; Downe et al., 2012; Heazell et al., 2012; Ben-Sasi et al., 2013; Kang et al., 2014; Lewis et al., 2017, 2019). Studies have consistently shown that the availability of minimally invasive techniques can be particularly beneficial in these cases (Ben-Sasi et al., 2013; Kang et al., 2014; Lewis et al., 2017). Only four parent participants in our study identified as being specifically religious (either Muslim or Anglican). It is not possible, therefore, to know the extent to which religion informed parental decision-making over post-mortem examination in our research. Professionals, however, spoke frequently about the role of religion and how it shaped parents' attitudes towards the body, and thus to post-mortem examination. As Maryam, a Muslim chaplain, commented, the availability of MIA was really important for Muslim parents:

> Religious leaders will say well it's the will of God so your baby was just born like that but then you think well if there's something that could be preventative or something that can help through this then is it not something that... So just given the choices to the families especially now that 'cause I know that they've got the MRI scan now haven't they at [the hospital] and I think that's made a massive difference.

One of the most common reasons identified by parents as to why they did not consent to a full post-mortem relates to fears over its invasive nature. This is something unanimously articulated by both parents and professionals in our research, and in existing studies on post-mortem examination (Ben-Sasi et al., 2013; Kang et al., 2014; Lewis et al., 2017). Parents did not want their baby's body being 'messed with' or 'cut up', often raising concerns about their baby's body wholeness (Sheach Leith, 2007). Keeping their baby's body intact through MIA might help parents maintain the sense of their baby's personhood during that interstitial phase between life and death, in the mortuary and before the funeral has taken place

(Reed et al., 2021). MIA appears to offer a clear alternative, therefore, for parents in such cases and where religious beliefs surround death and burial. In order to explore the post-mortem MRI experience more fully, the next section presents an in-depth analysis of the experiences of two participants – Amy and Victoria.

Minimally invasive autopsy: the cases of Amy and Victoria

Due to the limited availability of MIA in the UK at the time our research was conducted, not many parents in our study had had the opportunity to select MIA as an option. Amy and Victoria were two participants who did. Victoria's baby Daisy was stillborn at term two years prior to our interview with her. Amy's baby Clementine died in utero at sixteen weeks nearly five years before our study. While the MIA did not provide these parents with a definitive answer regarding their babies' cause of death, it did offer them peace of mind and they were both happy with their choice. We begin with a focus on how the examination was initially presented to parents by health professionals, outlining why they chose MIA as an option. Victoria articulated the process and rationale behind her choice:

> The staff gave us some leaflets about what different tests that they could do and post-mortem and things like that. And then they sat down and spoke to us about it all. So there were a few things where we automatically said I don't want to do this or that, we didn't really want... We wanted it to be as the least invasive as possible which is why we chose the MRI. Because I said I wouldn't want to do anything to her [...] And I think they told us a bit of information about what the MRI involved. And I think they did the skin scrape. I don't know exactly what that's called.

Research has indicated various reasons as to why parents *do* want their baby to undergo a post-mortem examination. In particular parents often consent to a post-mortem because they want to understand why their baby has died. They also want to find out whether the cause of death is something that could re-occur in future pregnancies and gain some reassurance that their baby's death was not their fault (Lewis et al., 2018). Where MIA was available, it was often the prefered option when parents wanted to find out further information about their babies' cause of death, but did not want their baby to undergo an invasive examination (Ben-Sasi et al., 2013; Kang et al., 2014; Lewis et al., 2017). This rationale was articulated by Amy:

> It was only then when they said, right. so what happens now, so you can have, like, a full post-mortem where, you know, she's chopped up, which obviously we didn't want, they said there's this new thing that's just come out where you can have an MRI scan, would you like that? And I jumped at that, because I wanted answers, I wanted to know why and I thought that is just not invasive at all. So I couldn't stand the thought of her being cut up, but they asked about the karyotype test[6] and they said they'd only need to take, like, a small tiny bit of flesh for that, so I said, yes, we'll have that, but I didn't want her being, you know, all chopped up.

The post-mortem MRI showed that Amy's baby had some form of ventriculomegaly. This is a medical term used to describe enlargement of the ventricles of the brain. The scan also showed that the baby had no corpus callosum. The corpus callosum is a bridge of nerve fibres joining the two cerebral hemispheres of the brain. MRI is often used in pregnancy to identify ventriculomegaly, both to confirm severity and detect and characterise additional anomalies (Cardoen et al., 2011). The clinician delivering this news informed Amy that this condition would not have caused the baby's death but would probably have led her to be born with a severe disability. Amy articulates this in the quote below:

> They had picked that up and everything else was normal and it … yeah, it listed everything else that's, like, you know, just normal and that was the only abnormality and he did say there are adults walking around in the world with that condition, so it's not necessarily that that killed her, but it's likely that it was and he did say, if she had lived, she would have probably been severely disabled.

The MRI post-mortem did not provide Victoria with a definitive answer about why her baby had been stillborn, which she found frustrating. She was told by clinicians that 'it was just one of those things' and it 'couldn't have been predicted'. Despite the post-mortem not offering a definitive answer, however, she still felt that they had made the right choice to opt for an MIA: 'so we were quite pleased actually that we'd not gone for the invasive approach because if we had and didn't get answers I think I would've been really, really upset about that. So actually it reinforced the fact that thankfully we made the right choice for us.'

Parental and professional interaction can have a huge impact on parents' decision-making about post-mortem examination (Reed et al., 2021). As Lewis et al. (2019: 1249) argue, parents often look to professionals to guide them, and desire a conversation about the post-mortem that is both 'open' and 'honest'. Parents in our study were strongly influenced by their interactions with professionals at all stages of the post-mortem journey. This included how and when they received the results of a post-mortem. Parents meet with consultant obstetricians six to eight weeks after decease, when all the results are complete and available to discuss with them. Victoria's positive view of the technology was strongly influenced by her interaction with professionals:

> I think it's easier when you're there with somebody and you can ask your questions and whatever. I think over the … I don't know why over the phone, but sometimes things seemed to get lost in translation, I don't know. So I thought it was quite good to have that face-to-face conversation, even though it didn't really answer any questions for us, it was nice for us to be able to speak to somebody like that I thought.

Although MRI had not provided either Amy or Victoria with definitive answers, both women felt positive about their experience. They also felt that the MRI post-mortem should become more widely available in the future, as articulated by Victoria: 'Yeah, I think it should definitely be an option for everybody. I didn't even realise that it wasn't.' The views of both Amy and Victoria support the findings of existing studies which have consistently shown that MIA, when available, could be a more acceptable option for parents than a full post-mortem (Ben-Sasi et al., 2013; Lewis et al., 2018). Both women's experiences of MIA illuminated in this section were, however, strongly influenced by their relationships with professionals. This highlights the need, when exploring individual experiences of technology in any given healthcare context, to acknowledge the importance of the social and cultural context in which it is being applied (Timmermans and Berg, 2003).

Parental choice, future options

At the time our study took place only a small number of parents had access to MIA. These were parents who lived locally to the study sites and whose baby had not died suddenly and unexpectedly. As part of the study, however, we wanted to garner a range of parental views on MIA, including the views of those for whom this type of post-mortem had not been an option. We found that all parents in the study were keen on MIA becoming a more widely available option in the future. For example, Dawn's baby boy Alex died in utero at twenty-nine weeks over thirty-three years before our study. Dawn has no idea whether her son underwent a post-mortem examination because very little information was given to parents at that time. She was very supportive of the development of MIA though, again because it does not involve significant invasion of the body:

> Personally I think, to have a tiny baby have any kind of a post-mortem is incredibly invasive on a tiny body and you can't help but think what happens during that. So an MRI post-mortem isn't as invasive and your baby's still whole and perfect and unmarked and hasn't had to go through the procedure, the normal one. So I think an MRI in that respect will bring a little bit more peace of mind to parents that their baby's fine. It hasn't had to be mutilated or damaged in any way.

Male as well as female respondents articulated concerns over the invasive nature of a traditional post-mortem and expressed interest in the development and availability of MIA. For example, Nathan's baby Aria died suddenly over five years before our study aged eleven weeks. She had to undergo a full post-mortem because MIA is not currently used as part of a coronial post-mortem. Nathan was very supportive of the wider use of MIA, provided that it was as good as a full post-mortem in terms of providing families with answers about why their baby had died:

> When I first saw it, I thought, that's interesting. The thing that struck me was, would it help give answers? So if I just leap straight to the assumption that doing an MRI based post-mortem is normally as effective as a traditional one, I think there'd be a huge number of parents that would take a massive comfort if you can just do an MRI, because obviously the thought of a post-mortem is pretty ghastly.

This was a sentiment shared by other parents such as Hannah. Her baby boy Simon died suddenly and unexpectedly three years before our interview, and therefore had to go through a coronial post-mortem. She was positive about MIA becoming more widely available in the future but also felt that she would need to be convinced that the quality of the limited post-mortem was as good as the full post-mortem. Hannah hoped that an MIA would allow her to spend more time with her baby before the funeral and that her baby would look better and more whole because there would have been no dissection:

> I can't speak for others, but I guess I would want to make sure that it was as accurate as an invasive process, but if there was a non-invasive process, then, yes, definitely, that would be good and I think that ... as I say, I don't know much about this, but I imagine that that would mean that you ... the body of your child looks better for longer and you have more time to come to terms with, you know, kind of, you don't have to give up on the physical seeing of the child as soon as you might have to do if there's been an invasive post-mortem.

Parents whose babies had undergone a full post-mortem were often concerned that their baby would look different after the examination. They saw MIA as enabling them to preserve their baby's body wholeness for longer (Sheach Leith, 2007). Parents felt that this would take the fear out of viewing their baby's body after the examination, allowing them more time with their baby as a whole person. Parents clearly wanted reassurance, however, that MIA could offer them the same quality of information and answers that they needed. If it could, then they saw it as a huge step forward for the future.

Post-mortem MRI: is the future visual?

In 2006 sociologist Kelly Joyce predicted that MRI would be used in the future to help clinicians diagnose a whole range of illnesses including fetal and breast imaging. At the time that she published her sociological monograph on MRI, the technology was most often used to identify problems with the brain during life. It has since become a routine technology used to aid the diagnosis of a vast array of conditions from torn ligaments to tumours. The use of MRI in fetal, infant and adult post-mortem examination was first reported in 1990. More detailed reports of its use followed in 1996 and 1997 which further delineated the value of MRI in this context (Whitby, 2009). As argued throughout this chapter, MIA using MRI is becoming highly acceptable for parents and professionals, and there is now widespread political support and public interest in its clinical implementation in the UK (Addison et al., 2014). A report by the Department of Health in 2012 recommended the development of an integrated, phased implementation programme for a national cross-sectional autopsy imaging service. This would be based on a regionalised service provided by thirty mortuary-based imaging centres in England (NHS, 2012). Despite this interest and support, however, there are currently very few centres across the UK that run an MIA perinatal post-mortem service. This penultimate section of this chapter focuses on exploring the potential future of this technological application, drawing on accounts from professionals.

Professionals often talked about the ways that the post-mortem service using MRI had improved over time. It had been a research tool initially – something that was out of the ordinary – but now it was run as a clinical service in the main hospital where this research took place. As highlighted by this chapter, although MIA was far from routine, it was becoming more common. Clinicians such as obstetricians and neonatologists felt that they had got better at referring babies for it and encouraging parental consent for it. As Dave, a neonatologist, commented:

> Yes [cough] and then there are some where the parents have declined a post-mortem but have said yes to an MRI. Then there are some who you specifically ask them, can they have an MRI at the same time and that's certainly helpful for some of the cerebral brain problems. On the whole, the more we've done the better I think we've got at getting the post-mortem MRI. Of course it has been a research thing in the past and you've needed to ask for it and now it's a service, you need to remember to ask for it.

Professional respondents interviewed in our study all viewed the increasing use of MRI in post-mortem examination as a positive development. Some pathologists, however, are against the use of imaging post-mortem because they feel it threatens the traditional practice of post-mortem examination. Ava, a very senior paediatric pathologist, noted this:

> I know that there are people that are completely against MRI as a tool or a future replacement of post-mortems. I think that there are people that say it's impossible. However, I think there are other people who feel that it will be the only way forward, and I think I am in between.

Some professionals in the study did feel that MRI would become a routine part of post-mortem examination. This was not just related to the possibility of MIA becoming more widely available; rather, professionals often referred to the increasing use of MRI as an adjunct to inform a full post-mortem so as to get better results. This was articulated by Ali, a specialist paediatric radiologist:

> I think it will become a part of post-mortem if you ask me, you'll have an MR on every child that dies before it has a formal post-mortem. It'll be just like any other clinical situation, you wouldn't operate on a child unless you've done an imaging, so you know it would be the same, to me in five years' time that would be the same, you would do an MR on every baby and then you do the post-mortem and collate between the two.

Most professionals felt that MRI would become an increasingly important adjunct, and an alternative option when parents did not wish to consent to full post-mortem. They all felt, however, that it would never replace a full post-mortem. They tended to feel that if it did, important information regarding certain types of death would be lost. This was illuminated by the neonatologist Dave, regarding SIDS deaths:

> My feeling is that if you start replacing post-mortems with post-mortem MRIs for SIDS you're going to lose a lot of information. The pathology of SIDS is, well, there is no pathology of SIDS. There are lots of things that are described and increasingly it's abnormalities in the brain stem. Well, I've asked the MRI people if they can pick those up and they can't. So I don't think that's going to be helpful and then you've lost that information forever. One of the things we're doing is looking to see if there are any genetic markers for SIDS. Well, if you haven't saved any tissue then you can't do that. So I suspect there'll be an awful lot of negative post-mortem MRIs for SIDS.

According to Addison et al. (2014), MIA using MRI together with ancillary investigations has been shown to be as accurate as conventional autopsy in fetuses, newborns and infants, and could be more widely available as an option across the UK. While most professionals in our study were supportive of the use of MRI post-mortem in the future, there was some caution over this. Professionals were often concerned, not just that the increasing use of imaging post-mortem would signal the decline of autopsy and pathology as a profession, but also that some important clinical information would be lost. What was clear, however, was that MRI would play a vital role in *informing* post-mortem examination in the future – whether through fetal MRI, MIA or using MRI as an adjunct to guide a full post-mortem. We will now explore this in more detail in the conclusion.

Conclusion

Scholars of death and dying studies have often sought to distinguish between physical and social death, discussing the ways in which social 'life' can extend beyond the boundaries of physical 'death' through various practices that continue to yoke the dead to the living (Borgstrom, 2017; Howarth, 2000). As Howarth argues, by facilitating life beyond the point where it might once have been viable, medical technology can also contribute to a confusion of the boundaries between life and death. We argue that fetal and post-mortem MRI is an emerging technology that blurs the boundaries between life and death in novel ways. The use and value of MRI post-mortem begins during 'life' with fetal MRI, which can be used to aid parents' decision-making over termination 'death' and assist professionals to plan for 'birth'. It can be used both to inform and cross-check the findings of a full post-mortem examination, thus reaffirming or refuting cause of death. MRI can also be used as an adjunct to a full post-mortem, guiding the full examination as well forming a crucial part of MIA. This not only helps to establish cause of death, but can also be used to inform life potential by helping parents plan future pregnancies and the creation of new life. MRI, therefore, appears to blur the boundaries between the start and end of life, or at the very least extends the liminal space between the two (Howarth, 2000).

MRI use in this context was very much an emerging technology in professional practice. Professionals in our study were all supportive of the development of MIA, and of the use of MRI as an adjunct to a post-mortem. They felt it was particularly useful when parents did not wish to consent to a post-mortem examination for religious or other reasons. The successful application of this technology, however, was strongly reliant on multidisciplinary teamwork. Professionals also identified various organisational challenges that could make its implementation difficult at times. Furthermore, in support of the findings of other studies, professionals continued to identify full post-mortem as the gold standard (Lewis et al., 2018). As sociologists and STS scholars have often argued, imaging technologies such as MRI and CT do not in themselves provide one truth. Rather, they must be viewed as part of a wider diagnostic jigsaw which is almost always incomplete (Prasad, 2005, Reed et al., 2016). As we have sought to show in this chapter, whether as an adjunct or alternative to a full post-mortem, MRI use in this context is one part of a wider assemblage of materials used to inform professional practice (Latimer, 2013).

Parents in our study were strongly supportive of the development and availability of MIA. This was the case even when it might not provide them with a definitive answer as to why their baby had died. When considering its potential wider availability in the future, however, they did want to be assured that the quality of MIA was the same as a full post-mortem and that they would get the answers they needed. Parents were often fearful of the invasive nature of traditional post-mortem examination and worried about their baby's appearance afterwards (Rankin et al., 2002; Sheach Leith, 2007). In support of the findings from other studies, our data shows that the availability of MIA in these cases could improve post-mortem uptake (Ben-Sasi et al., 2013; Kang et al., 2014; Lewis et al., 2017). Parents did not want their baby 'messing with' or being 'cut up' and were strongly drawn to the idea of MIA. Keeping their baby's body intact during post-mortem examination was clearly related by parents in our study to issues of personhood. The notion of fetal personhood in debates on reproduction is often contentious. For example, it has been used by pro-life advocates in US debates on abortion to argue that personhood begins from the moment of conception (Casper, 1998, Conklin and Morgan, 1996). In discourses around baby loss, however, parents are often encouraged to create a sense of personhood and social identity for their baby through memory-making (Lovell, 1983; Keane, 2009; Shaw, 2014). In this chapter we have shown that keeping their baby's body 'whole' by opting for MIA rather than a full post-mortem assists parents with the preservation of their baby's personhood in that interstitial space between life and death (Reed et al., 2021).

The potential use and value of MRI post-mortem has long been discussed and highlighted by clinical research. In 1996 Brookes et al. found that post-mortem MRI scanning could give information that was comparable diagnostically to that obtained by necropsy in twelve of the twenty cases they examined. This was followed by other key studies, all of which identified the value of MRI as an adjunct or alternative when parents do not wish to consent to a full post-mortem (Thayyil et al., 2011). While arguing that the full post-mortem examination must remain the gold standard, health professionals, coroners and parents are genuinely supportive of the development of MIA in perinatal and paediatric care (Cohen et al., 2008; Ben-Sasi et al., 2013; Lewis et al., 2018). Despite this continued interest and support, at the time of writing there are still very few centres in the UK that offer a clinical perinatal MIA service. According to Lewis et al. (2018), a detailed health economic analysis and further exploration of parents' views, particularly among different religious groups, are required before this can be rolled out more widely. Clinicians involved in developing this service across the UK have suggested that in the first instance a supra-regional network of specialist centres should be established to provide this service within the current NHS framework (Addison et al., 2014). In addition, based on the findings of our study, we suggest some further issues that might be considered before this service is adopted more widely in hospitals across the UK. These relate to both the logistical challenge of moving dead bodies around hospitals and the wider cultural taboos associated with death, dying and the handling of dead bodies. These issues should factor into any future multidisciplinary staff training on MIA.

In this chapter we have focused on exploring the specific role of technology in the post-mortem process. In doing so we have again sought to highlight the very emotive nature of this subject. We want to move on in the next chapter to broaden this focus and examine the role of emotion in more depth across the entire baby loss journey.

Notes

1 Autolysis (self-destruction) is brought about by the breakdown of the cells and tissues of the human body. For further information, see Shedge et al. (2020).
2 In our study, consent was mostly taken by mortuary staff (pathologists and APTs), and by gynaecologists, obstetricians and neonatologists.
3 In genetic terms, a carrier refers to a person who has a genomic variant associated with a genetic condition but does not have the condition themselves. In certain clinical contexts a person's tissue may be tested to see if they carry a gene known to cause a disease or condition. See https://www.genomicseducation.hee.nhs.uk/glossary/carrier/ (accessed July 2022).
4 Primrose Villa was an informal name given to the mortuary by hospital staff in order to make it seem a less daunting space.
5 For further information, see https://www.hta.gov.uk/guidance-professionals/regulated-sectors/post-mortem/guidance-body-storage (accessed June 2022).
6 Karyotype tests analyse the chromosomes inside human cells to identify anomalies. They are often used in pregnancy to identify chromosomal anomalies including Down's Syndrome and Edwards Syndrome. For further information about prenatal screening, see https://www.nhs.uk/pregnancy/your-pregnancy-care/screening-tests/ (accessed August 2022).

Chapter 4

Emotions

The sociology of emotions emerged as a sub-discipline of sociology in the second half of the twentieth century (Bericat, 2016). According to Holland (2009: 11), the 'dead hand' of Cartesian dualism (which set reason against emotion) served to keep emotions beyond the boundaries of sociological concern until that time. From the late 1970s onwards sociologists began to conceptualise emotions more explicitly and to develop theories and research programmes for their study. Emotions are difficult to define, because as Turner contends, they function on multiple levels including 'biological and neurological, behavioral, cultural, structural and situational' (2009: 341). Researchers will prioritise different aspects according to their own interests. Despite some variation in the way sociologists might approach emotions, however, many emphasise the importance of their embodiment. As Denzin argues, emotions are a 'lived, believed-in, situated, temporarily embodied experience that radiates through a person's stream of consciousness' (2009: 66). According to Barbalet (1998: 8–9), sociology is interested in emotions for two key reasons: first, because as a discipline, it seeks to explain social phenomena; and secondly, because emotion is crucial to understanding social behaviour.

Emotions do not occur in a vacuum but emerge and are experienced through social relations. In order to understand the articulation of different emotions, therefore, it is necessary to understand the situations and social relations that produce them. Furthermore, as Bericat notes, the sociological understanding of any given social phenomenon is incomplete, 'if it does not incorporate the feeling subject into its study of structures and social processes' (2016: 145). Since the 1970s, therefore, sociologists have sought to explore how emotions are triggered, interpreted and expressed through an individual's participation in social groups (Hochschild, 1983, 2009; Kemper, 1991), exploring the social conditions behind emotions, and their role in individual, community and organisational contexts (Pawłowska, 2020). With the emergence of a wider 'affective turn' across the humanities and social sciences in recent years (Hardt, 2007: ix), sociologists have become increasingly preoccupied with both researching emotions and exploring the role of emotion in research (Brownlie, 2011; Burkitt, 2012).

This chapter offers a sociological analysis of emotion in relation to baby loss and post-mortem practice. It focuses on examining parental experiences of emotion or *being* emotional as well as exploring emotion work in different types of professional practice. While parental and professional data provide the central focus of the chapter, we also offer a sociological exploration of the emotional nature of *doing* research in this area. Throughout the chapter we explore some of the acute trauma and sadness of experiencing and witnessing baby loss and post-mortem examination. The chapter also seeks to uncover some of the more life-affirming emotions often experienced in this context – for example, articulations of parental and professional pride – which often remain hidden from view (Reed and Ellis, 2019). Emotions, as we conclude, are indeed socially mediated (Barbalet, 1998; Bericat, 2016), their articulation and management contingent on the social relations and structures surrounding them.

Being emotional and doing emotion work

Losing a baby through miscarriage, late fetal loss, late termination of pregnancy, stillbirth or SIDS is an immensely emotional and traumatic experience for parents (Bennett et al., 2008; Murphy et al., 2014; Heazell et al., 2016). Emotional responses to the death of a baby are diverse and unique to each individual. In their systematic review of qualitative literature on perinatal loss, however, Dyer et al. (2019) found that the most common feelings expressed by parents were self-blame and guilt, loneliness and emptiness, anger, fear, failure, shame, sadness and grief. Less well documented in existing research perhaps are the small moments of pride and joy that parents can feel after giving birth and meeting their baby. As Burden et al. (2016) argue, such feelings can – at least temporarily – sometimes take over from the shock of the death. While studies on perinatal loss can include a focus on both parents (women and men), their analyses tend to be centred primarily on women's experiences. As we will seek to show in this chapter, men can also feel very emotional after the death of their baby. They tend to feel prohibited from expressing their feelings, however, due to the prevalence of more traditional ideologies around gender and emotion (Brody, 1999).

While experiencing baby loss is a hugely emotional experience for parents, caring for babies and families in this context can also be a very emotive experience for the professionals involved. Professionals are often required to perform a significant amount of emotional labour in this field of medicine. The concept of emotional labour was initially developed by Hochschild (1983) in the context of the commercial services, but has increasingly been used to explore the work involved in managing emotions in a range of different healthcare settings (Bolton and Boyd, 2003; Reed and Ellis, 2020). As several authors have pointed out, professionals often employ different types of emotion management strategies in various settings, and according to whether they take place 'frontstage' in the public realm or 'backstage' in the private sphere (Bolton, 2001; Boyle, 2005; Reed and Ellis, 2020). While the emotional strain that doctors experience is widely recognised by existing research (Larson and Yao, 2005; Nettleton et al., 2008), literature tends to focus on the ways in which certain professional groups – such as nurses – perform the bulk of emotional work. This work then becomes marginalised, feminised and devalued (McCreight, 2005). While several authors have tried to highlight the ways in which emotion work can be a productive and rewarding experience for professionals (Wouters, 1989; Purcell et al., 2017), it often remains institutionally undervalued and considered undeserving of financial reward (Lewis, 2005).

This chapter seeks to explore emotions from three different perspectives: parent, professional and researcher. It begins by exploring some of the mixed emotions that parents experience when they lose their baby – sadness and devastation at their loss, but also joy and pride at giving birth and becoming parents. The chapter moves on to explore some of the hidden emotional work conducted by different types of health professionals, highlighting the ways in which professionals such as midwives are often required to be 'emotion jugglers' (Bolton, 2001). The third and final substantive section of the chapter turns its attention away from examining emotion in the data to consider the role of emotions in the research process. As various scholars have shown, research in sensitive areas – including death and dying – can be an enormously emotional experience for researchers, often involving a significant amount of emotional labour (Valentine, 2007; Visser, 2017). Drawing on researcher fieldnotes, therefore, the penultimate section of the chapter considers the role of emotion in the research process. The chapter concludes by using the research findings and process to reflect more on key sociological themes relating, more broadly, to the changing nature of gender roles, emotion work and the social production of emotion.

Life, death and the mix of emotions

Throughout this book so far we have explored some of the emotions felt and articulated by parents after the loss of their baby. For example, in Chapter 1 on trauma, we explored some of the extreme and heart-breaking emotions that parents experience as soon as their baby dies, such as shock, devastation, sadness and grief. In Chapter 3 we touched on the feelings of regret that parents can experience after declining a post-mortem examination. We seek in this section to explore a broader range of parental emotion – from the joy experienced at the birth of their child to guilt over their baby's death. We will draw on wider sociological debates on gender and emotion to explore issues relating to fatherhood and masculinity as well as examining parental emotions in subsequent pregnancies. We begin this section, however, with a focus on the embodied nature of grief.

Unbearable and embodied emotion

Sociologists have often sought to emphasise the embodied nature of emotions (Denzin, 2009). According to Bericat, for example, 'we can state that emotions constitute the bodily manifestation of the importance that an event in the natural or social world has for a subject' (2016: 493). The overwhelming emotion felt by parents in our study was extreme sadness and grief. Such emotions often manifested themselves physically. For example, Penny, who lost her baby Dustin suddenly at six months, discussed the ways in which she felt physically ill with emotion.

> And then leaving him [Dustin] there was just unbelievable. That was really bad. It was like a physical pain. There wasn't anywhere I wanted to be. I couldn't sit down, I couldn't stand up. We tried to go for a walk but then I was like I don't want to... It was just like this total... I can't even describe it. For a few days I was just in absolute agony. Physically. It was weird. You don't think that you can feel physically ill with emotion, but I did. I don't really remember much. I remember my mum forcing me to eat something, and they wouldn't let me drink too much, which is probably a good thing. I didn't sleep. I smoked like a chimney.

Olivia lost her baby Ian suddenly, aged six weeks. She talked extensively about her overwhelming sense of sadness and grief and was visibly upset while talking about this during her interview. Olivia highlighted the ways in which her grief manifested itself physically. After her baby died, she would often find herself moving and swaying as if she were still holding him. Continuing to mother her son after he had died by doing physical activities for him appeared to provide Olivia with an important emotional outlet:

> It's because in that early phase of grief the empty arm syndrome that people talk about, I'd often find myself standing and swaying even though I didn't have my baby in my arms any more. So what I needed to do was to keep mothering him although he was gone and so I would... I spent a lot of time doing things for him. I really enjoyed, and this is awful, I enjoyed packing up his room because it gave me a licence to fold his clothes and pack up his toys and do all those things that make you feel like you're still a parent. I think in going to visit him it was an extension of that. You cling on to being able to do anything that you can do to still be their parent. [participant becomes upset]

Existing studies highlight the ways in which baby loss is an immensely emotional and traumatic experience for parents (Bennett et al., 2008; Murphy et al., 2014; Heazell et al., 2016). What we have also sought to show here, however, is the way in which such emotions are embodied and often manifest themselves physically.

This appears to reinforce the importance of what sociologists often refer to as the embodied nature of emotions (Denzin, 2009; Bericat, 2016). While sadness and grief were the overwhelming feelings articulated by parents in our study, we want to move on in the next section to explore some of their more hidden and often unanticipated emotions.

Unanticipated feelings of pride and joy

While parental feelings of sadness after the loss of a baby are well documented in existing research, what is less well understood are the momentary experiences of pride and joy at giving birth and meeting their baby. Such experiences – although hidden and often fleeting – are important, because they can reaffirm parents' role as parents (Burden et al., 2016). This was articulated by Anna, whose baby Lily died at twenty-three weeks. During her interview Anna talked about the ways in which the joy of giving birth to her baby would always outlive the pain of losing her:

> It's just really, that time will always be the best and worst of my life. Because I met my daughter for the first time, and I love that. Because that defines me now, as a person. Because now I'm not just Anna, I am a mum. And that made me. That time made me a mum. And I'm not sad about that. That doesn't make me sad. Those moments don't make me sad. Everything that happened after that, and everything that happened before that, made me really sad, but that time, if I could go and do that again and again and again, I would. Because the pain of losing her, was not as powerful as the joy I had to have her. So, I would go and relive that a million times over, absolutely, there is no way that I regret that in any sort of way.

In our study, these mixed emotions of joy and sadness were articulated just as powerfully by fathers as they were by mothers. Wayne, for example, whose baby Flo died at birth, talked about the entire experience as surreal. On the one hand he experienced pure devastation at the loss, on the other he felt joy at meeting and holding his baby:

> All of that was quite ... all of that spending time with her afterwards, right after she was born and going to see her again, was all very surreal. It's a really interesting sort of thing to stand outside of it,

because you know your child's dead, you feel absolutely bereft like one of them wrecking balls that's repeatedly slamming into you. But at the same time, you feel a sort of sense ... you still feel some of that sense of, dare I say, joy because you've still got your baby in your hands, it still looks real but you know it's not. So it's like a ... that's a really small thing. But you're not just sitting there weeping.

Existing studies have sometimes highlighted the ways in which parents can experience short moments of joy at having their baby with them after they have died. One mother in Nuzum et al.'s (2018) qualitative study about parental experiences of fetal loss in Ireland, for example, spoke very positively about having her baby son back with her after the post-mortem. The mother could not explain why, but she felt a sense of joy at seeing him again in his babygro. She felt he became more of a person to her. Our data emphasises similar experiences. For example, parents often expressed momentary feelings of joy at being able to bring their baby home after post-mortem examination. This was articulated by Ivy, whose baby Brian died of SIDS aged four and a half months:

And then I remember celebrating and ringing around all the family when the undertaker rang and said we can bring Brian home, as though he was coming back as him. So then he was then in his coffin in the bedroom and then we brought Chandler into our bedroom.

When their baby died, the overwhelming emotion experienced by parents in our study was deep trauma and utter devastation at their loss (Dyer et al., 2019). As shown in this section, however, parents did also experience other emotions which were perhaps not anticipated – including pride and joy. While these feelings might only be ephemeral, it is still important to understand and recognise the productive nature of these emotions. They can help to reinforce the baby's personhood and in cases of fetal loss or stillbirth help to establish parental status (Burden et al., 2016).

Loss and guilt, relief and post-mortem examination

As various studies have shown, after the loss of a baby parents often question whether their own actions and behaviours might have contributed to the death of their child. It is not unusual therefore for parents to experience feelings of guilt (Hale, 2007; Duncan and

Cacciatore, 2015; Burden et al., 2016; Gold et al., 2018). Guilt was also an emotion that was articulated by some parents in our study. Anna was taken to her local county hospital when she went into premature labour. Once hospitalised, Anna wanted to be transferred to a larger teaching hospital in a nearby city. She felt that her baby would have a greater chance of survival there because they had the facilities to treat premature babies at an earlier stage of gestation. The medical staff at her local hospital, however, said that physically moving Anna at that stage would pose a significant threat to her life. They also felt that her baby would be very unlikely to survive wherever it was born because it was so premature. Anna made the decision to stay at her local hospital, but in making that decision she felt that she had prioritised her own life over that of the baby and felt profound guilt afterwards:

> She's [baby] everything, and I would sacrifice anything, and not getting in that ambulance and going, on the surface of it sounds like I was perhaps prioritising my life over hers, that's how it feels sometimes, but actually it wasn't, I was fed information and had to make a decision, and in the end, really, my husband made a lot of the decisions, because he said, well I'm not losing you both. The odds are, she's going to die anyway, and the odds are you'll live, so actually, they're the odds that I'm going to go with.

While parents often felt guilt about why their baby had died, they sometimes expressed feelings of relief after they received the results of their baby's post-mortem. This was because post-mortem examination confirmed to them that their actions had not caused their baby to die. This was particularly important for parents whose babies had died through SIDS. In such cases parents were usually subjected to a multi-agency investigation into the cause of their baby's death. Parents felt that they were under extreme scrutiny and subsequently often blamed themselves for their baby's death. Lesley expressed her relief at receiving the post-mortem results:

> Well, my main memory of the post-mortem, apart from when we were told... I remember Mike [her partner] coming. It must have been within two days. Because Mike arrived one morning and said we've had the post-mortem results, and I remember him saying Mia died, they don't know why she died, there was absolutely nothing wrong with her. You didn't suffocate her, you didn't roll on her, there

was nothing broken on her, she was perfect when she died. And I
remember the immense relief. Because you thought you'd rolled on her.

As this account shows, post-mortem examination can play a crucial
role in helping parents deal with some of the emotional fallout of
their loss, potentially assisting them with the longer-term management
of their grief. Some parents in our study sought to have another
baby to help assuage their grief. We will move on in the next section,
therefore, to explore mothers' emotions during later pregnancies
after the experience of loss.

Emotions and later pregnancy

Parents often describe the loss of a baby as a void that can only be
filled by a subsequent pregnancy (Dyer et al., 2019). Research also
shows, however, that women often feel particularly emotional during
subsequent pregnancies, and that these can be fraught with anxiety
(Armstrong and Hutti, 1998; Côté-Arsenault and Morrison-Beedy,
2001; Armstrong, 2004). Research has shown that parents are often
unable to feel the same excitement, anticipation and bonding during
pregnancy as they did before they had lost a baby (Burden et al.,
2016). While some parents in our study could not face the pain and
trauma of attempting another pregnancy, several participants did
go on to have subsequent pregnancies and children. Some participants
said that they felt particularly emotional during these subsequent
pregnancies. Olivia, for example, already had a three-year old son
when she lost her second baby boy, Ian, suddenly, aged only six
weeks. When we interviewed Olivia, she was twenty weeks' pregnant
with her third child. She explained how she found her third pregnancy
emotionally challenging after the loss of her second child:

> It's an emotionally difficult pregnancy [pause]. It's scary, terrifying.
> We didn't … we couldn't really talk about it for a long time and I'm
> still not able to talk about it in the same way that I was excited about
> my last two pregnancies and I think that's because my mindset has
> changed. I used to see for myself a future and I'd think about what
> was going to come in the next few weeks, months, years and now I
> have very limited capacity for looking ahead […] So this pregnancy
> is different because I'm not excited at the moment because at the
> moment my brain is not thinking about when there's a new baby
> here because my brain is too busy thinking about how am I going to

survive the next month. So it has a very different … it means that you don't talk about nurseries and names and buying clothes and [pause] I focus much more on the present.

Some mothers also experienced the additional stress of anomalies being identified in their subsequent pregnancies. This caused them further anxiety and emotional distress. After losing her baby girl Daisy, who was stillborn at term, Victoria went on to suffer a miscarriage before becoming pregnant with her son Logan, who was one at the time of interview. Victoria's pregnancy with Logan was not straightforward and she needed to undergo invasive testing to make sure that he was not suffering from a genetic disorder. She talked about how emotional she felt during this time, but also about how she found it hard to express her emotions to other people:

> Oh, it's been a nightmare for me, because his pregnancy wasn't straightforward. They thought he might have a genetic disorder at one point. So I had to have the amniocentesis and lots of scans and everything. So it's not been straightforward… I think I did alright with it, and I think for me, I think people always think I'm not very … I suppose I'm not very emotional about it. But I think I just … I shut it off and obviously everybody has a cry. But I'll have a cry in private and I'll get all my feelings out and everything and then I feel able to talk about it. I think a lot of people struggled with that because they thought she's going to collapse at some point. She's been too brave or whatever.

Parents – women in particular – often felt a heightened sense of emotion and anxiety during subsequent pregnancies (Armstrong and Hutti, 1998; Côté-Arsenault and Morrison-Beedy, 2001; Armstrong, 2004). While women often wanted to be pregnant again, they could not bear to face the same level of emotional pain as they did when they lost their baby previously. Although it was mostly women who discussed emotion specifically in relation to subsequent pregnancies, men did talk extensively about their emotions after experiencing the loss of their baby. In the following section, therefore, we move on to explore fathers' emotions in more depth.

Men, masculinity and emotion

There has been a significant amount of sociological work on gender and emotion in recent decades (Shields et al., 2006; Simon, 2014;

Hess, 2015). As such literature shows, traditionally it has been seen as acceptable for women to articulate feelings of sadness and grief. By contrast, men have been encouraged to channel their energy into expressing powerful emotions such as anger and pride (Brody, 1999; Bericat, 2016). During the 1970s feminists sought to focus on the ways in which men's emotional inexpressiveness was influenced and supported by patriarchal privilege (Firestone, 2003). As more recent literature has sought to show, increased emotional literacy among men has been seen to play a crucial role in addressing gender inequalities (Kimmel and Holler, 2011). According to de Boise and Hearn (2017), a growing body of research has shown that men not only have an active understanding of their emotions but in many cases practise more emotional forms of masculinity.

Men in our study felt extremely emotional after the loss of their babies, but often felt that they could not express their feelings in the same way as their female partners could. They tended to feel external pressure to conform to more traditional masculine stereotypes of being strong and stoical (Brody, 1999). This is demonstrated by the quote below from Nathan, whose baby Aria died suddenly aged eleven weeks. Although Nathan felt pressure to be stoical, he did acknowledge the importance of his own emotions. He appeared to resist some of the gendered assumptions made by others about how he should feel:

> I had a few people, a few clichés, like oh you need to be strong for your wife, and well I was strong enough to tell them to bog off, quite frankly. Because obviously I've got my own emotions and I've got my own things that I'm dealing with. And so I knew that, occasionally, some men there might not be that support network, or they think they've got to be stiff upper lip about it, and one of the things the charity does is the befriending, and I thought well if I still feel that I'm up to that, when I become eligible, because you need to wait a certain number of years after the bereavement, I'll look at doing it.

Men spoke about how the emotions they felt after losing their baby were distinct from anything they had ever experienced before. Wayne, for example, articulated how no other life events compared to the depth and gravity of emotion he felt after losing baby Flo: 'but it's a pretty bad thing to happen. And the emotional impact of it for me was I've had other bereavements, I've had a few traumas in my life, but this was like hitting a wall in terms of emotion.'

Men were often extremely emotional after losing their babies and were overwhelmed with sadness and grief. They did appear to articulate an active understanding of their emotions and could be seen to be practising what de Boise and Hearn refer to as '"softer" or "more emotional" forms of masculinity' (2017: 779). As shown in this section, however, men found that certain gender norms prohibited them from doing this. They still felt pressure from others to be strong and stoical rather than completely expressing their emotions. We will reflect on gender and emotion more fully in the conclusion. We want to move on now, however, to begin to explore emotion as articulated by some of the professionals in our study, focusing our analysis on the ways professionals both express and manage their emotions in this sensitive area of medicine.

Emotion work across life and death

Work that involves dealing with the loss of a baby, infant or child is particularly sensitive and emotive. As Lewis points out in her research on neonatal nurses, emotions can run high 'in a work context where the potential for death is juxtaposed with the potential for life' (2005: 569). Research on other occupational groups such as paramedics has shown that attending jobs where a baby or child was dying or dead was particularly traumatic for the professionals involved (Boyle, 2005). Professionals who work at the intersection of life and death, therefore, are often required to draw on a range of different emotion-management strategies to cope. Such strategies are likely to vary according to whether they are 'frontstage' with parents and the public or 'backstage' in private (Bolton, 2001; Boyle, 2005). Bolton and Boyd (2003) usefully outline four types of emotional-management skills that professionals might draw on in different contexts. These are presentational (emotion management according to general social 'rules'), pecuniary (emotion management for commercial gain), prescriptive (emotional management according to organisational/professional rules of conduct) and philanthropic (emotion management given as a gift). In the next section, we explore some of the emotions articulated by professionals in our study, and, drawing on Bolton and Boyd's typology, also provide an analysis of the different strategies they use to manage their emotions.

Work that makes you cry

Professionals working at the start of the post-mortem journey (such as midwives and obstetricians) were often dealing acutely with issues of life and death (Reed and Ellis, 2020). They tended to be present when women gave birth prematurely or when babies were born stillborn. They literally work at the front line of life and loss. During her interview, Wendy, a senior midwife, described how she gets very emotional and often cries when a baby has died. As articulated in the quote below, however, Wendy felt that being emotional and showing empathy when dealing with the death of a baby was an important part of being a midwife:

> And I always think it's sad and I'm sad, but it's nothing to what those parents are going through. So .t's a case of like pull yourself together. But I think if you don't cry and if you don't feel something you're probably not doing the right job. And I said that to a more junior member of staff not long ago. It's like when you stop crying that's when you've got a bit too hard to everything and you need to take a step back. And if you can just brush something so sad and tragic off, why are you doing it?

Research on emotional labour has often drawn on Goffman's (1959) dramaturgical metaphor to highlight the different ways in which professionals show and manage emotions 'frontstage' with patients and the public and privately 'backstage' at home (Bolton, 2001; Boyle 2005). Healthcare professionals are often required to be emotion jugglers who need to be able to 'match face with situation' (Bolton, 2001: 86). In our study, midwives – such as Wendy – were often required to juggle their emotions. They could be dealing with mothers who had given birth to healthy babies on the one hand, while also trying to support parents whose babies had died on the other. As Wendy stated, when faced with the death of a baby, professionals sometimes had to find somewhere private to go to at work so that they could let their emotions out:

> But on the day, I mean say you're looking after somebody who's just come in to be induced and there's nothing strange about it in any way, shape or form, then it's just a case of... I mean often I've gone off and had a little cry in our dirty sluice or something like that, and people say are you alright? And I tend to say I'll be fine if you don't

ask if I'm alright. Because you've got to then go back in that room
and look after a woman.

It was not just health professionals in our study who felt emotional,
however; most professionals got very upset when dealing with parents
who had lost a baby, regardless of what kind of job they did. Martin,
the hospital chaplain, for example, made similar comments regarding
cases where a baby had died on NICU. He felt that it was often
particularly sad when a baby had been in intensive care on life
support, and the first time the parents were able to hold the baby
was after it had died. As he states: 'we find ourselves coming out
of rooms and crying'. Similarly, Nell was a medical photographer
who often took photos of deceased babies for families either in the
mortuary or the bereavement suite. She worked across the hospital
site. Her main role was to take photos of patients' injuries for
medico-legal cases. The only contact she had with bereaved parents,
therefore, was when she went to take photos of their baby as a
keepsake for them. She particularly valued this part of her job and
always sought to give parents the best image possible. She did,
however, sometimes find it awkward and upsetting and often felt
like crying after she had taken the photos. She described the process
of photo-taking.

> You'd say, hello, I've come to take a photograph. And they've got a
> consent card and you'd just photograph the consent card but quite
> discreetly, because it seems a bit, you know, clinical. And then I'd
> maybe try and ask them, would you like the teddy in with the baby,
> or would you like a picture of you with the baby? Because I don't
> know if they've asked that or if they know that can be done. So if
> they're there I would try and just talk to them a little bit, but make
> it focused on the baby rather than – I don't know – rather than the
> loss. It's hard to know what to say. But then that's the problem. That's
> almost easier going in, because you've got a task to do. It's the leaving
> that's quite hard, because you want to say ... do you say, thank you?
> I think I've said a few times, I'm really sorry for your loss, but then
> you want to cry. It's hard to know what to do when you're leaving.

Feeling sad and struggling to control these feelings was central
to working in this area of medicine – regardless of occupation or
gender. Professionals working at the intersection of life and death
often needed to juggle their emotions depending on whether they

were dealing with 'life' or 'death'. We move on in the next section to explore some of the emotion involved in death work, focusing particularly on post-mortems.

Emotion management in post-mortem work

Qualitative research on post-mortem practice has tended to focus on the forensic and scientific aspects of the examination – less is known about the role of emotions in this form of work (Reed and Ellis, 2020). When research does include a focus on emotion, it tends to concentrate on exploring the ways in which professionals try to avoid situations that humanise the body in order to create emotional distance (McCarroll et al., 1993). Professionals in our study who were directly involved in performing autopsy – APTs and pathologists – often felt very emotional about the babies in their care. Professionals frequently employed a mix of prescriptive and philanthropic emotion-management strategies to manage such emotions (Bolton and Boyd, 2003). The emotion-management strategies that professionals used were not so much about distancing themselves from the dead person per se. Rather, while performing the examination professionals often needed to distance themselves from the family and the social context surrounding the dead person.

Despite feeling emotional, professionals often felt it was important to maintain an appropriate balance between being caring and being detached. These sentiments were articulated by the APT, Carmen. She drew on a prescriptive form of emotion management to assist with the post-mortem examination. She talked about the need to switch her emotions off to complete her clinical work.

> I found that really you have to go in there with a certain mindset and so you go in and you switch off and you do the post-mortem with the child and then at the end when you come to reconstruct that child then that's when I can sort of think well my job's done now, but it's a really strange feeling while you're doing the post-mortem that you have to just get on and do the job because it's your job to be able to try and find out why that child has died and you can't afford to be emotional so you do have to try and switch off a little bit and look at the whole picture rather than as it being a child.

Switching off their emotions in order to perform the clinical examination, however, did not mean that professionals did not feel profoundly sad. Professionals attempted to hold their emotions in while they were performing autopsy. It was often through interactions with parents and families after the clinical examination that professionals felt able to release their emotions and often cried with families. It was in these instances that we saw more philanthropic forms of emotion management at play (Bolton and Boyd, 2003; Lewis, 2005). This was articulated by Ava, who managed her emotions by not meeting families before she had performed the autopsy on their baby/child:

> Because one trick for me is I don't want to see the family before the post-mortem, because if I see them before the post-mortem then I am emotionally engaged more with the families, when if I see the baby, and then I see the family, then it's done, and I'm there to help them. And to help them find the cause of death, helps me not to be emotionally involved. Of course, sometimes you cry, with them, and you hold their hands, and you become emotional. But you leave the room and you are detached. Of course you remember cases. I remember all my babies [some] ones more than others, but one trick for me is not to meet the family before.

During the interview Ava talked about incidences that were especially emotive for pathologists and mortuary staff. She felt, for example, that it was often especially hard for staff in the mortuary when they were dealing with babies or children who had died suddenly and unexpectedly: 'the cases that involve more emotions for the pathologist I think, and the staff in general, are the babies that are born and die suddenly. Because you are talking about a baby, that was not expected to die.' In these cases, as Ava explains, the baby is often already dead when they are brought into Accident and Emergency and the family are often understandably extremely distraught. The coroner will then order a post-mortem examination. There are also home visits to the family by a paediatrician/neonatologist and the police. The paediatrician will write a clinical report for the pathologist which will include a range of information such as family history, whether the baby was face down in the cot, whether the parents are smokers, whether it is a vulnerable family known to the police, etc. This tends to be a very emotional experience for the mortuary staff. Once the examination is complete some sort of emotional equilibrium is restored in the mortuary. Members of the mortuary team would engage in more philanthropic forms of emotion management such as reconstructing the body, washing and dressing the baby and making them look nice for the parents, as Ava explains: 'I will do the post-mortem, the body will be reconstructed, the family is invited to visit the child. They bring their clothes, they bring their toys and the baby is washed, hair is shampooed, so they look nice, in their clothes, so they look nice.'

As we have discussed, professionals in our study tended to draw on a range of emotion-management techniques throughout the post-mortem process. They often needed to draw on prescriptive forms of emotion management while performing autopsy, but then switched to more philanthropic forms in making the baby look nice for the families afterwards (Bolton and Boyd, 2003). Although professionals aimed to be emotionally detached while performing autopsy, they did not achieve this by distancing themselves from the dead body itself. Rather, they often needed to distance themselves from the family on a temporary basis until the examination was complete. Data from our study, therefore, appears to reinforce the argument often articulated by sociologists that emotions are strongly mediated by social relations (Barbalet, 1998; Bericat, 2016). We will pick up on this in more detail in the chapter's conclusion. In the following sections, however, we examine other, often hidden types of emotion – namely humour – and the way that this can be employed by professionals as a coping mechanism in the face of such distressing work.

Humour and repulsion: the role of other emotions

Several scholars have sought to show that humour in medicine is often used to relieve stress and create solidarity among health professionals (Coombs et al., 1993; Parsons et al., 2001). Gabbert (2020) explores the role of humour in medicine through the lens of suffering. She argues that in contexts of suffering, medical staff use humour as a traditional means of transformation. They assign comic meaning to various dimensions of suffering, and in doing so, temporarily transform it into something else, thereby shifting the actual experience of work-related suffering. In this chapter so far we have focused on exploring the various strategies that professionals use to manage their sadness when dealing with the trauma of baby loss and post-mortem examination – such as crying in private or not meeting the family before conducting the post-mortem. Occasionally professionals in our study used humour as a way of coping with the traumatic nature of their work. This was articulated by Nell, the medical photographer, who talked about the challenges of photographing a second trimester fetus. These fetuses are often very small and are not yet fully formed. As Nell stated, photographers try to produce the best images possible for the parents. This is often a very sad and traumatic experience for photographers. She talked about some of the dark humour used to try and cope with this: 'jelly babies we call them [fetuses] just in the office [laughs], you know. It's, sort of, I think a bit of black humour, isn't it?'

Regardless of how a baby might look when it is born, professionals were all clear that one set of emotions that should never be visible 'frontstage' with parents are feelings of shock or horror. This was something articulated by Wendy, a senior midwife:

> But once as a student I read a piece of research that a woman was talking about stillbirths and she said two things. She said she remembered the look on the midwife's face when she delivered the baby, and that's always stuck with me, that no matter what this baby looks like we should never look horrified. Because sometimes babies obviously don't come out in a very good condition. And that has always stuck with me for ever and ever, is that you should let them...

In her work on hospice care, Lawton (1998) wrote about leaky, smelly and disintegrating dying bodies and the need to sequester such bodies from mainstream society. In our study, humour was sometimes employed to deal with some of the more unappealing olfactory side effects of death. During her interview Linda, a bereavement assistant, for example, talked about a baby who had been in the bereavement suite for a long time. The baby's parents came to visit every day. Over time the baby's body began to deteriorate and smell. After getting the baby ready for a parental visit, Linda made a joke to one of her colleagues: 'I said to Phillipa, I don't want my dinner now.' Linda was an immensely caring member of staff who went above and beyond her role to help support parents. As we will see in the next chapter, she was also caring and respectful to the babies she tended. Humour in this instance, therefore, appeared to be used to help her cope with witnessing parental suffering and with the general sadness of her job. Similarly, Wendy felt very emotional about her work. During our interview she talked about how she and a group of midwives joked that they were the 'grim reapers', as they were always the ones dealing with the traumatic cases of stillbirth. This dark humour was again used as a coping mechanism for Wendy and her colleagues:

> And it tends to come in runs, it's very bizarre. So you might not have any [baby deaths] for a couple of weeks and then you'll have three ladies all at once that come in, or you'll have two stillbirths in a night or something really horrible like that. So I'd say you see a fair amount of it, I couldn't give you a figure. But I mean a midwife I was speaking with … we were talking about every year there's a remembrance service and there's a few of us that call ourselves the grim reapers sometimes, because we always seem to be involved in the ladies that who have stillbirths, and she's one of them.

Occasionally professionals drew on humour as a coping mechanism to deal with the traumatic nature of their work. It was also a way for professionals to try to deal with the parental suffering they had witnessed as part of the job (Gabbert, 2020). Humour was only used by professionals in a 'backstage' context, however, when they were in the company of other professionals – not 'frontstage' with parents and publics. It was not felt to be either socially appropriate or professionally acceptable to use humour in public in such a sensitive context. In this setting professionals felt they needed to perform both presentational (emotion management according to general social 'rules') and prescriptive (emotional management according to organisational/professional rules of conduct) forms of emotion management (Bolton and Boyd, 2003; Reed and Ellis, 2020). Despite the challenging nature of emotional work, however, professionals often placed significant value on this form of labour.

The value of emotion: celebrating life in death

The personal value professionals ascribe to emotional work is often emphasised in existing research, particularly in contrast to the increasingly bureaucratised nature of work (Bolton, 2000; Twigg et al., 2011; Reed and Ellis, 2020). Despite this positive experience, however, sociologists often argue that emotion management – particularly philanthropic forms – still tends to be viewed as natural and female, and as undeserving of financial reward (Lewis, 2005). While emotion work in our study was challenging and often hidden from wider public view, it was a form of work that professionals tended to value. For example, emotion work for professionals was not just about dealing with sadness and trauma, it could sometimes also involve celebrating life. This was articulated by Carmen who spoke about how families sometimes wanted to spend time remembering or celebrating their baby/child. The mortuary staff often facilitate and join in with this process, as she explained:

> We've sat there [with parents/families] and we've gone through like photographs on the phone, we've gone through videos on the phone, and just really just talk about life with their child and laughed there, we've had tea parties, we've done it all, we've had people playing musical instruments, we've had families that for a religious ceremony they've all come in and they've started singing, and I just think there's just, you know, that death's really so awful for some religions and some people just it's like a celebration of their life and sometimes although in the midst of it and it's really awful there can be so much joy as well, you know, that people are singing.

As shown in Chapter 3, mortuary-based professionals such as Carmen work exclusively with dead bodies, and are used to managing their emotions in this context. By contrast, some professionals in our study worked almost exclusively with living patients. These professionals often articulated mixed feelings about dealing with dead babies. Some radiographers, for example, articulated strong feelings of sadness at imaging dead babies and some of them felt unable to perform such scans. Others, however, felt that scanning terminally ill children was much more emotionally traumatic work. This was articulated by radiographer June:

> And obviously we have some quite sad cases here [in the hospital] who are not dead. So I tend to, sort of, think, well, there's nothing more we can do for them [deceased babies] really. So, no, it doesn't. But, I mean, I know some of my colleagues obviously don't feel the same as me and they are affected by it, so they don't want to see the babies.

Finally, despite the sadness of their work, most professionals in the study tended to talk very positively about what they did. During his medical career Dave, a neonatologist, had played a pivotal role in supporting families in cases of SIDS when a baby had died suddenly of unknown causes. These are complex cases often requiring the involvement of a multi-agency response team and a coronial post-mortem. Dave emphasised the importance of going to see families soon after the baby's death and before the post-mortem examination, ideally within twelve to twenty-four hours. There are three to five SIDS cases per year in the location where our study took place (at the time of writing). Dave emphasised the ways in which clinicians and charities had worked together to decriminalise SIDS over time, emotional support becoming an accepted aspect of multi-agency professional practice (Reed and Ellis, 2020). He was very proud of this aspect of his work and felt that helping parents in this way was beneficial to him as a clinician. He told us: 'what I get out of it is trying to help the parents. Of course these are sad situations, of course you might feel emotional about them but actually what you're trying to do is help the parents through that difficult time.'

Being emotional was a central and important part of professional practice in baby loss and post-mortem care, involving the articulation and management of a range of different emotions. While emotional labour in this context was 'hard' work, it could also be a productive process that was highly valued by professionals (Reed and Ellis, 2020). Furthermore, through the clinical examination, professionals could provide parents with important information about why their baby had died. This could offset some of the challenges of emotion work in this sensitive setting (Gassaway, 2007).

Before concluding, we would like to move on in the next section to explore one final aspect of emotion work that was central to the research on which this book is based: the emotion work of the research team.

Reflexivity and emotional research work

An increasing amount of literature has focused on the role of emotions in social research (Reed and Towers, 2021). This includes studies that have sought to shed light on the myriad of emotions that researchers experience when conducting perinatal research (Jones and Murphy, 2021). Existing literature on this issue has identified several factors (from the sensitive nature of the subject matter under study to prior personal experience) as evoking a range of emotions in researchers. These include frustration, loneliness, sadness, boredom, apprehension, guilt, exhaustion, fear, humour, relief and repulsion (Dickson-Swift et al., 2009; Jones and Murphy, 2021). Some researchers even discuss the physical pain and distress experienced during and after fieldwork (Emerald and Carpenter, 2015). While literature does acknowledge that emotions are an important and central part of knowledge production (Rager, 2005; Holland, 2009), the more life-affirming impact of emotions in research remains neglected (Jones and Murphy, 2021; Reed and Towers, 2021). It is perhaps no surprise, therefore, that literature in this area has tended to frame research as a form of 'emotional labour' and has sought to advocate a range of self-care and reflexive practices to help researchers cope with some of the emotional challenges they face. Drawing on fieldnotes from the study, we seek, in this section, to explore and reflect on some of the emotional challenges that we faced during the research. As we will show, although research on such a difficult and sad subject could be challenging, it could also be life-affirming, often reinforcing the value of social science research.

Both researchers on the project – Kate and Julie – spent a significant amount of time in the mortuary observing various practices and conducting go-along tours with key professionals such as Ava and Carmen. In order to fully explore the post-mortem journey, we asked the mortuary team whether we could observe an MIA post-mortem. We had ethical approval to conduct such observations, and the mortuary team gave their consent for us to do so. The APT and mortuary manager, Carmen, let us know when an MIA case was coming in so that we could go along to observe. We observed the MIA of a 22-week-old fetus. Another MIA post-mortem of a four-month-old baby was taking place in the dissection room at the same time. The mortuary staff were quite worried about how we would cope, particularly with seeing the autopsy of the older baby. In the fieldnotes below Julie describes how Carmen tried to prepare us for this process:

> She asks if either of us have seen a fetus before – and Kate explains she has but I say that it will be my first time. Carmen pulls a concerned face and I do my best to convince her that I'm prepared and I'll let them know if I'm struggling. She also tells us that there will be another baby in the PM room – one of the other pathologists, James, will be

doing the PM. She wonders if we'll be OK with that and says they can cover the face if we'd rather. I realise now that this baby must be at least full term – and recognisable as a baby. Carmen anticipates that we'll find that more difficult it seems. We don't ask for the face to be covered.

Witnessing the post-mortems was a heart-breaking experience for both researchers. What was often more emotionally challenging, however, was listening to parents talk about their experiences of loss during research interviews. Prior to interviews, we invited parents to bring memory items with them to help them talk through their experiences of loss. Parents brought different objects with them, from photos to a favourite cuddly toy. Some parents brought a memory box filled with different items such as positive pregnancy tests, knitted hats, babygros, locks of hair, condolence cards etc. Kate interviewed Esther and Ricky in a neutral location – an out-of-town café. Their baby boy – Oliver – had died one year prior to the interview. Esther gave birth prematurely to Oliver, who died at just twenty-five weeks. The couple brought their memory box and baby photo album with them and went through the different items and pictures with Kate during the interview. Going through both the photo album and memory box was an immensely emotional experience for Kate, as articulated in the fieldnotes:

> As we went through the different items from their memory box I felt really sad, from the positive pregnancy test to the congratulations and condolence cards. But it was looking at the photos of their baby boy in NICU that was really hard. We sat together, in an out-of-town café, just off a very busy road, and shared a tear.

Feeling and demonstrating emotion during the research was not necessarily a negative experience for either researcher or respondent. Knowing that both researchers cared about their experiences of loss was often very important to parent respondents. Feeling emotional with respondents could also act as a life-affirming experience for the researchers. These sentiments are articulated by Julie in the fieldnotes below in relation to her experience of interviewing Anna, whose baby girl Lily had died over three years previously at twenty-three weeks:

> There are times when Anna is speaking that I can feel my eyes become watery – and particularly when she talks about the moments she had

with Lily alive, I feel emotional and feel I need to point this out to Anna so she doesn't notice and worry. I explain I'm fine and she isn't making me sad, just that it is moving to hear her speak in this way. Anna understands and explains it sometimes gives her comfort to know others feel moved and care.

There has been a growing awareness in recent decades that conducting bereavement-focused fieldwork can be very emotionally challenging (Valentine, 2007). While both researchers had expected to feel emotional during parent interviews, what was less expected were the emotions they both felt when interviewing professionals. Listening to professionals talk passionately about their work could be an equally moving experience for the researchers. This was articulated by Julie in relation to her experience of interviewing senior pathologist Ava: 'I am struck by her warmth and care for families. At one point I am touched by something she says about a family and when I tell her hearing her speak about her work makes me feel emotional – she reaches out to touch my arm.'

As Reed and Towers (2021) have argued, while interviews can be a very emotional experience, researchers can be distracted by various tasks while conducting them. For example, during interviews researchers tend to concentrate their attention on following an interview schedule and being mindful of respondent emotions throughout the process. By contrast, after interviews have finished, researchers can have more time to stop and reflect on what has been said. It was often during these moments of reflection that Kate and Julie felt particularly emotionally exhausted. This is articulated in Julie's fieldnotes below, written after she had completed several interviews with parents in one week:

> After I leave and get back in the car the weight of the week (and its cumulative sadness) hits me. I feel very tired and tearful as I sit in the car and contemplate the drive into the office. I move the car away and then park up further away from the house. I call family and eat something before driving to the office to deal with the various post-interview tasks.

Both Julie and Kate sought to manage their emotions throughout the research process by adopting a range of reflexive self-care practices – from keeping a diary to peer debriefing (Rager, 2005; Borgstrom and Ellis, 2017). Such reflexive practices can be useful for drawing out unanticipated emotional responses in research. There is concern, however, that the voice of the respondent can be eclipsed through confessional-style approaches in favour of that of the researcher, potentially reinforcing rather than overcoming power relations in the research process (Finlay, 2002; Faria and Mollett, 2016). Furthermore, as Borgstrom and Ellis (2021) note, while such approaches can serve to heighten a researcher's emotional awareness, they do not always provide a proper outlet for researcher emotionality. This is something we will consider further in the final chapter of this book. In the next section, however, we provide a conclusion for this chapter.

Conclusion

Emotion was a key aspect of our parental and professional data, as well as being a core part of the research process itself. Being and feeling emotional in an embodied sense (Denzin, 2009) and conducting emotion work is central to the experience of baby loss and professional practice in this area. Conducting research on baby loss and post-mortem practice is also an immensely emotional experience for the researchers involved. In support of the findings of existing research, we found that the strongest emotions articulated by parents in our study were trauma, sadness and grief (Dyer et al., 2019). During interviews, however, parents also discussed some hidden and often unanticipated emotions. For example, bereaved parents did sometimes experience temporary moments of joy – when they gave birth and met their baby for the first time, or when their baby was returned to them washed and dressed after post-mortem examination (Burden et al., 2016; Nuzum et al., 2018). Furthermore, while sadness was the overwhelming emotion expressed by the professionals in the study, they did experience other emotions such as pride at having helped to support a family during their time of need (Reed and Ellis, 2020). We highlight the need, therefore, for sociologists to explore some of the more positive but hidden forms of emotions in sensitive contexts such as these. While such positive emotions may be fleeting, they are crucial to both parental and professional experience.

While losing a baby is obviously an intensely emotional experience for parents, it could also be very emotive for the professionals involved in caring for babies and families. Professionals in our study, therefore, all employed different types of emotion-management strategies to cope. These often varied according to roles. Professionals working at the acute intersection of life and death – such as midwives – were often required to act as emotional jugglers, changing their emotions to match face to situation (Bolton, 2001). Pathologists and APTs appeared to draw on different emotion-management strategies during different parts of the post-mortem examination. They tended to use prescriptive forms of emotion management during autopsy to maintain emotional distance. They would then switch to philanthropic forms afterwards through the process of making babies look nice for their families (Bolton and Boyd, 2003). Professionals did tend to moderate their emotions according to whether they were 'frontstage' with parents or 'backstage' in private areas of work (Bolton, 2001). For example, some professionals used humour to manage their sadness and transform their experience of witnessing suffering (Gabbert, 2020). Such humour could act as a source of solidarity but was only ever performed backstage, away from parents. In situations where professionals broke down and became emotional in front of parents, however, the boundaries between front and backstage often became more blurred (Reed and Ellis, 2020).

Sociological research has often highlighted the ways in which the articulation and experience of emotion and emotion work are gendered (McCreight, 2005; Shields et al., 2006; Simon, 2014; Hess, 2015). Drawing on data from our study, we have sought to show a more complicated picture. While mothers in our study did tend to talk about their emotions more freely, fathers also suffered extreme sadness and grief after the loss of their babies. Men often felt that they could not fully express their emotions as they needed to be strong for their partner. This reinforces the argument we made in Chapter 1 about masculinities in transition (Robinson and Hockey, 2011), and to which we will return in Chapter 7 on relationships. Men in our study were both active fathers and partners, but also sometimes reverted to more traditional masculine roles of breadwinner and protector (Reed, 2012). Professional data explored in this chapter also supports the notion of gender roles in transition, or what Lorber (1994) refers to as the paradox of gender. Female professionals often appeared to be more vocal about emotion work than men. However, this was not just the case with nurses, midwives and allied health professionals but also with senior doctors. Furthermore, while female participants were generally more vocal about their feelings, male participants did indeed talk about and practise more emotional forms of masculinity (de Boise and Hearn, 2017). We suggest that these findings emphasise two key issues: first, that the relationship between gender and emotion is continually evolving, and secondly, that emotion work is becoming a more acceptable part of professional practice in healthcare.

As well as focusing on emotions in the data, we have also sought to show how researching such a sensitive topic can be an intensely emotional experience for the research team. During the research, both researchers experienced a myriad of emotions – from extreme sadness to more life-affirming and positive emotions. The emotions experienced by the research team were mediated through their social relationships with research participants. This serves to reinforce a wider point, that emotions do not occur in a vacuum but emerge and are experienced through social relations. To understand the articulation of different emotions, therefore, it is necessary to understand the situations and social relations that produce them (Bericat, 2016). In all cases explored here, the experience of emotion is strongly mediated by the social relations that surround them. This is something we will continue to return to throughout this book, beginning in the next chapter with a focus on the issue of care.

Chapter 5

Care

The notion of 'care' has a long history in Western philosophy and culture (Fine, 2005). Over the past forty years there has been a significant body of work on care from feminists and others writing from a sociological and social policy perspective (e.g., Freidson, 1970; Parker, 1981; Graham, 1983, 1991; Hochschild, 1983; Waerness, 1987; Abrams, 1989; Arber and Gilbert, 1989; Ungerson, 1990; James, 1992; Thomas, 1993; Daly and Lewis, 2000). Care, however, has remained neglected in the work of major contemporary social theorists. As Fine argues, since it is impossible to imagine a world without care, such neglect is 'a serious shortcoming and distortion of their approaches' (2005: 249). Social relations are foundational to the notion of care. It is based on a social relationship between a person who gives care and another who receives care (Krause and Boldt, 2018). According to Fine (2005), care is a necessary social response to bodily vulnerability and a foundation for the patterns of social solidarity that underlie human societies. In her work on care, Thomas has questioned the extent to which it is 'a *theoretical* category' in its own right, 'or whether forms of care are *empirical* entities which must be analysed in terms of other theoretical categories' (1993: 650). Fine, however, makes a strong and compelling case for it to be considered a core concern in sociological theory and research.

According to Twigg, 'the word "care" is notably a slippery one that elides normative and analytic elements' (2000: 393). The difficulty of the concept of care begins, according to Thomas, with the verb to care, which can mean two different things. It may refer to 'either a *feeling state* (emotion, affection, love) – "caring about someone", or an *activity state* (work, tasks, labour) – "caring for someone"'

(Thomas, 1993: 652). In sociological research, care has often provided a route through which to analyse the welfare state, its ideologies and systems. Building a greater understanding of the needs and interests of certain vulnerable groups in society through research on care can also have practical implications relating to its delivery (Thomas, 1993). Regardless of how the concept has been defined and approached in sociology, however, feminist authors have consistently shown that care remains a predominantly female activity, and as such they argue that its analysis must be rooted in the gender order (Graham, 1983, 1991; Ungerson, 1990; Thomas, 1993). While the meanings attributed to the concept of care are diverse, so too are those associated with the concept of 'carer', which can include paid professionals, paid non-professionals, volunteers, and care that arises from unpaid domestic work (James, 1992). It is no surprise therefore that the social relations of care are difficult to research and understand.

Despite the difficulties of defining and theorising care, the concept has been used by sociologists to explore a range of issues (for example, nurture, treatment, protection, containment or work) in various settings – from children's homes to residential care for older people (Oakley, 1974). Care is also often the central focus of sociological research on palliative and end-of-life 'care' (James, 1992). There is also a significant amount of literature that has focused on exploring the professional care of children in health and palliative care settings (Committee on Bioethics and Committee on Hospital Care, 2000; Shields and King, 2001). While sociologists have often analysed the role of care in various formal healthcare settings (Allen, 2019; Krause and Boldt, 2018), research has yet to focus on care in certain specialties such as post-mortem and mortuary work.

In this chapter we seek to shed light on the role of care in post-mortem work, referring to care in this context as an activity state (Thomas, 1993: 652), a range of practices with purpose and intention. Drawing on data from the study, we explore the various care practices enacted by different types of health professionals. Although hidden from the view of the public and some other clinical staff, such practices are often crucial to parental and professional experience of the post-mortem process. By uncovering some of these hidden care practices, this chapter seeks to extend existing sociological literature on both care and post-mortem work.

Bodies, care and death work

In recent years there has been an increasing interest in sociology and social policy on the links between the body and care (Twigg, 2000, 2004; Fine, 2005). As Twigg has argued, at the most fundamental level, care involves a relationship based on intimate physical tending. When care includes attendance to the physical needs of others through body work it is generally treated as dirty work, a hidden and often devalued form of labour (Twigg, 2000). Body work is often viewed as a form of dirty work because it involves the negotiation of leaking bodies and boundaries (Twigg et al., 2011; Nettleton, 2021). Care work is governed by a division of labour, with those professionals able to distance themselves from body work being accorded the greatest prestige (for example, managers, counsellors) (Twigg, 2000; Fine, 2005). In the context of death and dying work, care is often mediated through the body of the deceased. For example, as Howarth (1996) argues, care is often articulated in the profession of funeral directing through attempts to 'rehumanise' the corpse with embalming and individualised presentation. Care of dead, dying and disintegrating bodies tends to be particularly sequestered labour (Lawton, 1998), viewed by many as a form of dirty work (Ashforth and Kreiner, 1999).

As Thomas (1993) argues, the way care is delivered varies according to context and the institutional and organisational setting in which it is administered. Care in death and dying work can take place in many settings: in the home, the hospital, hospice or at the funeral directors. In healthcare, for example, care of the dead is administered in an institutionalised and professionalised context. In contrast to care that takes place in a domestic context, care actions in healthcare are often standardised and subject to assessment, often creating a source of normative tension (Krause and Boldt, 2018). Care can be in direct conflict with commercial interests in certain private-sector contexts (for example, funeral directors) (Bailey, 2010). By contrast, care of the dying in a hospice setting is based on a family model (James, 1992), whereby care is understood in terms of family relationships in which 'caring for' someone is assumed from a relationship of 'caring about' them (James, 1992; Allen, 2019). The division of labour in hospices replicates hospital labour divisions, however, resulting in a form of hospice care which is often incompatible with the 'family' model. As several sociologists have pointed out, regardless of variation in context, care work must be seen as an activity shaped by similar factors to those affecting other paid employment, including, for example, time pressure and a resistance to formal definitions of the work (Twigg, 2000).

This chapter will centre its analysis primarily on care performed by professionals in a hospital context. Throughout the chapter we examine various care activities embedded in different forms of professional practice. We explore the importance of different locations of care, paying attention to the ways in which care in this context is often performed as a form of body work. We will also examine some of the constraints that professionals face when attempting to care. Central to the chapter, however, is an exploration of the hidden care that takes place in the mortuary. This includes an exploration of the ways in which professionals frequently sing to and dress babies. We acknowledge that care delivered in this context is a form of gendered work (Graham, 1983, 1991; Ungerson, 1990; Twigg, 2000) and that hierarchical divisions of care operate both within and across occupations (Daykin and Clarke, 2000). Our data shows, however, that care in post-mortem work is performed by both women and men across occupational groups and status positions. We seek to make the case, therefore, for a more fine-grained analysis of these issues in the future. Furthermore, while highlighting the ways in which care conducted in this context is often hidden work, we do not see this necessarily as a form of 'dirty' and devalued labour. Rather, we highlight some of the ways in which professionals take immense professional pride in this work.

It's just part of the job: the role of care in professional practice

Existing literature on care in healthcare has traditionally focused on examining the occupational and gendered division of labour in care, centring its analysis on the relationship between certain occupational groups – doctors and nurses. It tends to highlight the ways in which (male) clinicians often perform the scientific, diagnostic work, while nurses and other allied health professionals perform the direct care and body work (James, 1992; Twigg, 2000). Our study included a wide range of occupational and professional groups, from midwives through to police officers. Care often took different forms depending on our respondents' occupational group and status. It was not, however, something that was just performed by women in allied health occupations. It was performed by a whole range of different professionals – from hospital chaplains and administrators to consultant neonatologists. The aim of this section, therefore, is to introduce the reader to some of these different forms of care in this setting.

Over the past forty years, nursing in the UK has undergone significant change, largely driven by a professionalisation strategy which began with Project 2020.[1] This has led to a medical division of labour in which nurses have mostly divested themselves of hands-on care, while being held increasingly accountable for its quality (Allen, 2019). We interviewed two nurses as part of our study – a consultant obstetrics and gynaecology nurse and a paediatric surgical nurse. As articulated at the start of the chapter, care must be seen as an activity state, a range of practices with intention. This is illustrated by Tracey, a surgical nurse. She talked at length about the ways in which she felt that care was central to being a paediatric nurse. In the quote below she demonstrates how her care for her patients goes beyond the hospital context, as she often attends the funerals of babies and children who have died:

> Quite a few people [professionals] want to go to the funeral. So, I think part of it is, as your job, but part of it is it's just personally, it's personal because you're that sort of person who does nursing, do you know what I mean? You wouldn't be doing nursing. It's just part of what you do.

Care in our study was not just the province of healthcare professionals, however, but was also performed by professionals from other occupational groups. Hospital chaplains, for example, performed spiritual and pastoral forms of care. As Cunningham et al. note, chaplains have an ability to connect with patients on a different level than healthcare professionals, providing a form of care and perspective that would not be expected from physicians or nurses

(Cunningham et al., 2017). One of the hospital chaplains in our study, Frank, outlined his role:

> So we're employed to care for the religious, pastoral and spiritual needs of patients, staff and relatives, carers. So basically the whole hospital. And in that sense we're not a dedicated resource anywhere. So we can be called anywhere. What we tend to do in practice is have areas where we're proactive and say we know there will be particular need in these places. Neonatal, labour ward are obvious places when a baby's dying. There can be issues that parents may well want support with and a provision of ritual being an obvious thing.

Existing literature on care work in healthcare tends to focus on the ways in which allied health professionals – such as nurses and nursing assistants – tend to perform most of the care (Twigg, 1999, 2000; Daykin and Clarke, 2000). Although it often took different forms, care in our study was also a fundamental part of the work of doctors – regardless of medical specialty or gender. Brian, for example, a consultant neonatologist, articulated what caring meant for him in his work. He spoke about the importance of looking after families and respecting their wishes:

> Well, it's obviously a lot of communication, supporting parents, making sure other team members are involved. Following the family's wishes, the ways they want to say goodbye, whether they want to consider moving to another place, whether they want to go home to die, whether they want to go to a hospice.

Parents, as already noted in earlier chapters, were often very fearful of their baby undergoing a post-mortem examination. One of their chief concerns was knowing who the professionals were who would be looking after their baby during the examination. Care was central to the work of the mortuary team – the pathologists and APTs. As Carmen explained, addressing parental fears over who would be caring for their baby was crucial to post-mortem work: 'I think the concerns that most parents have is are you going to look after them [baby], can you make sure they're alright, and I think really by meeting us as a team you can see that we're not that scary, you know.'

As we will see throughout this chapter, there was diversity in the types of care practices conducted by professions in the study. Such practices tended to vary according to when and where they were taking place and who was doing them. In all cases, however, care consists of a range of practices with purpose. Most professionals in the study, regardless of occupation or gender, did perform some form of 'care' work and saw it as an integral and valued part of their job. As others have argued, context and setting are crucial to how care is performed in both an informal and formal context. In the following section, therefore, we will focus on the role of care and space.

Labour and loss: the private/public locations of care

As Gregory and Urry argue, spatial structures provide 'a medium through which social relations are produced and reproduced' (1985: 3). In the context of care, as various scholars have shown, social relations are produced across both private and public spaces, often reconfiguring spatial structures in the process (Twigg, 1999; McIntosh, 2008). Twigg (1999) has shown how domiciliary care often transgresses the boundary between the public and private realm, involving intimate body work within the home, reordering this division in different ways. According to McIntosh (2008), in the context of formal healthcare, facilities often become both public and intimate spaces simultaneously. He argues that this is because the therapeutic interactivity that occurs in them challenges existing structures, creating new spaces in the process. Such spaces can be experienced by patients and professionals as both authentic and inauthentic, as caring and supportive, or as reinforcing separation and isolation (Griffin and Yancey, 2009; Glenister, 2012). As we will explore in this section, care work in our study around post-mortem practices tended to challenge the boundaries between the public and private realm in different ways.

Professionals worked hard to create a caring and supportive environment for bereaved parents in the hospital. This work often began on the labour wards. In the maternity hospital where part of the study took place, there is a special room, the butterfly room, which is decorated like a hotel room, with suitable relaxing colours. It was created in this way to provide a space where parents could spend time with their baby after stillbirth. However, the room was not clinically equipped and therefore women could not give birth in it. Mothers would have to give birth on the labour ward and then walk down the corridor to the butterfly room. In response to parent feedback about the trauma surrounding this experience, the midwives reordered the space to create a more appropriate environment for parents whose babies were stillborn, as articulated by Wendy:

> But what we've recently done, because we used to tend to put ladies who were having stillbirths in the room next to the labour ward office, so we have an office and then we have a labour room right next door. But unfortunately somebody must have commented once, a parent, that you can hear … well, the phone ringing at the desk all the time. You can also hear laughing and joking quite a lot [...] So we then decided to move the room next to the Freesia [special labour] room and try and aim to deliver people in that room. And that cuts down on them having to make the awful walk down the labour ward corridor. It's also at the end of labour ward so they're less likely to be able to hear people with either crying babies or laughing and joking.

The midwives and bereavement support team sought to make the butterfly room as soothing a space for parents as possible. There were sometimes institutional and organisational challenges related to this. Heather, the bereavement services manager, for example, explained that the special bedding used in this room often got mixed in with the general hospital bedding, meaning she ended up buying replacement bedding with her own money:

> Yeah, which the bedding from the butterfly room upstairs is supposed to go to special care for washing, but sometimes I think they just forget. They must be on autopilot, take the bedding off and chuck it in the regular hospital … and then it disappears, so again I have to go and buy more linen, I have to buy it out of my own money and then claim it back [laughs].

In the mortuary there were several family spaces for parents to spend time with their deceased babies. These included the family room with chairs and a small kitchenette, the viewing room with crib and bed, and a conservatory space with sofas and views on to a small courtyard outside. Professionals sought to make these family spaces appear more 'homely' and less institutionalised for families.

This is illustrated by Kate's fieldnotes relating to the conservatory space in the mortuary:

> The conservatory was built by charitable donations and was decorated by Bletchley's (non-standard NHS). This is actually problematic as it does not meet NHS fire safety requirements but the professionals insisted that it be decorated (they tend to keep quiet about the issue of decor) in this way to make it more of a 'home' from 'home' rather than an institutionalised space.

In their research on palliative care, Driessen et al. (2021) suggest moving away from associating a singular notion of death with unproblematic ideas of place. Rather, they suggest that a more dynamic relationship exists between a patient and their location as they approach the end of their life. This was something that was reflected in our study. While the care of dying or dead babies often involved bringing the 'home' into the 'hospital' to create a less institutionalised space, it could also involve bringing the hospital into the home. For example, professionals in the hospital would often support parents to take very poorly babies home to die. This included setting up a ventilator in the parents' home and ending life support in the home context. Professionals (such as funeral directors) also often supported parents to take their babies home so that they could spend time with them in their own home environment after they had died. This was particularly articulated by one of our mothers, Rosie, whose baby Camilla had suddenly died age four months while in foster care. The funeral directors encouraged Rosie and her partner to bring their baby home before the funeral. As Camilla had not been in Rosie's care for some time, this was vitally important to her:

> Rosie: So we had her home for the afternoon. Which was, yeah, it was nice. It was one of those things where I said, I had to do that, she had to come home, because she'd been in foster care for several weeks, I said, she's got to come home before we lay her to rest. I didn't budge on that one. Some people might think it's strange, but I don't care.

> Interviewer: And was that something that was offered to you, or is that something you asked for?

> Rosie: They offered, yeah, our funeral directors offered, yeah, and brought her home in a little white Moses basket. So, it was nice.

Care work around baby loss and post-mortem examination, therefore, did appear to transgress the boundaries between private and public realms in various ways (Twigg, 1999). Professionals sought to make hospital spaces more authentically 'homely' and caring in different ways: by creating and moving rooms so that parents did not have to endure the sounds of healthy babies being born to other mothers, and by furnishing certain locations with bespoke bedding and decor (Griffin and Yancey, 2009; Glenister, 2012). At other times, professionals sought to bring the hospital into the home so that babies could die at home with their family around them. In the context of our study, therefore, both home and hospital were often simultaneously private and public locations of care (McIntosh, 2008). We move on in the following sections to explore in detail some of the care practices that take place in these settings, shedding light on their social nature in the process.

Hidden forms of care: singing and talking to baby

The notion of care work as a form of hidden work is not novel. Studies on informal care, for example, have often focused on the ways in which this is a hidden and gendered form of work (Graham, 1983), with informal carers often struggling to gain access to appropriate resources and support (Knowles et al., 2016). We seek, however, to uncover and explore a different form of hidden care work. We will focus on exploring how professionals often talked and sang to babies as they cared for them, treating them as if they were still alive. These practices were often hidden from public view and from the view of professionals working in other parts of the hospital. The reasons professionals gave for engaging in these specific care practices were twofold; first, they felt it was respectful to the babies in their care, an important way of maintaining the baby's dignity and personhood. Secondly, it was often a coping mechanism for health professionals, an important way for them to deal with the sadness of the situation. This form of work began on the labour ward with midwives caring for stillborn babies. Wendy explained how she talked to the babies when she was getting them ready for parents:

> And I mean if I wash a baby after it's died or I do anything with it and I dress it or I'm taking its hand and footprint, I talk to the baby,

because I have to. Because I can't treat it like it's a dead baby, it has to... I keep it alive in my head.

After death, babies would often be taken down to the bereavement suite in the maternity wing to be stored in fridges before either being moved to the mortuary for post-mortem examination or being picked up by funeral directors in preparation for the funeral. Babies were cared for in the bereavement suite by members of the bereavement support team, including Linda, a bereavement assistant. She would dress and care for the babies, getting them out of the fridge in advance of parental visits to ensure they were not too cold. Linda spoke of how she often talked and sang to the babies and wanted to keep them warm and snuggled up while they were in her care. This was partly because she cared deeply for the babies and the parents. As with Wendy, it was also a way for her to cope with the sadness of the situation:

> When I see the babies I just say, are you going to sleep now? Has mummy said that you need to go to sleep and I just sing to them, that's my way of thinking, they've not passed away, they're just asleep and I love to get them out and make sure that they're wrapped up.

This form of care work continued as babies were moved to the mortuary. The mortuary manager Carmen commented on how she sang and talked to the babies as she was doing reconstruction work after post-mortem. She felt that the mortuary team were like child-minders, looking after babies while they were in their care:

> I think by meeting us and seeing that we're quite normal really, I just like them to think of us as a childminder that, you know, just because their child's died it's no different to us, and yeah, we do go and I mean I talk to them, I have the radio on so sometimes I sing, which my singing is awful [laughs], but I think just that normality of being with them [the babies].

This form of care work – talking and singing to babies – was central to the work of certain allied health professionals (such as APTs), but it was also a crucial part of care work performed by clinicians during post-mortem examination. For example, Elena, a radiologist, talked to the babies as she was scanning them as part of an MIA. These kinds of care practices, however, were often completely hidden from parents. When parents received information about the post-mortem prior to consent being taken, it tended to be focused on the clinical examination. There was no mention of care practices in this literature. The senior midwife Wendy felt, however, that it was important for parents to know that this kind of care went on:

> And Elena [the radiologist] was saying she talks to the babies and I was thinking that's nice. And if parents knew that and knew how kind people were, because I'm sure they've just got this image of this like ... just like you see on TV, isn't it? I mean we're just ... that's all the experience a lot of ordinary people have got, is a metal table in a cold room, usually with a police officer stood watching.

Existing studies on baby loss have explored the role of professionals in working with parents to create and maintain their baby's person-hood by obtaining footprints, a lock of hair etc. (Layne, 2012). Less is known, however, about some of the professional care practices that take place after a baby has died – such as singing and talking to babies – and the function that these activities perform for babies, parents and professionals. We have uncovered some of these hidden practices in this section. In what follows we extend this focus on hidden care work, this time focusing more explicitly on care and body work.

Dressing and handling baby: administering care through body work

As argued in the introduction, in recent years there has been an increasing focus on care work as a form of body work (Fine, 2005; Twigg, 2000, 2004). Sociologists have shown how such work tends to be gendered and treated as a form of dirty and undervalued labour (Twigg, 2000; Twigg et al., 2011; Nettleton, 2021). As Nettleton (2021: 241) argues, in the context of healthcare, body work performed by professionals further up the social hierarchy (such as doctors) tends to be mediated by other factors. For example, the patient's body might be prepared prior to interaction, and contact limited to discrete interventions and investigations. Body work was a central activity for professionals in our study who were directly involved in looking after babies once they had died. This section focuses on exploring some of the intimate care and body work that takes place in this context once a baby has died. As we will show, although mostly performed by women, this form of care work was conducted by doctors as well as by allied health professionals.

In the first instance, professionals – such as midwives – talked about some of the sensitivities around holding or handling a baby after it had died in the maternity unit. They emphasised the importance of being led by parental wishes in this context. This was articulated by Wendy:

> But I personally don't go in and go 'oh, can I hold your baby, is that alright' kind of thing. But I will just automatically handle the baby and do whatever I need to do and obviously do that in an appropriate way. But yeah, some people say oh, do you want to look at my baby? Some people are quite open about it [...] And then I've had the other extreme where parents are too scared to hold their baby. So you've said let me show you, this is how you can do it.

Parents could often be quite fearful of what their baby might look like after birth, especially when there was a very visible physical anomaly. In these instances, professionals sought to assist parents in getting to know their baby and its body in the most appropriate and respectful way possible. Consultant obstetrician Gina gave an example of this. One mother in her care had given birth to a baby who had died due to a significant cranial anomaly. Gina gently and carefully helped the mother to get to know her baby's body, while being respectful of the parent's wishes and fears:

> I remember one lady in particular who actually had a baby with anencephaly[2] where the back of the skull hasn't formed at all and she was quite an intelligent lady and didn't want to see her baby at all and I said are you sure you don't want to see your ... and she said 'I don't know, I don't know what I think', I said well look why don't we just gradually take it step by step and just tell me if you don't want it ... I literally just undressed baby from feet to ... and she held her baby's feet and ... and the hands and so on but she then didn't feel she could go to the head [...] I remember her saying to me afterwards I was so pleased you spent that time and did that with me.

As Shaw (2014) has argued, until recently it was standard practice for British hospitals to dispose of the bodies of miscarried and stillborn babies as if they were clinical waste. In response to the pregnancy loss support movement, however, it is now largely recognised that miscarriage and stillbirth bring deep and long-lasting grief for parents, grief that could be reduced by socially acknowledging the loss (Shaw, 2014: 87). As we explore further in Chapter 6, families are now encouraged to spend time bathing, dressing and holding their dead baby (Layne, 2012). Many professionals in our study were involved in supporting parents in this process. On the labour ward, for example, this could often be a strongly relational process as midwives sought to involve parents in these most intimate care activities, as Wendy articulates:

> Bathing the babies and dressing the babies and helping parents choose clothes for the babies. And I know a few of us will take great care in picking appropriate things for the babies to wear, and not just... But we're lucky we've got an army of little knitters that make hats for us and little dressers and cardigans and things, so that's always good.

In other locations, such as the bereavement suite, certain professionals would take babies out of the fridges to thaw a little and then dress them in preparation for a visit from parents. Linda, the bereavement assistant, described a family who came to visit their baby every day while he was in the bereavement suite. Linda would dress the baby in a different outfit every day before the parents arrived. This was something that the family greatly appreciated. It did become problematic after a while though, because the baby's skin began to deteriorate As Linda commented:

> Yeah, I mean, I dressed the baby five times and it wasn't fully formed in any case, so it's skin was all, like, deteriorating and that, they thought it were marvellous, because I dressed it like a proper baby and there was only one thing I couldn't put on it and that was its vest. So what I did was, I got a babygro and cut its little legs of the babygro and put that on.

Intimate care performed through certain body work practices such as washing, dressing and holding the babies was indeed a form of gendered work (Twigg, 1999, 2000). It was not work, however, that was performed solely by allied health professionals as often argued in existing literature (Daykin and Clarke, 2000). Rather, as Gina's account shows, this intimate form of body work was also performed, in some instances, by doctors. As articulated earlier in this chapter, care must be viewed as a set of practices with purpose.

Professionals performed this form of care out of respect for the babies and families, and by providing this form of care, they sought to create and reinforce the baby's personhood (Layne, 2000, 2012).

In the following section, we move on to explore more care practices performed by professionals through body work, this time focusing specifically on the post-mortem examination.

Care in clinical work: the post-mortem examination

As already argued elsewhere, death work is a form of hidden work. Corpse dissection and post-mortem examination, for example, have remained closed to public eyes over the last century. Mortuaries are locked, regulated places largely hidden from members of the public and from some hospital staff (Stephens, 2011). While the clinical aspects of post-mortem work such as dissection remain a taboo subject (Horsley, 2008, 2012), care practices during and after the post-mortem examination remain particularly hidden. As we will explore in this section, such practices are, however, central to this form of work, despite being concealed from public view (Reed and Ellis, 2019, 2020). During our ethnography we spent a significant amount of time with the most senior paediatric pathologist in the hospital – Ava – conducting interviews and observations. She was upfront and open about the dual nature of her role as a pathologist. She made it very clear to us during our fieldwork that her role as a pathologist was twofold; to find out the cause of death and to provide care and support to parents during their time of need:

> So I think my double role there, I think once, to try to answer, yes I found the meningitis or infection, or I think it's sudden infant death, and at the same time giving them the words that they need, the reassurance that they need to support their grief. Like, did he suffer? No he didn't, he was just sleeping. He didn't suffer, he was not in pain, he didn't realise what was happening. And that is incredible, it's a small thing, but it helps them.

When she conducted a post-mortem examination Ava felt that it was important to be respectful to the baby, treating them as a living person rather than as deceased. This could involve, for example, covering the baby's face and genitalia to maintain their dignity. It was interesting that Ava linked these care practices directly to gender:

> When the baby is in the mortuary and we are about to have the post-mortem, I always make a note of how beautiful the baby is, or look at its hair, or look how sweet... I think most of us are women in the mortuary and it's making a note of this particular face of this baby and just paying attention. Not taking the body as a body, but just thinking, this is a baby, how beautiful the baby was. And, sometimes we cover the face, so we don't want the baby to watch what we are doing, or if it is [...] we tend to cover the genitalia, because it's paying respect.

As well as interviews and respondent tours, we also observed post-mortem examinations – specifically two MIA post-mortems, one on a 22-week-old fetus, and the other on a baby who had died at four months. During our observations we were struck by the care and attention that both pathologists and the APT gave to the babies as they were performing or assisting with the examination (Reed and Ellis, 2020). In her fieldnotes Kate described the importance of touch and care in post-mortem work: 'I notice as James (pathologist) talks and tells us about this little girl who is four months old and who has been ill for much of her short life (latterly receiving palliative care) that he gently taps the child in a reassuring way.'

Once all aspects of the post-mortem process were complete, Carmen, in her role as APT, would wash and dress the babies and do any reconstruction work needed. She felt a significant sense of professional pride in making the baby look as good as possible for the parents after a post-mortem. For her this was the best part of the job:

> Yeah, that part of the job I always enjoy putting, or making the child look nice at the end because I think that the mum or the parents just deserve to see that child at their best that you can do; and it might be that it is a macerated baby and it didn't look very nice when it came but when you've reconstructed and put it back together then it just looks lovely, it's all dressed and it smells nice, we've washed its hair and things, and I think that that's the best that we can do for that family; and a lot of parents want a photograph so we organise photographs for them and we obviously dress the baby, if they don't come in clothes then we put some on, we've got wardrobes full of

babygros and things like that so none of our babies wear shrouds and none of them go out naked.

Our ethnographic research highlighted the importance of the hidden care work that took place during and immediately after post-mortem examinations. While this form of care work, as Ava highlighted, was often gendered work, men also did intimate care work as illustrated by our fieldnotes. It was not just work that was conducted by allied health professionals but also by senior clinicians. This again appears to challenge much existing literature, which tends to associate care and emotional labour with certain professional groups such as nurses and midwives (James, 1992; Daykin and Clarke, 2000). Furthermore, while care work in the mortuary brought together two forms of hidden labour – body work and death work – it should not be seen, we argue, as a form of dirty work. It was a part of their job that professionals often got the greatest value from doing. This is something we will explore in the penultimate section and the conclusion to this chapter.

The limits and constraints of caring

According to Allen (2019), the kind of care that can be provided in healthcare contexts rests on the social organisation of care work. This, in turn, depends on what we – as a society – are prepared to pay. Furthermore, the amount of time professionals can allocate to individuals is limited by the number of cases they are expected to manage (Krause and Boldt, 2018). As we have demonstrated throughout this chapter, care was a fundamental part of professional work in this sensitive area of baby loss and post-mortem examination. There were limits, however, to the kinds of care that professionals could perform. This was related by participants in our study to a range of issues. For example, time appeared to be a huge constraint on health professionals' (nurses, midwives, doctors) ability to give care. In these instances, other professionals – such as hospital chaplains – stepped in to provide care and support. This was articulated by Frank, one of the hospital chaplains:

I think sometimes it's talking things through, that we're people who've actually got time to sit in a way that staff haven't [...] it's not that other staff can't listen, but we've got time to listen [...] Whereas the doctor and the nurse, they always come with a particular agenda. They have an input into their story, this is your diagnosis, this is what I think you should do with the treatment. I've just come to put this medicine or I've come to put this catheter or whatever into you. So there's always a slight agenda. And of course, we have our own agendas, but we can sit there and at least say to the patient, well, you tell me what you want to talk about. So it can really be patient driven in that sense.

While time often limited professionals' ability to deliver the type of care that they wanted to provide, so too did monetary constraints. Professionals often wanted to offer more care to parents than they currently did, but were unable to because of the cost implications. Heather, the bereavement services manager, for example, talked about how budget constraints impacted on the hospital's ability to provide parents with good follow-on care after their baby had died and they had been discharged from hospital:

I would say most of the time my role stops after the funeral's taken place. I mean, there are some families that come back [...] so sometimes they'll come back and they just have a bit of a chat or ... a lot of them do ask me for counselling and ask me for support, and then I just have to signpost them on to their GP, and then a lot of the time they say, I've already been to my GP, and my GP says it's you. So we go round in this vicious circle and I have to explain, well, actually, it's not us, we don't have the budget for counselling.

While parents in our study tended to feel very positively about the care they had received in hospital, they did also identify areas for improvement. Some parents, for example, felt that professional care practices sometimes lacked sensitivity. This was articulated by Nathan. He was generally positive about the care he and his wife Loretta had received when their baby Aria died. He did, however, talk about how the clumsy and well-meaning comments from one healthcare assistant in the hospital really distressed them both:

And she [healthcare assistant] knocked on the door, opened that and said, oh just want to check if you're okay? And then she wheeled in her tea trolley and made us a cup of tea. And my wife was obviously massively distressed. And she said, 'oh lovey, what's the matter?' And Loretta said, our daughter's just died. And she went, 'oh darling', and I remember she threw her arms around her and she said, 'oh it

will be alright, she said, you're young, you can have lots more babies'
[...] And we were still processing everything that was going on, and
it's easy for me to look back and go, I should have yelled at her and
told her to get out of the room, but actually, we were still in that
stage of shock, and I didn't say anything [...] Pretty much everyone
we dealt with that day, and in the day after were absolutely top notch,
there was one person who stands out, and she clearly didn't mean to
offend anyone.

As well as raising issues around insensitivity and care, parents
were also sometimes critical of the lack of care from certain professional groups – for example, the police. By law, sudden infant death
involves a multi-agency response, including a police investigation.
According to multi-agency guidelines, the investigation of the death
of a child is an extremely complex and emotive area of police work.
However, even in cases where there are no apparent suspicious
factors, the police contribution to the investigation must be detailed
and thorough (RCP, 2016). Parents in our study often found their
interactions with the police in these instances to be lacking in care.
This is shown in the interview extracts from Tom and Sam, for
example, a couple who lost their baby Aurora suddenly over three
and a half years before our study. They felt that the care provided
by the police, and in particular the family liaison officer,[3] was poor:

Tom: Yeah, it is, the aftercare is awful and even with those police
officers I was chasing them up, what do you call it...?

Sam: Oh yeah, she was our family liaison officer but she never seemed
to get in touch with us and keep us updated, it was just poor Tom
was constantly having to get ... that's the last thing you wanted but
he was just constantly having to ring them just to see what was the
latest.

The issues raised by Sam and Tom about a lack of care from the
police was supported by an account from one of the police officers
we interviewed. Pete was a retired detective chief inspector with
thirty years' experience in a large urban police force. He talked in
detail about police involvement in cases of SIDS over the course of
his career. He was keen to stress that, as a profession, the police
were not heartless, but that the protocol-driven nature of police
work makes it hard to demonstrate care to members of the public,
including bereaved parents:

I didn't think at any stage that the parents were dealing with heartless, cold, clinical officers, people who had no heart and who didn't want to speak to people, because I know that they did because I was working with them and supervising them every day [...] And the police, or people in general dealing with traumatic situations aren't necessarily cold, heartless people. In a lot of cases it's the complete, exact opposite. But what they do get bogged down in – which has never changed, still the same today [. .] the police are very procedurally controlled, and they're controlled very much by process and protocol.

Professionals caring for babies in the context of baby loss and post-mortem examination appeared to face the same constraints identified in healthcare more generally – namely lack of time and money (Krause and Boldt, 2015). Parents were generally very positive about their experiences of care, although some did identify negative and often unintended consequences of care – as illustrated in Nathan's account. Furthermore, while most professionals in this study demonstrated care in some form, for some occupations such as the police, substantial barriers to care persisted. This was something that was further supported by parental accounts regarding police involvement in cases of SIDS. While these limits and challenges did exist, however, professionals often greatly valued the care they provided for babies and their families. We will move on to explore this in the penultimate section of the chapter.

Professional pride and the value of care

Although care work is often perceived as a gendered and financially undervalued form of labour, it can be personally valued by the people who engage in it (Bjerregaard et al., 2017). As Stacey (2005) argues, for example, by forming deep emotional connections with clients, care workers can find dignity in routine care work (dealing with hygiene, incontinence etc.). In our study, despite the many constraints and challenges that professionals faced, most really valued this aspect of their work. They felt a strong sense of professional pride about the care they performed for babies, parents and families. It was not uncommon for professionals to say that they felt privileged to perform this work. This was articulated by Heather, a bereavement services manager:

I do love my job, and lots of parents say to me, 'how can you do this job?' And I try to think very carefully about how I answer that [...] I feel very honoured that I can contribute to these patients ... parents' journeys, and that hopefully I've made that really awful journey a slightly bit easier by helping them, and I know ... and I think the reason that I love it is because I know that I do make such a big difference to the families, from the feedback that I get from families, and they just say, I wouldn't have been able to get through the last few weeks without you, because I just didn't know what to do, because often times they just ... a lot of them don't know, they've never been to a funeral, let alone planned a funeral.

Some of the doctors we interviewed also discussed the fulfilling nature of longer-term care, as a few clinicians built deep emotional bonds with parents over a longer period. Gina, an obstetrician, got a great deal out of supporting parents beyond their pregnancy loss through to future healthy pregnancies. She felt it was a privilege to work as an obstetrician:

It's a really good thing to be in, it's incredibly satisfying looking after women when they're pregnant and following them through, and also following women through from this point of view in terms of women who've had a poor outcome and then seeing them have a good outcome, do you know what I mean, of a pregnancy.

Regardless of what professionals did, and what their caring role involved, for many it was often one of the best parts of the job. For example, Nell, a medical photographer, emphasised the importance of being technically accurate in her job. She would often take photographs of deceased babies for families before post-mortem examination, either in the mortuary or the bereavement suite (Reed and Ellis, 2020). It was, however, often the hidden side of her job that she enjoyed most – the caring patient-facing side:

And the caring side, if you work with patients you generally want to be with the patient. That's the side I really enjoy [...] If we could just give them something nice, pretty, you know, attractive, just a nice memory, a better way of looking at it than mobile phone pictures I suppose, if we could add something that we're good at and our strengths into that that's what we would want to do. But it's hard.

Looking after families and supporting them through a post-mortem is clearly emotionally challenging work for professionals. It is, however, a form of work that tends to be personally valued by professionals. The social relations of care are clearly at the heart of this professional fulfilment. Caring for babies and being with parents – building relationships with them over time where possible – clearly provided our professionals with a strong sense of professional pride. In the final section of the chapter, we move on to reflect in depth on our findings in the context of wider debates on the role of care in healthcare.

Conclusion

In this chapter we have sought to shed light on a range of hidden care practices that take place in the hospital context when a baby has died and has been sent to the mortuary for post-mortem examination. Care is viewed here as a range of practices with purpose and intention. It is administered, in this context, by a range of different professionals in various ways – from creating a soothing environment for grieving parents after they have given birth to talking and singing to babies while performing essential body work tasks in the bereavement suite or mortuary. Although this form of work is often concealed from members of the public – as well as from some professional groups working in other parts of the hospital – it is an essential part of post-mortem work.

Care was obviously performed differently according to occupation and role within the post-mortem process. For example, while pastoral and spiritual care was provided by hospital chaplains, intimate care of the baby's body both before and after a post-mortem was mostly administered by health professionals (with the exception of administrators who were part of the bereavement support team). Care was also context-specific and could vary according to location. As Twigg (1999, 2000) has argued in her own work on domiciliary care, however, care also has the potential to reorder space – transgressing boundaries between the private and public realm. Although care work in post-mortem practices is often hidden, this type of work does challenge the boundaries between private and public realms in novel ways. For example, at times professionals demonstrated care by attempting to create a sense of home in the hospital, while at other times the hospital was taken into the private sphere so that parents could spend important time with their baby at home. We have argued that this created simultaneous private and public locations of care (McIntosh, 2008).

Feminist authors researching care in various settings have consistently shown that it remains a predominantly female activity (Graham, 1983, 1991; Ungerson, 1990; Thomas, 1993). Daykin and Clarke (2000) have also sought to argue, however, that discourses of care can reflect and reinforce class, status and other divisions within and between groups of healthcare workers. In addition, sociological research has increasingly sought to examine care work as a type of body work (Twigg, 2000, 2004; Fine, 2005), a form of labour that is often labelled as 'dirty', unskilled and undervalued (Twigg, 2000; Twigg et al., 2011; Nettleton, 2021). We have sought to use the data from our study in this chapter to highlight a more complex picture. Female professionals in the study were more likely to perform intimate body work care practices, such as dressing and washing babies. Men, however, also performed care in different ways – from providing pastoral and spiritual care through to tender body work during the post-mortem examination. Furthermore, although allied health professionals – such as nurses, APTs and bereavement support workers – do provide a significant amount of intimate body work care (e.g., dressing babies), so too did senior female doctors. This was illustrated by the very powerful account from Gina, the obstetrician who helped one bereaved mother to navigate her dead baby's body. We make the case in this chapter, therefore, for sociological research to develop a more fine-grained analysis of care work as performed in healthcare, one that allows for the increasing complexity of the gender order and the changing nature of medical work.

As argued in the introduction, care is central to contemporary social life. It is an essentially social activity resulting from a relationship between different parties in which mutual respect and support of the recipient are paramount (Fine, 2005). We have sought to use our data in this chapter to show how care conducted during post-mortem is a fundamentally social activity. While fostering autonomy can obviously no longer be the main aim of care when the recipient is deceased, this does not make the practice of caring in this context any less of a social activity. Despite babies being deceased, professionals continue to care for them as if they were alive, holding, talking and singing to them while performing the clinical death work that is required. Care is performed in this context by professionals for babies both *with* and for parents. As other research has shown, it is this social relationship and the resulting deep emotional bonds that are formed between carer and the recipient of care that often provide fulfilment in this type of work (Stacey, 2005). This was certainly the case for many participants in our study. Despite the various constraints on care, it was a form of work that was highly valued by professionals. Such value, we argue, undoubtedly contributes to professionals in this context being able to reject the label of dirty work (Woodthorpe and Komaromy, 2013; Gassaway, 2007).

Notes

1 Project 2000 refers to a professionalisation project in the UK whereby nursing education moved into the realm of higher education. For further information, see Francis and Humphreys (1999).
2 Anencephaly is a life-limiting condition in which the baby's brain and spinal cord (the fetal nervous system) do not develop properly. For further information, see 'Anencephaly: information for parents', https://www.gov.uk/government/publications/anencephaly-description-in-brief (accessed February 2022).
3 A family liaison officer is an investigator whose role is to gather evidence and information from the family to contribute to the investigation, providing support and information in a sensitive and compassionate manner. See https://profdev.college.police.uk/ (accessed February 2022).

Chapter 6

Memory

Over the last couple of decades, interest in memory and memorialisation has grown significantly among academics studying the social aspects of death, dying and bereavement (Woodthorpe, 2012). The popular understanding of memory, however, draws from the individual perspective of psychology, where it is conceptualised as a 'body function ... commonly characterized as a container wherein a lifetime of images, thoughts and experiences are archived' (Green, 2008: 156). Social theorists have sought to complicate the idea of memory as 'storage capacity' by highlighting its collective, moral and social dimensions, arguing that it is a 'more active and creative process than mere recall' (Green, 2008: 157). A sociological understanding of memory, therefore, recognises it as a dynamic phenomenon of perspective, rather than a static window on the past.

Scholars in the field of death studies have also argued that memory is a 'cultural process and a social experience' (Hallam and Hockey, 2001: 1). Often their work highlights its intersection with material and embodied practices of everyday memorialisation and mourning (Gibson, 2008; Woodthorpe, 2010; Richardson, 2014). In recent years, sociologists have focused less on large-scale, formalised acts of public commemoration, identifying instead a shift towards diverse, personal and spontaneous forms of memorialisation (Prendergast et al., 2006; Howarth, 2007; Cann, 2014; Holloway et al., 2019). Some empirical studies have explored what Miller and Parrott (2007: 150) describe as the 'domestication of death ritual', focusing on personal commemorative practices in the home involving material items pertaining to the deceased (Hockey et al., 2005; Richardson, 2014). Others, such as Cann (2014) writing about the US context in particular, document 'grassroots' memorialisation practices that are emerging routinely in public spaces such as symbolic tattoos, commemorative T-shirts, roadside ghostbike memorials and internet mourning rituals. These 'popular expressions' of memory represent a significant shift in the private management of grief because their presence in everyday life helps to disrupt the societal silence surrounding loss. Cann argues that by 'transforming public space into a bereavement space' these new rituals demand social recognition for the bereaved, as well as the deceased (2014: 14). Social geographers are developing even more encompassing conceptualisations of the spatial dimensions of mourning and remembrance by identifying a range of places that are significant for bereaved people and that reveal 'the messy, shifting, multi-layered geographies of living with loss' experienced over time (Maddrell, 2015: 19).

This chapter provides a sociological analysis of memory and memorialisation in the context of baby loss, and expands on themes identified in this introduction, such as space and materiality. However, unlike much of the previous literature in this area which tends to focus on the experiences of bereaved parents and to a lesser extent other family members, this chapter also seeks to highlight how professionals working in the baby loss landscape, such a midwives, medical illustrators and bereavement workers, understand and experience memory. Our primary aim is to demonstrate how memory and memorialisation in this context are both processual and dynamic, and we realise this by showing how parents and professionals actively shape and create memory across time and space.

Baby loss, personhood and memorialisation

When a baby dies during pregnancy or just after birth, parents have limited memories of the child because they leave behind so few 'material traces of social life' (Layne, 1997: 300). While this is less often the case with SIDS and may explain the lack of sociological literature on memorialisation in this context, there is still only a relatively short amount of time to establish a social identity for the baby beyond their immediate family. Much of the existing literature on baby loss, therefore, has been concerned with the intersections between memory and personhood (Layne, 2000, 2003; Keane, 2009; Rosenberg, 2012; Brierley-Jones et al., 2015; Cadge et al., 2016).

As we discussed in the previous section, memories are neither fixed nor passive, and memory itself is more than preserving and recalling experiences from the past. Rather, as Garattini (2007) has argued in her paper on infantile deaths in Ireland, parents '*create* memories' in the face of death to *make* identities, and to help with their feelings of loss. To this end, bereaved parents actively engage in a range of memorialisation activities, often involving material objects such as photographs (Godel, 2007), everyday items such as ornaments (Murphy and Thomas, 2013) and consumption and gift-giving practices (Layne, 2000, 2003; Garattini, 2007). It is argued that these 'symbolic activities help embed painful memories, thoughts, and feelings, into a narrative structure' both to create meaning in the face of loss (Blood and Cacciatore, 2014: 225) and to mitigate feelings of powerlessness (Cacciatore and Flint, 2012). Material objects are significant because memories relating to the deceased are often embodied in physical things (Garattini, 2007), with artefacts supporting the enduring biographical narrative that parents strive to develop about their baby (Murphy and Thomas, 2013). Crucially, as Layne (2000) has argued, the tangible properties of material objects confer 'realness' to the ambiguous identities of both (non-) parent and deceased child.

Much of this work on memorialisation also draws upon the current 'dominant academic discourse' (Valentine, 2008: 4) that emphasises the importance of continuing bonds between the living and the deceased (Klass et al., 1996; Walter, 1996). Although there is a body of work that explores the private nature of these ties and their embeddedness in personal spaces such as the family home (Murphy and Thomas, 2013), empirical studies have also observed the manifestation of continuing bonds in physical public space (Woodthorpe, 2012; Cadge et al., 2016; Faro, 2021), as well as online forums (Davidsson Bremborg, 2012; Davidson and Letherby, 2019) and virtual remembrance sites (Godel, 2007; Keane, 2009). In their study on ritualisation after child death, Cacciatore and Flint found that bereaved parents often changed their mourning rituals from public to private because people did not understand their need to 'continue bonds in this way' (2012: 167). Similarly, Brierley-Jones et al. (2015) explored UK mothers' experiences of stillbirth and argued that the stigma associated with this event reduced memory-sharing opportunities for women and that this negatively impacted upon their mental health. Indeed, much of the literature suggests that baby loss is disenfranchised (Doka, 1989), mostly hidden from societal view (Layne, 1997; Weaver-Hightower, 2012), with parents experiencing shame (Keane, 2009) and feeling that their loss is devalued because there is no 'person' to grieve (Lovell, 1983). As Keane points out, 'the dominance of the model of inherent biological personhood ... has strict requirements for what counts as a real and socially recognized person, one of which is an embodied existence' (2009: 157). Physical absence, therefore, presents a challenge for parents seeking ongoing social recognition and personhood for their baby.

So far, this book has explored what happens when a baby dies across time and space to understand parents' experiences as a journey from pregnancy through to loss. This chapter aims to advance this approach by exploring how memory-making is a process that happens over time. Accordingly, we explore memory through three processual lenses, beginning in the first section with an analysis of how decisions and actions at the time of a baby's death shape what is possible to remember in the future. Here the focus will be on professionals' accounts of supporting parents to *prepare* for 'good' memories; something that is underexplored in the sociological literature on loss. Then we move on to describe how parents *make* memories with their baby during the period immediately after death and before the cremation or burial, emphasising the impact of contextual factors such as space on this experience. Finally, the focus shifts to ongoing life without the physical baby and to *materialising* memory in their absence. Here we explore how physical objects and parents' multifaceted relationships with these in daily life can evoke memories as well as facilitate the creation of new social connections with the deceased child. The chapter concludes by connecting the research findings with broader sociological concerns surrounding social identity and post-death relationships, materiality and everyday practices, and the social production of memory.

Preparing for memories

When a pregnancy ends or a baby dies in the current UK context, the impetus for memory-making usually begins in hospital with the routine provision of memory boxes and the preservation of physical traces of the baby such as handprints and footprints (Fuller and Kuberska, 2020). In the absence of an established cultural script to navigate this experience (Layne, 2003; Frost et al., 2007; Kuberska and Turner, 2019), existing research has identified the influential role that health professionals and baby loss charities can play during this time (Lovell, 1983; Komaromy, 2012; Mitchell, 2016; Smith et al., 2020; Fuller and Kuberska, 2020). Acknowledgement of how professionals and their practices can shape the *possibilities* of memory, however, remains largely implicit in this work. Therefore, we begin this section on preparing for memories by considering how the support offered to parents is influenced by a sense of responsibility to protect and preserve memories for the future.

Decision-making and the possibilities of memory

As we explored in Chapter 2, when parents experience the loss of a baby, they usually need to make a range of decisions very quickly. Most participants in our study felt unprepared for this and found the process overwhelming. Heather, a bereavement services manager at the hospital, considered guiding parents during this uncertain time to be a key part of her role.

> I like to think of myself as an advocate for the parents, because I try to encourage them to think about things that they wouldn't necessarily think about, and that's around making memories [...] There's a big thing at the moment about photographs and things like that, and most parents want photographs, but some parents say they don't, and then I try to get them to think about how they would think in five years' time, say when it's their [baby's] fifth birthday, for instance, how will you want to go back and remember her or him, and if you don't have any photographs taken are you going to regret that in five years' time.

Heather explains that it is her job to prompt parents and prepare them to think about memories; to make the connection between how decisions made at the time of loss create possibilities for what can and cannot be remembered in the future. Her concern about photographs resonates with Gibson's (2008: 81) point that 'it is not just what they represent now but what they could and may yet represent' in the future.

As discussed in Chapter 1, another important decision that parents usually need to consider is whether they want to see and handle their deceased baby's body. Most recent research suggests that viewing is beneficial for parents' longer-term well-being (Kingdon et al., 2015)[1] and that this contact might present a rare opportunity for parenting to be performed (Murphy, 2012). If a baby has had a post-mortem, however, there are potential implications of seeing the body for future memories. Heather commented:

> I've had a couple of families in the last month or so that wanted to view their baby [...] and they've said to me I'm not sure about viewing the baby after the post-mortem, but I really think I want to, so I said, well, let me get the baby back to the [hospital] [...] then I'll have a look at baby and let you know what kind of condition the baby's in, and the last two babies [...] I've done that for, I've had to phone the families and say, I'm not telling you what to do, at the end of the day it's your choice and it's your baby, but I personally don't think that they're viewable any more, and I want you to think very carefully about what your last memory [...] I just try to make them think about how they want to remember baby and what they want their last image in their mind to be.

Some parents in our study also described occasions when professionals offered advice regarding decisions to be made. Although a few parents felt that they had not been adequately supported – as in one case where decisions had been completely 'taken out of our hands' – many found it helpful. For example, Victoria only realised the significance of advice offered at the time of making decisions about her baby's funeral when she was seeking ways to be reminded of her daughter afterwards.

> We'd decided at one point to have no music, because we just couldn't think of any music that we wanted to use and we didn't plan to be there very long. But they said in the chapel you might regret that decision because you might feel like you want to spend some time and the silence might not be very nice. So are you sure you want no music? So we [said] right okay, just pick some music for us because we can't think of anything. And they did. And actually it's quite nice to have a piece of music now that we can listen to and it reminds us of her.

While existing studies have identified the role that professionals can play in guiding parents who experience baby loss, what we have demonstrated here is the importance of this work as a form of *preparation* for the protection and facilitation of future memories. As we go on to explore in the next subsection, professionals often tried to align their work practices to help prepare for the creation of 'good' memories for parents and families.

Preparing for 'good' memories

Writing in the *Lancet* in 2021, Tamarin Norwood recounted the precious moments that she and her husband spent in hospital bathing and caring for their stillborn son. She describes these interactions as 'something good enough' in the painful absence of a living child. In the piece she explains that, with time, she has 'come to understand that these memories of [her] son's birth and death were not formed by accident at all, but were crafted ... by the efforts of many, many people' (2021: 2306). Beautiful and raw, this personal account is Norwood's tribute to the professionals who knew that, for her, the years ahead 'would turn on those memories' (2021: 2306). As we showed in Chapter 5, professionals often undertake an array of care practices as part of their work with deceased babies. In this section we extend this discussion to show how care is enacted with the production of 'good (enough)' memories in mind. For instance, Tammy, a doctor training in paediatrics, spoke about the meticulous need to plan prior to the withdrawal of life-sustaining support for gravely ill neonates.

> You have to be efficient, you can't be uncomfortable with it, that's the worst thing you can do with the family, you have to be sure you're doing the right thing in terms of this is ... there's nothing more we can do for that baby [...] So you have to plan every single silly thing perfectly before you do it and how you manage that family during that process will go a long way in how they cope with it for the rest of their life, every single thing will be in slow motion, in detail for them as they close their eyes [...] they will remember it so vividly for them, so you have to plan with the nurses.

The moment of death is understandably a hugely significant time for parents, and it is very clear that Tammy and her colleagues recognise the implications for future memories if this process is not managed carefully. However, safeguarding the time parents have with their baby after death is also something professionals actively plan to achieve, as Maryam, a Muslim hospital chaplain, explained. She positions herself as a 'counter-influence' to community dynamics that may inhibit how some Muslim parents feel they can interact with their deceased baby's body.

> Then it's facilitating that, if they see you speaking to the baby they think oh wow this is normal, I can do this, 'cause they want to do it but because the elders have always said oh you do things like this, this and this it's now just empowering them and saying to them actually you can do a lot of this yourself [...] What I try and do is kind of take a step back and talk the families through what they need to do [...] And I'll say of course you can wash it [the baby], I'll talk you through it. Because it's such an important time [...] you're never gonna get that back.

Maryam's recognition that this time together as a family is painfully finite (see Heineman, 2014) underpins her commitment to make it as 'good' as possible for parents.

Another way in which professionals attempt to assuage a baby's impending absence is by creating a more durable memory of the child's physical form using hospital photographs (Hochberg, 2011). Data from our study suggests that this work involves careful preparation and can be challenging when the baby's physical body might be less developed or show signs of trauma (Layne, 2012). Nell, a medical photographer, pointed out that taking pictures of babies requires a particular set of technical and emotional skills.

> There's two parts of it, because it's taking the picture and it's then editing the picture, which we can do with digital which is a really good thing. For this type of image it's really useful. I think you do, you're thinking of the person who's going to look at it and you want to make it as kind for them as possible to make their memory – I don't know – it's never going to be a good memory, but, yeah, so it's less traumatic I suppose.

It was evident that for some professionals in our study their work was guided by a sense of how parents would feel in the future about the physical form of their deceased baby. Often, enabling the creation of 'good' memories was conflated with being able to make the deceased child appear 'presentable' and as baby-like as possible (Komaromy, 2012) – in other words, to establish *a person* to be remembered; a foundation upon which (good) memories can be made.

As noted previously, existing research consistently shows that constructing a social identity for a deceased baby is important for continuing bonds with the child (Godel, 2007; Rosenberg, 2012; Murphy and Thomas, 2013) as well as for legitimising the loss and making the baby 'real' to others (Layne, 2000; Keane, 2009). What data from our study adds to this understanding is an appreciation of the intentional role that professionals play in this process by planning for future memories as a routine part of their work. In many instances this involves striving to ensure that babies appear 'baby-like' and that parenting activities such as nursing and bathing can take place. We will return to parenting in the latter part of the following section, where we turn our attention to *making* memories during the period after a baby's death and before their physical body becomes permanently absent via cremation or burial.

Making memories

In Chapter 4 we discussed the unanticipated feelings of pride and joy parents experienced when holding and spending time with their deceased baby. In one of those accounts, Anna described meeting her 23-week-old daughter as both the 'best and worst time' of her life. Her words echo the sentiments of other parents in our study. Their reflections highlight the strange and at times contradictory nature of contact with a deceased baby's body. For instance, Victoria remembered that it was 'nice' but also 'difficult' to spend time with her stillborn daughter.

> So it was quite nice to see her and just be with her. But at the same time obviously it was very difficult thinking we're never going to watch her grow up and we're never going to really see her again after this point. Because at the hospital we'd made the decision that we'd just say goodbye and then not see her again. But we soon changed our minds [...] and I think we did end up seeing her another three times after that [...] at the chapel.

We want to begin this section by acknowledging this emotional complexity, appreciating that many parents had multifaceted memories of this time. It is important to note that while the majority did see their baby's body after death, not all parents wanted contact and some required encouragement as they felt apprehensive about what the baby would look like (Weaver-Hightower, 2012; Ryninks et al., 2014; Brierley-Jones et al., 2015). As Victoria's account implies, place was also a relevant consideration. A few parents felt more able to spend time with their baby in certain settings – for instance, in a chapel of rest rather than the hospital. Therefore, as some parents identified place as having particular significance for the memories they made, we shall explore this issue in more detail.

Place, space and memory-making

We sought to acknowledge the connection between trauma and space in Chapter 1. A growing body of literature influenced by geography (Maddrell, 2015) and sociology (Hockey et al., 2010a) has conceptualised spatial aspects of grief and memorialisation. However, as Collier and Broom (2021) have recently argued, there has been limited consideration within the social sciences about spaces in which dying and death take place. Aside from valuable work on baby memorial gardens (Woodthorpe, 2012), there has been even less research that explores place, the death of a baby, and any subsequent implications for memory. Yet when we spoke with Lesley and her husband Mike about the sudden death of their two-week-old baby Mia, the hospital bereavement suite featured positively in their memories.

> Lesley: My biggest memory of that is the fact that when we got to [the hospital] ... Have you been to the bereavement suite?
>
> Interviewer: Yeah.
>
> Lesley: Absolutely beautiful place. They sat us down and they said we're just getting Mia ready for you now, because they put them in a little crib in a bedroom don't they? It's like a little house. And they said to us she's going to have a hat on because due to the procedure of the post-mortem [...] Basically they told us don't take the hat off because you'll be upset, which basically means they've cut into her little head. And I remember that, because she was dressed in the outfit I gave them, apart from the hat.
>
> Mike: That's right, yeah.

Lesley: But they'd matched the hat. I remember thinking oh, they've matched the hat, it matches her outfit. And I remember when I had her in my arms that the hat [crying] ...

Interviewer: It's all right, take your time. Do you want to stop for a while?

Although recalling Mia's post-mortem was clearly very painful for Lesley, her recollection of the bereavement suite as a 'beautiful' place and the thoughtful attention her daughter experienced there are intertwined in her memory. This entanglement of space and care (Milligan and Wiles, 2010) was also evident when Victoria spoke about how, despite the best efforts of the midwifery team, the physical environment on the labour ward negatively impacted upon the time she and her husband spent with their stillborn daughter Daisy.

And I don't think they had a proper cold cot at that point. So they did have to keep taking her. So they said right, well, we'll just take her away for a little while, while you have a shower or whatever, and then we'll bring her back. That was a bit ... the way it was back and forth and ... I mean they were really good about the way that they timed it, because it never felt like they were taking her away from us [...] And that was the other thing, there was not really an appropriate place to sit with her. So I was laid on the bed and I had Daisy, but then [my husband] was having to perch on the side of the bed, and it wasn't comfortable. It wasn't ever really comfy. So you were phaffing about having to pass her backwards and forwards.

As articulated in Chapter 5 on care, our fieldnotes are replete with references to the 'homely' touches that we encountered in these spaces, such as cushions, brightly coloured mugs and non-standard NHS tissues. These items typify what Buse et al. (2018: 243) describe as mundane 'materialities of care' – the 'often unnoticed aspects of material culture within health and social care contexts' which were intended to create a less clinical environment. Despite this, for a few parents it was important that they were able to take their babies home to spend time with them there as a family (Heineman, 2014). Ivy's son Brian (who was a twin) died suddenly thirty-seven years prior to our study when he was four and a half months old. Bringing Brian home for a few days allowed the family to create a less traumatic final memory.

It was like he was there one minute and then he was ... it felt like he was taken from us. And I couldn't bear that as a last memory. So by having him home it was like that's where he left from. And it was a comfort for us. Maybe partly there was a not accepting. Not accepting he was dead and that... Especially before he came home. So it helped actually to see him [...] And I don't know just having him in his bedroom and that just felt right.

Despite the potential comfort that parents such as Ivy might derive from having their baby at home, a midwife in our study explained that this is not something that parents are routinely made aware that they can do. Sadly, this was the case for Charlotte, who expressed regret at not being able to place her stillborn son 'in his nursery to feel like that's his nursery rather than a nursery that we made'. For both Ivy and Charlotte, the baby's bedroom was a particularly significant space for memory production after death. Indeed, as Charlotte suggests, it is often the space in any home that belongs primarily to the child and is therefore a site for their identity construction. It is also the place most associated with embodied care practices such as nursing, changing and dressing that are central to the 'doing' of family life with young children as well as the embodiment of being a parent (Morgan, 1996).

Having demonstrated some of the ways in which parents experienced making memories with their deceased baby via the nexus of space and care (Milligan and Wiles, 2010), in the next section we explore further the importance of acts of parenting. Here we consider how routine tasks that are customary for nurturing a living child are also performed by parents of a deceased baby when spending time together.

Being a parent: doing things for baby

Recently, sociologists have sought to theorise relational aspects of death and to consider how families are actively produced via practices at the end of life (Ellis, 2013, 2018; Borgstrom et al., 2019; Almack, 2022). Murphy and Thomas (2013) utilised a similar conceptual lens to explore how parents create a lasting identity for their stillborn baby and continue to include them as members of their family in the years after their death. What our data adds to this small body of existing scholarship is an appreciation of the importance of post-death parenting practices for the more immediate memory-making process, which we found can differ depending on the circumstances of the loss. For those parents who experienced miscarriage or stillbirth, the period between death and burial or cremation was their only opportunity to create memories of doing things with their child physically present that made them feel like parents, and which legitimised their status as such (Murphy, 2012). For example, Charlotte spoke about the importance of 'getting to do some things' to care for her stillborn baby, despite 'missing out' on others because of the effects of diamorphine taken during her labour.

> I wish I hadn't been so out of it when they bathed him because I would have quite liked to [have] bathed him, and by the time I was okay and I'd slept and things like that, it would have done too much damage to him to bath him then later, so I kind of missed out on that. But then when he was at the funeral directors, one day I put a nappy on him and then the next day I took it off, and I put him into a babygro and then I changed him into his funeral clothes, so I feel like I got to do some things.

Previous research about caring for preterm babies has identified that the symbolic nature of breast milk in a context where mother and baby are physically separated is significant for the social construction of motherhood (Sweet, 2008). This embodied connection can also be meaningful in cases of baby loss, however, as was Esther's experience when her son died in neonatal care. She described placing breast milk on his lips, using the term 'we' – meaning herself and her husband. Importantly, her account hinted at the importance of this memory for making them both feel like his parents.

The emotional consequence of being able to act like parents was somewhat different for interviewees whose babies had died suddenly and unexpectedly. For these participants, rather than helping to define them as parents, being able to 'do' parenting in the immediate aftermath of the death was about a continuation of their role and everyday routines (Ellis, 2013). We found that when institutional settings were able facilitate this, it helped parents to create post-death memories that involved normality and gave some comfort. For instance, Hannah's baby died suddenly when he was sixteen months old, and she described for us the moments after the medical team at the hospital informed her that they had been unable to resuscitate him.

> I just remember I was able to sit and hold him for ages and I sang to him and told him it would be fine, because I didn't know what else to do [...] and then, as I say, they let us stay with him for as long as we wanted to and they let us carry him through to the mortuary, which was really lovely, because he just looked like he was sleeping, he was still in his pyjamas.

Many existing studies have focused specifically on the acts of seeing and handling a deceased baby and the longer-term implications of this for pathological issues such as 'psychological morbidity' (Kingdon et al., 2015). What we have sought to provide here is a more contextual, social sense of what spending time with a deceased baby can be like for parents. In doing so we have also emphasised the active part that parents play in memory-making by engaging in care practices that either affirm or re-establish their identity as parents. We will return to this issue again when we reflect more fully on identity and post-death relationships in this chapter's conclusion. What we move on to explore now is how memories are negotiated in the longer term by parents – in the weeks, months and years after their loss. When we asked parents about this, they all discussed material objects, and so we focus our analysis on physical things and how these are used to evoke memories as well as to create a social identity for, and ongoing connection with, the deceased child.

Materialising memories

In his autoethnographic account of the stillbirth of his daughter Matilda, Weaver-Hightower (2012: 475) includes a catalogue of the physical things that his baby touched or that were part of her. He describes these items as 'sacred' – things that he 'hoards' and treats with meticulous 'reverence' such as locks of her hair, a hospital arm band and a baby book containing writing and photographs. Weaver-Hightower's feelings about these items exemplify Turkle's claim that 'evocative objects' become 'companions to our emotional lives' (2011: 5), and his analytical reflections provide a useful introduction to the final data section of this chapter. He writes that 'things function as the tangible, early connections these parents have with their babies, a means of creating memories of and social identities for their children since the corporeal child no longer exists and often goes socially unrecognized' (Weaver-Hightower, 2012: 475).

In the subsections that follow, we explore three different forms of materiality that were pertinent in our study – written words, photographs and memory 'spaces' such as boxes or shelves. In doing so we also examine the concomitant processes of materialising memory afforded to parents by each physical medium – that is, writing, displaying and keeping or collecting. As we discuss these in turn, we seek to expand on the issues of identity and social recognition identified by Weaver-Hightower, and to show what material things signify about memory as an active process negotiated in parents' ongoing, everyday lives.

Written words

For some time now, voices in the academic and baby loss communities alike have highlighted the distress experienced by some parents due to a lack of legal recognition for babies who die before twenty-four weeks of gestation (Kilshaw, 2020; Smith et al., 2020). Presently in the UK, the state does not require parents to register the birth/death of these babies and therefore they do not receive an officially sanctioned certificate as a physical record of their existence.[2] Given the authenticity that this document can bestow for parents who have limited means of demonstrating that their baby was 'real', this can feel like a painful erasure of their experience (Layne, 2000; Keane, 2009).

While official records as 'artifacts of civil society' (Layne, 2000: 335) were a concern for a few parents in our study, what we focus on here are examples of personal, everyday memorialisation involving written words. Although text has received limited consideration in the scholarly literature on material culture, memory and baby loss when compared to visual representations such as photographs, we found that parents used writing in a variety of material forms to memorialise their baby and to make connections with them. Finding ways to write their baby's name in public space was one example, as Charlotte explained: 'Yeah, we write his name everywhere, everywhere we go we always make a L (for Leo) or write his name or whatever.' Similarly, Amy and her husband Bobby talked about a trip they had made to a historic church when Amy was pregnant with their daughter Clementine. During the visit they wrote their names in the visitors' book, but not long after returning home, Amy had a miscarriage. She spoke about their desire to visit the church again.

> And in the visitor book, I wrote Amy, Bobby and Clementine and that's the only time I'd ever written it and the weekend after she was dead and since we've been back to that church and we've found that page in the visitor book and we've taken a photo of it, because that's the only time she's written down, you know, as existing.

For both these sets of parents, being able to see their child's name as a physical impression in the world made an important social connection (Finch, 2008; Cadge et al., 2016). For another participant, however, the act of writing was a more private affair. During her interview, Yasmine discussed three experiences of loss – an early miscarriage followed by two pregnancies which she and her husband chose to end at around twenty weeks due to serious physical abnormalities in each case. When asked about whether and how she remembered these babies, Yasmine said she did not do anniversaries, but nonetheless she told us that she remembered the losses with a mark on a calendar each year: 'I mean, I did, initially, I think, write on the calendar the dates of when they were born and things like that, which was kind of difficult, because it's not really the thing you want to remember because that was the end of their lives.'

Charlotte's experience was very different to Yasmine's. She wrote about her (still)birth[3] and produced a booklet commissioned by her local hospital to be used to support other parents. Telling us about the birth story and why she had wanted to write it, she explained:

> And it is a bit like therapy, getting it down, I felt like I didn't have to keep going over it, because all I have of him is his story, and when I came out of hospital I was a bit like… I was scared I was going to forget parts of it […] So then by writing my story then it was there […] So I did write it for myself, but I also wanted everyone else to know what went on, you know like you have random people on Facebook, I didn't want them to pity me, and I didn't want them to think that there was something wrong with Leo.

Charlotte identifies a further motivation behind her writing relating to the process itself, rather than the finished product; it allowed her to keep her memories of Leo as a central focus in her life and to have a demonstrable reason to mention him to others. Walter's (1996) 'new model of grief' identifies that the purpose of grieving is not to accomplish emotional separation from the deceased but rather to create a 'durable biography' that can foster continuing bonds (Klass et al., 1996). To create this biography, Walter argues that bereaved people need to be able to talk about the person who has died. After Charlotte completed the booklet, she told us that she experienced a 'meltdown' because finding ways to speak about a dead baby is not easy – without her writing, she was struggling to know how she might continue to mention Leo in a legitimate way to others. Whereas for Wayne, whose baby died during delivery, it was actually written words composed by other people that helped to validate his daughter's existence and personhood: 'That's one of the other things about it that – it's very easy to think that person (the baby) didn't exist for other people. And both our parents have been really good about it, so they send us cards every year on her birthday.'

At the start of this section, we began by highlighting the lack of legal recognition for deceased babies under twenty-four weeks, because this issue demonstrates the powerful connection between physical documentation and individual social identity. We broadened our focus beyond this matter, however, to explore less formal examples of writing and documentation that have been helpful for parents seeking to legitimise, honour and process memories of their deceased child. In the next section we extend this focus on recognition to include physical visibility, as our analysis shifts to the material form of photography, and to parents' experiences of looking at images and displaying or sharing them with others.

Photographs and displaying baby

In their research with parents bereaved of a child, Riches and Dawson found that photographs offer 'concrete records around which conversational remembering can take place', and they 'provide resources that can be used to construct and maintain biographies of lost children' (1998: 134). Existing literature on baby loss supports their findings (Godel, 2007; Murphy and Thomas, 2013; Blood and Cacciatore, 2014) as do many of our parental accounts where photographs played an important role in memorialisation. For instance, Sam's daughter died suddenly when she was seven weeks old, and she told us: 'from the moment she died I just printed out photos I just wanted her to be on show in some form. So, yeah, that's her there in the centre for people to see.' Similarly, Georgia's baby died unexpectedly at six months, and being surrounded by 'amazing' memories of him that she could see helped her to focus on his life rather than his death.

> We needed to get those pictures [printed out] and have them here and look at them and see really. Because although you can say to yourself oh, we had an amazing six months, but when you've got the pictures you can see them having those amazing six months, and I think that's the thing.

For other parents, however, photographs could be difficult to look at and challenging to share. Sam and Georgia had several photographs of their babies when they were alive, but for parents such as Victoria whose daughter Daisy was stillborn, opportunities to share her photographs happened infrequently.

> And [this person] said if you're comfortable with it I'd love to see a picture of her. Which I loved because everybody gets to show off what their children look like [...] we're never going to get to do that, and I find that quite difficult that I had this child and nobody... A lot of my family don't even know what she looked like because they didn't want to see pictures of her, which is their decision.

Having been denied the opportunity to take part in typical parenting conversations about which of the family's physical characteristics her baby shared, Victoria's ability to use images to memorialise Daisy as part of her family was limited (Godel, 2007). This was compounded by the fact that she was unable to do this with her husband.

> I've got a picture of her on my phone, on my lock screen, so that when I unlock my phone I can see her. And [my husband] gets very upset about that to be honest because he doesn't think that there should be pictures of her. But for me I feel a bit like she was my daughter and well, I don't have the luxury of being able to watch her grow up, so actually I'd quite like to see her a bit and look at photos of her. But he finds it very strange.

As we will explore in more detail in the next chapter, it was not unusual for couples to have different approaches to managing their grief. However, the point we seek to make here is that photographs depicting a deceased baby are transgressive of social norms of display; they can be distressing to view and therefore challenging to show, even within family spaces (Murphy and Thomas, 2013; Heineman, 2014: 99). Indeed, memory objects are not always experienced in ways that bring comfort and connection with the deceased – they can be multifaceted and affect people in different ways (Fuller and Kuberska, 2020). As we did not speak with Victoria's husband directly, it is impossible to know why he felt it 'strange' that his wife kept photos of their baby, although sociologists theorising the intersections between death, material culture and memory have pointed out that when a death is 'bad' or untimely (as in the case of stillbirth), objects associated with these deaths may feel like 'matter out of place' (Hockey et al., 2010b). In other words, they can be a disruptive, unpredictable and at times difficult-to-negotiate presence in the ongoing lives of the bereaved (Hallam and Hockey, 2001; Fuller and Kuberska, 2020).

The complex emotional relationships that some parents have with photographs was made especially apparent by Amy and Bobby. Almost five years after Amy's miscarriage, we interviewed the couple at their home. During the meeting Amy asked Julie if she would like to see pictures of their baby Clementine, and before handing over the photo album Amy issued these instructions: 'there's things in here that have got post-it notes stuck on and I've not just stuck them on for you coming, they're like that … they've been like that from day one. So I'd rather you didn't look under the post-it notes.' The photos that Amy had carefully placed sticky notes over included one image of a letter she wrote for Clementine, which the couple buried with her in a special box in their garden. While Amy found the emotions expressed in her letter too painful to see, the act of taking the picture and its subsequent preservation in an album suggests that it was important to know that her words had been captured and could be revisited again at some point in the future.

A particular photograph served a similar future-oriented purpose for another participant, Nathan. His daughter Aria died when she was eleven weeks old, and Nathan's wife had tried to resuscitate her while their older child, three-year-old Yari, was in the house.

Nathan spoke about a picture taken by his mother which, despite its being displayed prominently in his brother's home, Nathan chose to keep hidden from view in a memory box until such time as Yari might want to learn about his sister.

> When [my mum] visited the hospital with my nan, for my nanna to see the body and come to terms, she took a picture [...] And she had it printed off, and in my mum's opinion she looked very peaceful, beautiful. And she does [...] And I can actually picture in my mind's eye what it looks like, but it's in the box, because it's quite hard to look at [...] it's there if I ever want to go back to it [...] or there might be a point of time in the future where Yari is trying to make sense of some of the stuff.

In her historical analysis of taking pictures of dead bodies, Ruby (1995) explains that this kind of photography became a hidden practice from around the 1890s onwards, and therefore social taboos might account for some of the challenges our participants discussed. Nonetheless, we found that parents had multifaceted relationships with photographs that depict the 'reality' of their baby's deceased body. While photos might be an important conduit for memory (Edwards, 1999) and a tangible means of establishing identity and social presence for the baby, they can also be contested and materialise memories that are painful and emotionally disruptive (Fuller and Kuberska, 2020). As we found in the cases of Amy and Nathan, sometimes photographs required negotiation and 'strategic' concealment (rather than destruction) to accommodate their presence at a more manageable distance from day-to-day life.

Before concluding, we would like to move on in the next section to explore further how memory objects are practically arranged and made present (or not) in everyday life. Thus, we shall consider briefly what kinds of items parents kept or collected and where they chose to keep them.

Keeping, collecting and memory boxes

In an earlier section of this chapter on preparing for memory, we noted that encouragement of memory-making and specifically the collation of material things often begins in hospital. During our fieldwork we attended an annual memorial service for families and hospital staff in a church close to the main hospital site. By doing so we were able to see how this remembrance service not only connected with the initial act of offering parents a memory box, but also gave institutional recognition to the ongoing nature of memory-making. Describing the event, Heather, a bereavement services manager, explained that symbolic rituals involving objects are at the heart of the service.

> At the memorial service they [parents] get something every year to take away, so there's what we call an act of remembrance in the middle where they place something down on the ... whatever it is in the middle of the church [...] and then they take something away, and that's a memento that they get to keep [...] a lot of families that come every year say that they add that to their memory box each year, and a lot of families, I think they get their memory box out around the birthday or the due day or any particular anniversary where they're thinking about the baby and pull things out and look at them.

The conversations we had with parents confirmed that most did collect and keep a variety of different physical items. Some of these objects were things one might expect, because they were either physical traces of the child or had an embodied connection to them, such as locks of hair, blankets, soft toys and photographs (Layne, 2000). Symbolic trinkets and little ornaments were also popular, as were books and cards. However, parents also kept items that were more idiosyncratic, such as a hospital parking permit, a copy of their baby's post-mortem report and a container of expressed breast milk (Fuller and Kuberska, 2020). In terms of interaction with material items, a few parents had preserved things from the time of their loss, but they found them (or at least some of them) too difficult to look at. For the majority, however, these memory objects were mostly a source of comfort and a way to remain connected with their child. For instance, Bev's son George died suddenly when he was two weeks old, and this is what she said during her interview.

> Oh, I've got a box [...] But I just thought... I think it was yesterday when I was thinking of coming [to the interview], and I just thought... To talk about him, I just wanted to bring something to show you, to personalise it I suppose, to be like that. That's who he was for two weeks.

In explaining her actions in this way, Bev's words signify what Layne (2003, 2000) has observed about material artefacts and baby loss – that these are used by parents to establish an identity for their child and to demonstrate its 'realness' as a social being. Like Bev, many parents not only spoke about physical objects in their interviews, but also handled and showed us these items. Some produced entire memory boxes and proceeded to empty the contents as they talked about the significance of the objects and their experiences of keeping or collecting them.

> We need a bigger box actually, but her box is now made up of things that we've done after [...] I add to it all the time. It's got all her birthday cards. We buy her a birthday card every year. We buy her a Christmas card. We do something on her birthday every year. We do things that we think we perhaps would have done [...] I buy her things, every so often I'll buy her something.

Anna here emphasises the 'liveness' of her daughter's memory box and its ongoing place in her everyday life. She suggests that the box is always in the process of becoming, as different items are added that represent the passage of time since Lily's death and her parents' ever-evolving imaginings of the person she might have become (Cadge et al., 2016; Mason, 2018).

Charlotte also spoke about the potential of material objects to enliven the time since her son Leo was stillborn. She told us about Leo's shelf in her home, which is dedicated to displaying newly purchased seasonal gifts that allow her to feel as though she is still able to do something for him (Garattini, 2007).

> Yeah, because that's the thing, you don't get to buy him anything because you have to just keep it [laughs] whereas doing it like this I feel like... I love it when say Easter's coming up or Christmas is coming up and I can clear it all off and it's an empty shelf, because it's like a world of opportunity to buy him stuff, we can go out and buy him stuff, and it's nice to feel like we're doing that for him.

For Charlotte, clearing the shelf, sourcing and buying new items and then arranging these seasonal gifts became a means of embedding her continuing relationship with Leo within the rhythms of her ongoing life. What is also powerful about this example is the 'world of opportunity' she finds in the emptiness of the shelf, which offers an interesting contrast to the more familiar idea of parents filling up a memory box. While Charlotte did also have items concealed in a box upstairs, being able to shop for her son and display these gifts more prominently in her home offered her something beyond 'just keeping'. By purchasing, interacting with and displaying these items, Charlotte makes new memories that demonstrate to herself, Leo and visitors to their home that he is still a member of her family, that she continues to be his parent, and that he is not forgotten (Finch, 2007).

As this last example and many of the other parental experiences shared throughout this section on materialising memory have illustrated, physical artefacts can be 'active partners with bereaved people' as they try to make sense of their loss and maintain pertinent social identities for themselves and the deceased (Turley and O'Donohoe, 2012: 1333). As the existing literature on material culture, memory and loss has shown, objects have an agentic potential to shape ongoing relationships between the living and the dead (Hallam and Hockey, 2001; Miller and Parrott, 2007; Gibson, 2008; Horton and Kraftl, 2012), and what we have explored here regarding experiences of baby loss is no exception. Indeed, data from our study has shown how material objects engage parents in different everyday processes of materialising memories – writing, displaying and keeping or collecting – highlighting the active role that parents *also* play in negotiating memories as a dynamic presence in their ongoing day-to-day lives. We now consider these themes further in the conclusion, which includes reflection on the material turn in sociology and the ways in which physical objects shape, but are also shaped by, everyday practice (Miller 2010, 2008).

Conclusion

In this chapter we have acknowledged that when a pregnancy ends and/or a baby dies, mourners often have few memories with which to grieve for the life that has been lost. Therefore, memory-making and memorialisation were important, multifaceted aspects of the baby loss journey for parents in our study. We have been concerned throughout this chapter with the processes through which they *actively* made memories and managed ongoing bonds with their deceased child. Unlike many of the sociological accounts on baby loss and memory, our findings also allowed us to recognise the role of professionals in this process. While some research has identified the part they can play in guiding parents in decision and memory-making activities (Komaromy, 2012; Smith et al., 2020), to date the notion of *preparing for memories* has remained implicit and under-developed in this work. For this reason, we have highlighted the experiences of professionals who actively sought to protect future memories of deceased babies and to make these as 'good' as possible for families. As social actors working in the baby loss landscape, they have the potential to shape the production and possibilities of memory through their work. And so, our findings contribute to a wider sociological concern with the social production of memory, having shown it to be a dynamic process (Hallam and Hockey, 2001) that takes place across time and space and potentially involves multiple people.

In support of findings from existing research, in the sections on making and materialising memories we found that material objects (such as photographs) (Godel, 2007; Gibson, 2008; Blood and Cacciatore, 2014) and physical spaces (for instance, the family home) (Hockey et al., 2005; Murphy and Thomas, 2013) are pertinent for experiences of memory production. In addition, we noted the significance of some forms of materiality that have received relatively less attention in the baby loss literature, such as written words. We also reflected on *how* objects are displayed or concealed as part of managing memory in the ongoing flow of everyday life, signifying the disruptive or challenging potential of photographs in particular (Fuller and Kuberska, 2020). Therefore, our findings are illustrative of the broader material turn within sociology where, on the one hand, scholars have noted the agentic potential of physical things to shape human emotions and actions, while on the other demonstrating how objects themselves and the physical spaces they inhabit are shaped by social practices (Miller, 2010, 2008; Buse et al., 2018).

Finally, memory production, as we have sought to show, is also about constructing identities. Writing from the perspective of relational sociology, May has argued that our sense of self is interpersonal 'because it is constructed in relationships with others, and in relation to others' (2011: 7). We found this to be the case for parents making memories in the immediate aftermath of their baby's death, as well as later in their bereavement journey. Although parents had mixed feelings regarding spending time with their child's deceased body in the days and sometimes weeks after death, as much of the existing literature suggests, many were pleased to have seen and handled their baby (Kingdon et al., 2015). Talking to parents about the strange, liminal period between the death and subsequent burial or cremation (Van Gennep, 1960), we found that parents often valued opportunities to actively do things for their baby. For some, this became a focus around which to develop memories that either affirmed or re-established their identity as parents and validated their relationship with the child. Our observation that the enactment of post-death parent–child relations is important for identity construction is not novel. However, much of the existing literature on death and social identity has been inspired by Hallam et al.'s (1999) work entitled *Beyond the Body*, and therefore tends to focus on future social identities constructed for (and by) the deceased, in the absence of their physical presence. Our analysis pushes this thinking in a slightly new direction by highlighting how, in the immediate aftermath of loss, some parents sought to 'perform' their relational identity as a parent *with* the physical body of their deceased baby present.

In the next chapter we take forward this focus on relationships and consider the impact of baby loss on relations between the living, exploring relational dynamics within families and with those in the wider social network.

Notes

1 Although not all research has found this (see Hughes et al., 2002), and this has led to contradictory guidelines in the UK's NHS in recent decades (Ryninks et al., 2014).
2 Sands (a stillbirth and neonatal death charity) encourages all UK hospitals to offer the option of a 'Certificate of Birth' to parents of a baby who dies before twenty-four weeks.
3 The use of parentheses here reflects Charlotte's feeling that sometimes people failed to recognise that she had given *birth* and that she had a legitimate claim to this experience.

Chapter 7

Relationships

Sociologists have often talked about a relational turn in the discipline, beginning with the publication of Emirbayer's 'manifesto for a relational Sociology' in 1997. Relational theory insists on the points of connection between things rather than the things themselves. Its main aim is to 'overcome the abstract and static categories of philosophy and the common-sense reduction of social relations, process and structures to individual physical things' (Law, 2015: 276). Although relational sociology has its roots in classical theory, there are a wide range of contemporary approaches, from those favouring critical realism (Donati, 2011) to approaches underpinned by phenomenology and interactionism (Crossley, 2011). The general aim of relational approaches, however, is to move beyond the notion that one can posit pre-existing units (such as the individual and society) as the starting point of sociological analysis. Rather, a transactional or relational approach is interested in the processes, actions and interactions from which the participants in this process emerge (Emirbayer, 1997).

In recent years, the concept of relationality has been particularly popular among British sociologists researching intimacy, family and personal life (Roseneil and Ketokivi, 2016). According to Smart (2007), the word 'relational' is particularly useful in this context because it acknowledges that people relate to others who are not necessarily kin by blood or marriage, thus allowing for greater flexibility in approach. It has also been used as part of a broader critique of individualisation and transformation of intimacy theses (Giddens, 1991, 1992; Beck and Beck-Gernshein, 1995, 2002). Mason (2004) for example, used the term to assert the continuing significance of family relationships against the social theorists who understand them to be in decline. Sociologists frequently combine relationism with the term 'family practices' (which focuses on the ways in which families are constituted through practice) (Morgan, 1996; Finch and Mason, 1993). In doing so they seek to emphasise the active nature of relating, moving away from understandings of the family and relationships as fixed and unchanging (Smart, 2007).

While sociologists have increasingly focused on exploring the family and intimate relationships through a relational lens, scholars of death and dying have also sought to show how cultural forces are involved in the shaping of dying as a social and relational process (Seale, 1998; Howarth, 2007; Kellehear, 2008; Broom and Kirby, 2013). Central to this focus is the continuing bonds thesis, which is based on the premise that relationships can survive the life–death boundary through an ongoing process of negotiation and meaning-making (Valentine, 2008). According to Kellehear (2008: 1540), social relationships can continue to evolve at the point of death and beyond, through memorial practices and other activities. As Ellis (2013) argues, the maintenance of bonds can enable relationships and self-identities to be sustained or redefined even 'beyond' death and physical existence. While social relationships with the deceased can continue long after they have died, the death of a loved one can also have significant effects on relationships between the living (Gilbert and Gilbert, 2017). More specifically, family dynamics are often reconfigured after the loss of a child, grandchild or sibling, as those left behind must learn to adjust to new forms of family practice (Morgan, 2011; Funk et al., 2017; Towers, 2019).

This final substantive chapter seeks to explore perinatal loss through a relational lens. While most of the chapter focuses specifically on the impact of baby loss on family relationships, it also seeks to examine the role that friends, work colleagues and health professionals can play. This is because, as Towers (2019) argues, bereavement is embedded in all social relationships. The chapter concludes by highlighting the socially embedded nature of baby loss, reinforcing the centrality of social relations across the entire baby loss journey.

Family, relationships and loss

Existing research has highlighted the ways in which reproductive and perinatal loss can have a profound effect on family dynamics

(Fernández-Sola et al., 2020). As Cecil (1994) notes in her study on miscarriage in Northern Ireland, while miscarriage as a physical occurrence happens to an individual woman, it is also an event that can impact those close to her. The baby that would have been born would not only have been a child, but also often a sibling, grandchild, niece or nephew. In the context of stillbirth, Cacciatore et al. (2008) make the point that family members may struggle for years to find answers to a series of complex and inherently unanswerable questions about why a baby died, with the loss changing the make-up of the family to some degree. Several studies have shown how family events can be especially challenging for parents who have experienced the loss of a baby, particularly those with religious significance (such as baptisms and funerals) which often cause distress. While the family can be a source of comfort after baby loss, therefore, it can also cause further pain and sorrow (Cecil, 1994; Cacciatore et al., 2008).

While research has shown that baby loss affects general family dynamics, it has often highlighted its impact on specific relationships – for example, on the relationship between bereaved parents. According to Fernández-Sola et al. (2020), while the loss can increase the bonds between couples, it can also cause significant conflict and dispute. The loss of a baby can also impact on parenting practices and sibling relationships. While some parents feel unable to talk openly about the loss, others continue to make their deceased baby an ongoing part of family dynamics (Cecil, 1994; Cacciatore et al., 2008). Research on child loss has, for obvious reasons, tended to focus predominantly on the experiences of parents and siblings. Less is known, however, about the experiences of grandparents. According to Gilrane-McGarry and O'Grady (2011) grandparents can experience 'double' or 'cumulative' grief after the loss of a grandchild, grieving for their own loss as well as that of their child. It is hugely important in an analysis of family experiences of perinatal loss, therefore, to consider intergenerational aspects. While the death of a baby can have profound effects on family relations, it can also impact on parents' wider social networks and relationships with friends and work colleagues (Cacciatore et al., 2008).

This chapter examines the ways in which social relationships often provide an important source of support for bereaved parents during and after the loss of a baby. It also examines the ways in which such profound loss can cause key relationships to break down.

We begin our analysis by focusing on the impact of loss on the intimate relationship between mothers and fathers, highlighting the differential experiences of men and women. Through parental accounts, we also explore the impact on children. Parents did not always feel able to tell their other children about the loss. When children did know, however, they often sought to maintain a bond with their sibling, engaging in a range of meaning-making activities to reinforce the sibling bond (Kellehear, 2008; Davies, 2019). As we move on to show, grandparents often provided parents with an important source of support after the loss of a baby. Conflict could, however, sometimes occur between parents and grandparents, leading in some cases to a complete relationship breakdown. While family relationships are the main focus of this chapter, we also seek to highlight the importance of wider social networks – from work colleagues to health professionals. As we show, such relationships often play a fundamental role in shaping parent experiences of short- and longer-term grief.

This chapter seeks to combine and contribute primarily to the sociological literature on the family, intimacy and personal relation-ships, *and* to the interdisciplinary field of death and dying studies. It lends weight to existing research on the family and bereavement, analysing baby loss through a relational lens and acknowledging the diversity of contemporary family forms (Smart, 2007; Allan et al., 2011). By considering the impact of loss on a wide range of social relationships, however, the chapter also seeks to offer a broader contribution to the existing literature on relationality and bereavement.

Couple dynamics after loss

Research has frequently shown that when a baby dies, men often feel pressure to be strong and to act as a pillar of support for mothers and the rest of the family (Cecil, 1994; Obst and Due, 2019; Fernández-Sola et al., 2020). McCreight (2004) argues that men are often forgotten mourners of pregnancy loss and have limited access to appropriate means of support. While mothers acknowledge that men can and do fall apart after the loss of a baby (Fernández-Sola et al., 2020), fathers often perceive their pain as undervalued (Nguyen et al., 2019) and can experience a sense of disenfranchised grief (Doka and Martin, 2002, 2010). Baby loss can also affect the dynamics of intimate relationships, increasing bonds while also causing conflict (Najman et al., 1993; Cacciatore et al., 2008; Fernández-Sola et al., 2020), leading, in some cases, to divorce (Gold et al., 2018). In this section, we explore the effects of baby loss on the relationship between mothers and fathers, focusing on the ways in which such intimate relationships can be both a source of support and conflict. While we recognise the importance of considering the impact of baby loss on same-sex parents (Peel, 2010; Peel and Cain, 2012), due to the nature of our research sample we are only able to comment on the experience of parents in heterosexual relationships.

Mothers and fathers in our study often experienced and processed their loss differently. Some women felt that their partners initially repressed their grief after their baby had died, only for it to resurface later. Men's suppression of emotions often affected a couple's relationship, as articulated by Anna. Her partner Mark seemed to get straight on with his life after the traumatic loss of baby Lily at twenty-three weeks, pretending to the outside world that he was OK. Anna found his different way of grieving very difficult to deal with:

> So we had the funeral on the Friday, he [Mark] was back at work on the Monday. And he just suppressed the whole lot, to the point where, it did affect our relationship [...] So I was at home a lot, and he was at work, and he seemingly, to the outsider, I knew he hadn't, but to the outside eye, he'd seemingly got over it, kind of thing, in very inverted commas, very much sort of said, and I didn't ever really feel I could talk about her. We talked about her on special occasions, and we talked about her on her birthday, and he would always be happy to go along with what I wanted, but never initiated that conversation, never, I always had to bring her up, and it's not that he didn't want to talk about her, he just didn't.

Existing studies have frequently found that closeness between parents increases after the loss of a baby (Najman et al., 1993; Fernández-Sola et al., 2020). This was articulated by several respondents in our study, including Rosie. She felt that she had become much closer to her partner Liam after their baby Camilla died suddenly while in foster care. Rosie felt that the trauma that they had both experienced had really brought them together as a couple:

Definitely pulled us closer together. All the stuff we've been through, if I have a bad day, he picks me up, if he has a bad day I pick him up. 'Cause he's clinically depressed, he takes three tablets a day for that, he went through quite a bad patch before we lost her last year, so he's had a rough time of it. And when one of us is down the other one is normally up, and then the other way around, so we sort of pick each other up.

While the loss of their baby drew many couples together, there were exceptions. Some couples ended up separating after their baby died. They blamed themselves, or sometimes each other, for the death of the baby, and then felt unable to move forward together as a couple. This happened in the case of Penny. Her baby Dustin died suddenly aged six months. Penny's ex-husband, George, turned to drink after Dustin died. She felt that George really blamed himself and his drinking for the baby's death. Penny was so concerned with George's behaviour that she insisted that he visit the doctor to seek help and support. The couple eventually split up:

> I think he [George] was on kind of autopilot. I think that's how he dealt with it. One of the things I think is that he's never dealt with it. I remember him saying … he continues to drink very heavily, but I remember him saying to me one night when he was drunk, I [he] could have killed him, we don't know that I didn't. And I think the level of guilt and anxiety and stress I feel around it all... I remember George saying that as well, how can you feel guilty, you're not the one who could have killed him. But if he's sober he won't talk about it. He's like I've dealt with it, I've done it, it's fine. But I've found things he's written when he's been drunk that show he's clearly not. But I've walked into the psychiatrist, I've physically taken him to the doctor, I've threatened to leave him if he didn't go to the psychiatrist. He actually went into hospital...

Although there were exceptions, as shown by the quote above from Penny, most couples in our study appeared to become closer after the loss and saw each other as an important source of support. This clearly reinforces findings of other studies which highlight both closeness and conflict between couples after baby loss (Najman et al., 1993; Fernández-Sola et al., 2020). Mothers in our study often talked about the ways in which men reacted very differently to the loss, at least initially, often bottling their feelings up. In the following section we explore men's experiences in more detail, focusing on the ways in which they feel that their grief is marginalised and that there is a lack appropriate emotional support (McCreight, 2004).

'He was just his daddy': likeness, loss and lack of support

As literature on perinatal loss has shown, fathers are often forgotten mourners; their pain can frequently be unrecognised by family, friends and health professionals (McCreight, 2004; Nguyen et al., 2019). This can lead to some men expressing a desire for targeted emotional support for fathers (Fernández-Sola et al., 2020). Data from our study tended to reinforce these findings. While all the men we interviewed strongly felt that their partners should be the main recipients of support (from friends, family and professionals), they did tend to feel, as men, that they had no one to turn to and were left to deal with their grief alone. Men often desperately wanted to open up to other men, but didn't know how to find men in similar situations. One father, Mike, decided to take matters into his own hands and develop some designated resources for fathers, in consultation with his local hospital:

> I really need to speak to another dad. And I appreciate that the woman carries the baby round and I can't even imagine what that must be like, but it doesn't mean the dad doesn't love the baby as well. So I just needed to speak to... So we thought because there was nothing else ... well, there was nothing at all in this... Well, you get leaflets from the hospital and things like that, but because of that, I wanted to speak to ... we sort of started our own thing up. The hospital knew about it. We spoke to them about it, do you think it's a good idea and all of that, and it was just a little leaflet thing we did [...] Coping after losing a baby. We used to have maybe once a month group meetings just to talk really, just to talk about it.

All the fathers we interviewed appreciated that their experiences of losing a baby were very different to those of their female partners. They clearly recognised the physical and embodied differences of loss and grief (Murphy, 2012), acknowledging that their female partners had been through the physical experience of pregnancy and, in some cases, labour. Some men in the study found this hard because they genuinely wanted to be able to share in their partner's physical as well as emotional pain. In this sense men could feel as though they had failed in the traditional male protector role (Fernández-Sola et al., 2020). This was articulated by Ricky:

> There's things I'll never understand about how it physically feels to carry a baby, just as Esther won't understand what it feels like to want to be able to physically do something and be almost restricted. It's like having a barrier in front of you and no one will let you past it. For me who's somebody who likes to protect, and be proud about … you know, look after my wife and the kid and family and friends, it's like that is quite a big thing to overcome, and I don't think I ever will, to be honest.

Although men could not share directly in their partners' physical experiences of pregnancy and pregnancy loss, women often sought to reinforce the biological connection between men and their baby through 'resemblance talk'. Social anthropologists have shown how resemblance talk can be a valuable tool for understanding representations and meanings associated with kinship in various cultural and historical contexts (Martin, 2019). In our study, resemblance talk appeared to be a way of including men in the physical experience of both pregnancy and pregnancy loss (Reed, 2012). Several mothers made comments about how the baby physically resembled their father, as articulated by Ricky's wife Esther:

> Yeah. And I see pictures of him with his hands. You can see there he's not tiny. There's two sets of hands on him there. He was lovely and long. Like you see there with my hands on him, thinking it's that kind of spread. He wasn't tiny at all. He had the longest gangly legs. He was just his daddy.

Discourses on resemblance constitute a kinship or family practice and help to 'construct connectedness' (Nordqvist, 2017: 874), bringing individuals 'into a significant and permanent group of people that is expressed in a kin idiom' (Howell, 2007: 63). Resemblance talk in our study was a way for women to try to connect their male partners with their baby, bringing them out of the margins and connecting them more centrally with their own experience of life and loss.

While baby loss affected parents and their relationships, it also had an impact on their existing and future children. We move on in the next section, therefore, to explore the impact of baby loss on siblings.

Baby loss, siblings and family secrets

As Davies (2015) has argued, sibling relationships are a fundamental part of our identities and sense of self. The loss of a sibling significantly alters family dynamics (Clarke et al., 2013; Rostila et al., 2017). Unsurprisingly, therefore, the loss of a baby can have a profound effect on older siblings as well as on the way that parents continue to parent those siblings. As Bornemisza et al. (2021: 2) show, after a baby dies children lose not only their sibling but also their parents as they knew them before the loss. While the act of caring for children after baby loss can be an important source of comfort for mothers (Cecil, 1994), parents often feel as though they are neglecting their older children due to grief. They also don't always feel able to tell their children about what has happened (Fernández-Sola et al., 2020). When informed about the loss, research has shown that children tend to respond in a range of different ways. For example, some children refuse to acknowledge the situation, while others want to talk about what has happened, though sometimes to other adults (not their parents). Research has shown that the loss of a baby brother or sister can result in somatic distress and lead to a range of physical symptoms in children, from insomnia to loss of appetite (Cacciatore et al., 2008). This section focuses on exploring the impact of baby loss on older and subsequent siblings. We did not interview children themselves as part of our study; our analysis, therefore, is based solely on parental interpretations of their children's experiences.

According to Davies, family homes are often a site for children's previously unexplored embodied, sensory and material engagements with death, bereavement and remembrance. These engagements occur through children treasuring and displaying keepsakes. She argues that family becomes constituted through such temporal and spatially located practices (Davies, 2019). During our interviews, parents highlighted the ways in which their children continued to include their baby sibling in games and activities. This appeared to be a way for children to continue to 'display' their relationship to their baby sibling and to place them in the wider family context (Finch, 2007). Sam, for example, whose baby girl Aurora died suddenly aged seven weeks, talked about how Aurora's older sister – Anouk – still included her baby sister in various activities:

She often wants to buy things like matching things, it's one for her and Aurora. She puts stickers, there might be one ... yeah, there's bits of it ... any stickers Anouk's into stickers, little comics and things then she's going to put a sticker on Aurora's ... she puts it up on the photo. She is funny. Anouk is sweet like that at night when you've got a nice clear sky and the stars are out she always likes to say which is Aurora's star?

While it was not uncommon for parents in our study to talk about how much children missed their baby sibling, this was particularly acute for one of our respondents. Ivy lost her son Brian to SIDS when he was four and a half months old. Brian was a twin, and Ivy talked at length about the power of twin bonds, and how Chandler, the surviving twin, had continued to feel that something was missing after Brian's death:

And he [Chandler] said he always had a feeling, still does, that there's something different about him and something's missing. And he was very unsettled when Brian died, until ... Brian came home before the funeral and when I was putting Chandler to bed, I took him in to see Brian and said come and say goodnight to your brother. And he looked in the coffin, saw him, and his face changed completely. And it was almost like a relief. And after that he settled. So I don't know if there's anything in that. But it was quite powerful at the time.

According to Cacciatore et al. (2008), although various grief symptoms can be identified in older children after their baby sibling has died, it is harder to know how and in what ways the loss would affect siblings born after the death. Many parents in our study went on to have other children, and several used a range of practices (displaying photographs around the house, attending memorial services etc.) to continue to place the baby who had died within the family (Murphy and Thomas, 2013). One of our respondents, Wayne, felt that it was important to continue to integrate baby Flo within the family context. He and his wife, Sherene, went on to have two more daughters, and they told the girls about their sister Flo:

So she's [Flo] sort of incorporated into life. Early on when the kids were really small, we talked about them having a sister and they used to talk about her. I suppose other people could think that as odd because they've never known her, but they talked about having a sister. And they do that less now but they sort of know. And it was never in a morbid way, it was always, you know, there'd been this other child. And it's just normal, so that's just part of our family.

Other parents felt that their children were too young (at the time of our interview) and were therefore waiting until they were older to discuss their deceased sibling with them.

While most parents in our study felt that they would tell their children about their baby sibling once they were old enough to understand, some parents never felt able to tell them. In such cases the baby who had died remained a secret. Dawn's baby Alex, for example, died in utero at twenty-nine weeks over thirty-three years before our study. Dawn also has a grown-up son who is not aware that he had a baby brother. Dawn has never felt that it was the right time to tell him. Her son's wife was expecting a baby at the time of our interview, however, and so Dawn felt it was perhaps the right time to finally tell him.

> When he [her son] was small it's not something you would discuss with a little boy anyway. As he got a little bit older I thought, oh, yes, I will and then before you know it he was doing exams. Then it was like O-levels, A-levels, then at university studying, then his finals and it just, sort of, has never, ever come around. The fact that I don't have anything, as you say, tangible to give him, like his [baby Alex's] blanket or a shawl [...] Obviously it doesn't make it any difference for me but I think when I do finally tell him and I will, like when his own child's born, I think he'll be quite taken aback. I think he'll be sad that he's never known his brother. Yes, I do intend to tell him.

This section has focused on examining parental interpretations of children's experience of baby loss. It has sought to highlight the relational nature of death, grief and bereavement. As Towers (2019) has argued, sibling grief should be located in the wider context of family relationships. Family dynamics can significantly affect the course of sibling grief as well as expressions of continuing bonds (Packman et al., 2006), as articulated by Bornemisza et al. (2021) in their retrospective qualitative study on sibling grief resulting from perinatal loss. We recognise that our analysis is limited because it is based on parents' accounts of sibling experience, rather than data generated by interviews with children themselves. Parental accounts, however, do indicate the potentially profound effect that baby loss can have on sibling relationships. The kinds of relationships that siblings could form with their dead baby brother or sister appeared to be contingent on how, whether and when their parents told them about the loss. They were also impacted by the extent to which parents continued to place their deceased baby within the wider family context.

While siblings can be significantly affected by baby loss, so too can grandparents. Therefore, we move on in the following section to explore their experiences.

Double the pain? The impact of baby loss on grandparents

There has been a limited amount of research focusing on the grief experienced by grandparents at the loss of a grandchild. Parental and sibling grief tends to be the primary focus in research. Existing literature has suggested, however, that grandparents can experience a double pain or cumulative loss when a grandchild dies. They often feel pain and sadness at their own loss as well as bearing witness to the pain and suffering of their own child (Reed, 2000; Gilrane-McGarry and O'Grady 2011). As our study focused almost exclusively on interviews with bereaved parents (although we did include one set of grandparents at their request), we cannot talk in depth about grandparent experience. Therefore, in this section, we focus mostly on exploring the various roles that grandparents play after the loss of a baby. While highlighting the importance of the support that grandparents often provide to parents, we also show how the death of a baby can lead to intergenerational conflict. In some cases this leads to longer-term changes in the relationship dynamics between parents and grandparents.

We interviewed grandparents Kath and Gerry as part of our study. They were the parents of one of our participants – Georgia – who lost her baby boy Charlie to SIDS aged six months. In support of the findings of existing studies (Reed, 2000; Gilrane-McGarry and O'Grady, 2011), Kath talked about the double pain that grandparents often experience after the loss of a grandchild. She emphasised the ways in which grandparents grieve for their own loss as well as that of their child: 'and then thirdly you look at your own loss and your bereavement. I've read bits and bobs about the grief for grandparents, and how that difference, you're not just grieving the loss of him [grandchild], it's your baby [child] as well.'

Some respondents felt that their own parents really suffered after the loss of their baby. Such respondents often found it difficult to cope with their parents' grief as well as their own. Anna, for example, felt that her mother was deeply traumatised by the early birth and death of baby Lily. Anna found her mother's sadness and pain too difficult to cope with, and felt the need to keep an emotional distance from her mother:

> They grieved the loss of Lily in a very unique way, as grandparents, because they have to watch their baby say goodbye to their grandbaby if you like, and I suppose only as a mother you can realise how much you can love somebody else. It's bizarre. Even when I was pregnant I thought I loved her [Lily], but nowhere near as much as I do love her now that I've had her. And I can't imagine, then, watching her in any sort of pain. And I think my mum, especially just found the whole thing so unbelievably overwhelming, because I wouldn't let her be there at the birth. I wouldn't have them at the funeral because I couldn't deal with anybody else, I couldn't have her crying, 'cause I couldn't stand it. And that's not being cruel, and that's not to say that I don't want her to feel that, and share that with me, if you like, but I couldn't stand it. Everything was irritating to me. I couldn't stand anybody else's pain, because I was in too much pain of my own.

Anna went on to discuss gender differences in the way that her mother and father grieved for baby Lily. While her mother was very honest and open about her own pain and sadness, Anna's father was more private about his grief. Anna never knew about her father's grief until some time after the event: 'My dad, I mean, I talk to my mum more openly now about it, and she had never told me [at the time], but my dad cried every day for longer than she can remember.' To date there has been a limited amount of research focusing on grandfathers' experience of grief after the loss of a grandchild. What little research does exist, however, tends to reinforce Anna's father's experience. For example, in their study on grandfathers' experience of grief after pregnancy loss or neonatal death of a grandchild, Lockton et al. (2021) found that grandfathers expressed grief in a range of ways, but that emotional expressiveness often did not reflect the extent of their grief.

When discussing the role that their parents played after their baby died, respondents tended to refer to their biological parents. There were a small number of parents in the study, however, who highlighted the importance of step-parents. Ricky spoke about the role that his stepfather Carl played after baby Oliver died. Ricky felt that Carl had been particularly devastated when Oliver was born prematurely and was fighting for life in NICU. Ricky also felt that despite being completely shattered by the death of baby Oliver, Carl had been a huge support to him and his wife throughout their ordeal:

> No, Carl didn't stay. Because Carl were really scared of losing Oliver. He came up on the Saturday, he came in but he were just torn apart. I think Carl were quite realistic probably knowing the consequences. He were taking on board what we were saying probably more than what others were. I think he were preparing for the worse but hoping. After we lost him Carl were ... he still is now, he's a rock to us.

This quote from Ricky about the role of step-parents resonates with broader sociological accounts of the family which argue for the need to recognise the diverse nature of contemporary family forms (Allan et al., 2011). It also reinforces the value of studying the family and bereavement through a relational lens, because, as argued earlier, family connections are not always based directly on either genetics or marriage (Smart, 2007).

In support of the findings of other studies, parents in our research tended to see grandparents and wider family members as an important source of support after their baby died (Cecil, 1994; O'Leary et al., 2011). Ricky, for example, went on to talk about the importance of family support and how invaluable that can be. He felt that extended family members all loved and mourned baby Oliver, and that it was this family love that helped both him and Esther get through it. As he states:

> Everybody who kind of cares for him [Oliver] were hit by it, especially his immediate family were very stunned. Even now they're all feeling it in October. They all know it's coming up [the anniversary of Oliver's death]. But the support they've given for us, I mean, I suppose in some respect we had to ... not ignorant in a malicious way, but you probably didn't have chance to appreciate what they were going through as well. Until afterwards. In hindsight, you thought, God,

they came and picked us up and they lifted us when we really needed it, but I think what were they going through from that... Especially mums [grandmothers].

The death of a grandchild can have profound and wide-ranging effects on grandparents. While it can bring families closer together (Gilrane-McGarry and O'Grady, 2011; Moules et al., 2012), it can also create tension, strain and emotional distance throughout the family (Nehari et al., 2007). Data from our study highlights a range of different ways in which baby loss impacts grandparents, indicating subtle differences according to gender in certain cases (Doka and Martin, 2002, 2010). As shown in this section, most respondents in our study saw extended family members (especially grandparents) as being an important source of support. There were, however, also intergenerational differences and conflicts between bereaved parents and grandparents in our study. We will go on to explore this in the next section.

Intergenerational difference and family conflict

According to Breheny et al. (2013), an individual's positioning within a family has a strong influence on identity. While family solidarity and connectedness are desired across generations, intergenerational conflict can and does occur over a range of issues (Pahl, 2007; Breheny et al., 2013). In the context of baby loss, differences of opinion and conflict can emerge in relation to attitudes to grief. In her study on miscarriage, for example, Cecil (1994) found that mothers who had miscarried felt that their own mothers placed a time-limit on their grief, often encouraging them to get over it. Data from our study sometimes appeared to highlight similar intergenerational differences. Jade, for example, whose baby Scott died suddenly aged four and a half months, described how she was told by her grandmother 'to get over it'.

In our study, however, intergenerational differences did not just relate to appropriate length of grieving time, but also to how parents chose to remember their baby. As Murphy and Thomas (2013) have shown in their research on stillbirth, the presence of objects (such as photos) in or around the house often serves to remind family members of the continued place of the stillborn baby in the family. In our study, however, some older relatives found the open 'display' of death, grief and loss in the home unpalatable. This was articulated by Dawn, whose sister had also lost a baby. Her sister displayed photographs of her deceased baby around the house. This is something that Dawn's mother found unacceptable:

> My mum was a bit upset when my sister had a photograph [of her own baby who died] [...] I think my mum being, I mean, my mum was always a cool mum really. She was not fuddy-duddy but I think my mum thought that was a step too far to have a photograph of a dead baby. She didn't say too much because she wouldn't say it to my sister but I know she just couldn't understand why anybody would want a photograph of a dead baby. Being a mother of four and going through it with both of us she wasn't insensitive but for a lot of people it's distasteful but on the other hand it's all you've got. It's all you've got [...] but I know my mum was a little bit, she didn't really understand.

The loss of a baby did not just relate to differences in attitude to grief or remembrance. In some cases, intergenerational conflict could occur over emotional and physical closeness to the deceased baby. This was especially the case in our study between mothers and their in-laws. Lesley, for example, was furious with her partner Mike's mother after baby Mia died. This was because Mike's mother took Mia for a walk around the mortuary. Lesley was furious because all she wanted to do was spend precious time alone with her baby. This is articulated in the interview extract below:

> Lesley: Because I remember when we went into the bereavement suite and your mum walked off with her and I about punched her.
>
> Interviewer: [Laughs].
>
> Lesley: His mum walked into another room with her, took her out of my eyesight, and I went mad, went bring her back, what you doing. I could have...
>
> Mike: See, I don't remember that.
>
> Lesley: ... killed her, which is totally irrational.
>
> Interviewer: But you just needed her near.
>
> Lesley: Yeah. She's mine. Give her back.

Denial was another issue that often led to conflicts between parents and grandparents. Charlotte talked about conflicts between herself, her husband and her in-laws after the loss of baby Leo. This, however, appeared to be for completely opposite reasons to the case of Lesley. Rather than wanting to spend time with baby Leo, Charlotte felt that her in-laws appeared to be in denial that the baby had ever existed. This was deeply upsetting for both Charlotte and her partner John, and led to a total breakdown in their relationship with John's parents for some time, as articulated below:

> John's mum and dad are a bit more standoffish about Leo, they're not very good ... they see it as our loss, whereas my mum and dad see it as their loss too, they see it as they lost a grandson, whereas I think John's mum and dad see it as it's just a very sad thing that happened to us and we'll be better when it's all better [...] They're just kind of, let's just pretend he didn't exist, do you know what I mean, and I can't be doing with that [...] We did stop talking to John's mum and dad for quite a while because it just got that it was kind of affecting us, how we were dealing with it. But yeah, I feel like my side of the family are a lot more open to it.

While conflict relating to baby loss often arose between different generations, it did also sometimes occur between siblings. This was articulated by Sam, who had fallen out with her brother after her loss. He and his partner had other healthy children, one of whom would have been a similar age to baby Aurora, who died suddenly at seven weeks:

> We don't even speak to my brother now, it's hideous. My brother and his partner have three children and they actually had a baby, a little girl, she was born four weeks after us, so it was really hard for us at the time, we couldn't for us ... but me especially I suppose to be around. I'm not really good with babies now I must admit. Having Marlow [after Aurora's death] I think as a baby I found it a bit easier but now he's getting bigger I actually ... that's like a trigger for me almost to be around tiny babies and sleeping babies I find really quite...

As sociologists have argued, while family can often provide individuals with an important source of cohesion and unity, it can also be a strong source of conflict and division (Pahl, 2007; Breheny et al., 2013). The death of a family member is a major life event and often constitutes a significant change within the family (McCarthy et al., 2013; Davies, 2019). While it can bring family members close together, as Breen and O'Conner (2011) argue, it is more common for social relationships to deteriorate following bereavement. It is therefore inevitable, perhaps, that such a devastating event as the loss of a baby can lead to conflict and longer-term changes in family relations. Our data shows that family was undoubtedly a significant source of support for parents after they experienced the death of a baby. It was also clear from our data, however, that baby loss could lead to family conflict over a range of issues (including post-mortem examination), leading (in some cases) to a total breakdown in family relationships.

Having explored the different ways that family can shape parental experiences of loss, we now want to move on to consider the effects on other social relationships, including friends and work colleagues. We argue that to explore baby loss through a fully relational lens we need to move beyond a focus specifically on the family to examine the impact on wider social relationships.

'God, I'm so sorry': navigating other relationships

Research has often highlighted the impact that bereavement can have on wider social relationships, from friendships to work colleagues (Towers, 2019). Studies focusing specifically on different forms of perinatal loss have sometimes included a focus on friendship in their analyses. According to Cacciatore et al. (2008), for example, bereaved parents can often become distant from previously close friends after the loss of a baby. Bereaved parents often felt that their friends had moved on with their own lives, frequently forgetting special events and anniversaries (for example, Mother's/Father's Day). Parents in our study did talk about the effects of their loss on their wider social networks, on friendships, work colleagues and broader acquaintances. In most cases parents felt that other people distanced themselves after their baby died, both emotionally and physically. This was articulated by Ivy, whose adult daughter had died recently. She had also lost her baby boy Brian to SIDS almost forty years ago. She talked about how, in both cases, people would walk across the street to avoid having to talk to her:

I think a lot of people keep away, they don't know what to say, even still. And as I say, my oldest daughter died in summer this year, and people tend to talk around me and not to me. So you feel a bit alienated and I think that was the same. And when Brian died people would cross the road. And there were one or two people that didn't and they're the ones you remember.

These sentiments were also articulated by Lesley and her partner Mike, who also had school-age children. They spoke about how other parents treated them, after baby Mia died, during the school run or at school-related events. Although some other parents did offer their condolences, many parents just went quiet whenever Lesley and Mike were present. As with Ivy, Lesley talked about the way in which some people would cross the road to avoid them:

I remember when we walked into school and everyone went quiet, and then loads of people that came over ... even people that I didn't know and never spoken to before came and said God, I'm so sorry. But I remember this particular woman, I remember walking down the ... I don't think you [Mike] were with me. I think I took the kids on my own. And she physically crossed the road in front of me not to speak to me, and I remember thinking okay. Even now I won't forgive her. I see her now sometimes, and if she ever spoke to me...

Many of our respondents – both female and male – talked about the effects of their child's death on work relationships. It was particularly common for fathers to discuss work during our interviews with them. In particular they often talked about the importance of establishing a 'new normal' work routine after losing their baby. Nathan, for example, went to work specifically to attend a meeting after his baby Aria had died, but before the funeral. Although his colleagues were shocked to see him there, being with colleagues and doing work helped him to achieve some form of normality. That was important for Nathan, a watershed moment:

I ended up going back in on the Tuesday. I'd actually been in work in the period between Aria dying and the funeral, even though it had been made hideously clear I didn't have to go into work, there was one day where I thought, actually I just want to go into work, because there was a meeting, and I said to Loretta [his wife], I'll go into the meeting, it's an hour long, and then I'll come home again. And that was sort of useful for me, to sort of, everyone looked at me like I was mad for coming in, there was none of this sort of eggshell walking that some people get. We weren't a massive business at the time and there was only forty people in the company, so I went into the meeting, and then went home again. But still, that first Monday back just felt quite monumental, to go back.

While some parents felt supported by both their employers and work colleagues, several others found going back to work an incredibly difficult experience. This echoes the findings of broader research which focuses on the experience of returning to work after bereavement (Pitimson, 2021). Participants often felt that their line managers, in particular, lacked sensitivity. Lesley, for example, worked as an admin assistant for a major retail and financial services company. When she returned to work after losing baby Mia, her direct line manager set up a meeting between Lesley, herself and someone from human resources. Both her boss and the human resources manager told Lesley, rather callously, that in her current state she was not good for the work environment:

> Lesley: And in the end I had to go to a meeting with my employer and they got someone in from human resources down, and I had this interview and my boss… No, this woman from human resources said to me you're not very good for the place of work …
>
> Mike: Oh yeah, I remember this.
>
> Lesley: … because you're not the happy, jolly person you used to be. I looked at her and I went, I've lost a baby. She said, yes, but you're not the happy person that everyone … we all rely on you for a laugh and a joke. And then my boss said to me, I know what it's like, Lesley, my dad died last year.

In some cases, parents had to fight to receive the appropriate maternity/bereavement leave from their employer. For example, Anna was a social worker employed by a large city council. Her employer did not realise that, although Anna's baby had died at twenty-three weeks, she was still entitled to maternity leave. Her employer had assumed that Anna would take sick leave because she had not given birth to a healthy baby.

> I had to go and do the research myself, because they didn't want to pay me my maternity, because they didn't understand about what had happened. And I had to go to government departments, and get

quotes from them, about what I'm entitled to, and relate that back to an HR department within a massive city council. Isn't that the most ridiculous thing?

While the workplace can offer bereaved individuals a productive context for facilitating relational connection (Bauer and Murray, 2018), existing research has tended to show that grief is often silenced in the workplace (Bento, 1994; Eyetsemitan, 1998; Thompson and Bevan, 2015). According to Hazen (2006), women's experiences of infertility, pregnancy loss and stillbirth significantly shape their lives and careers, affecting team interactions and work processes. Despite these effects, however, such experiences tend to be particularly silenced at work. Although not a key focus of our study, work and work relationships were important to participants. In some cases, going to work and interacting with colleagues appeared to help parents deal with their loss; in other cases, relationships at work seemed to heighten the trauma of baby loss. Our data strongly highlights the powerful influence of social relationships on parents' experiences of grief, thus reinforcing the need to examine the relationality of loss beyond the family. We will extend this focus further, moving on in the next section to consider relationships between families and professionals.

Family and professional relationships: care, conflict and continuing bonds

Attempts have been made in recent years to advance family-centred practices in medicine, bringing the family directly into an ill person's medical care and decision-making (Northouse, 2012; Zaider et al., 2016). Such practices have been implemented primarily in critical care and paediatric settings, where family members are often surrogate decision-makers (Kazak et al., 2007; Tomlinson et al., 2012). Despite attempts to develop family-centred care, however, conflicts can and do occur between health professionals and family members. They can arise for all sorts of reasons, from differences in expectations and desires regarding information and data, to differences of opinion over what constitutes 'good care' (Moore and Kordick, 2006; Van Keer et al., 2015). As research has shown, although professionals frequently describe their relationships with families as rewarding, dealing with conflictual family dynamics can generate considerable stress (Zaider et al., 2016). This final section explores the complex but very important relationships between families and professionals. When a baby is dying or has died, close and extended family members will often be present in hospital, on labour wards, in intensive care and in the mortuary. As we will seek to convey in this section, looking after families at this tragic time takes a lot of care and planning by professionals. Although it can be hard for professionals to manage family dynamics, especially conflicts between family members, relationships between the two are often significant and can be enduring.

As highlighted throughout this book, caring for and supporting families was a core part of professional work in this sensitive field of medicine. Professionals often talked about how they needed to 'manage' families through the deeply traumatic experience of baby loss in the best way possible. They felt that the way that parents were treated by professionals at the time of their baby's death would stay with them for the rest of their lives. Research in oncology and palliative care has shown how nurses learn to support the needs of families. Often they function as a relational bridge between the medical system and the lived experience of illness, and between family members themselves (McLeod et al., 2010). This was reinforced by data in our study. Certain professionals – such as nurses – often felt as though they acted as a relational bridge between doctors and families, attempting to keep the lines of communication open. This was articulated by surgical nurse Tracey. The extract below relates to one instance when Tracey was trying to reassure some parents about the post-mortem examination and the care that their baby would receive from staff in the mortuary. Tracey felt that it was her job to talk through and almost translate information given to parents by doctors:

> The way you'd be involved is just supporting the family [...] So, if a doctor came in and said, we've got to do this post-mortem because of this, this and this, you'd probably then sit and talk to them if they had any questions or worries. And they were worried about how they were going to look afterwards, and you go, no, the other family, and I was going, no she'll be fine, she'll look lovely, she'll look just the same. And they'll look after her. 'Cause Carmen [the APT] does a

really good job down there. And all the staff down there are really lovely.

Professionals tried to create a calm and caring environment for parents in the mortuary. Because of the deeply traumatic nature of their circumstances, however, parents sometimes became agitated when they were in the mortuary. In such situations professionals often became very distressed themselves, finding it difficult to work. Pathologist Ava, for example, talked at length during the interview about how parents often arrived at the mortuary deeply traumatised, some screaming in distress. Not only is this deeply upsetting for mortuary staff, but it also makes it challenging for them to perform crucial tasks. She talked about how vulnerable families (especially where drugs were involved) were often particularly agitated:

> It's difficult, sometimes you have families that are in shock, sometimes you have families, usually the more educated the families, the better they take things, so they take everything less agitated. When the families are less educated, they tend to be more agitated. And, I don't know why but some of the most vulnerable families, involving drugs, they may be screaming.

Some professionals, such as Carmen, also spoke about family conflict in the mortuary context. Emotions between family members often run so high during this traumatic time that relatives sometimes fight with one another both verbally and physically. Carmen stated, however, that no matter what happened, it was essential that staff in the mortuary remained professional:

> I mean very often you'll get split families, mum and dad don't talk, or grandmas and granddads, we've had fights in here, and we've had all sorts of things, but I think the more chaos just adds to the day really, I mean we just deal with it so whatever comes our way we deal with it in a professional manner and hopefully we get through it [laughs].

Dealing with families, therefore, could be hard work for professionals, often requiring – as argued in Chapter 4 – a significant amount of emotional labour (Reed and Ellis, 2020). Despite the challenges that professionals often faced when dealing with family members, however, most professional respondents felt that working with families and trying to do something to help them through this truly horrific time was one of the best parts of their job. This was articulated by Karl, a funeral director:

> I like to meet families, that's what I do, arranging funerals. So I've probably arranged more funerals than anyone else on the premises, probably not twice as many but nearly that, I arrange a lot of funerals, that's what I like to do, so engaging with families and getting a feeling of what they want, it in some ways helps.

As highlighted at the start of this chapter, existing literature has frequently emphasised the importance of continuing bonds between the living and the deceased (Kellehear, 2008; Valentine, 2008; Ellis, 2013). Such studies often focus on the continued bonds between family and friends. We would like to end this section, however, by using one example from our study to illustrate the ways in which parents and professionals can continue to maintain bonds with each other over a baby's death, even long after the child has died. Carmen, the APT and mortuary manager, talked about how some parents would send thank you cards to the staff, acknowledging the care and support they had provided in the parents' hour of need. As Carmen articulated, sometimes these parents would come back years later to visit the mortuary, bringing pictures of the healthy babies that they had gone on to have after their loss: 'we do have families that bring their babies back years later, oh, I've just brought you so and so, you know, and that's really touching because you've helped them to sort of … because it is a natural thing of life and death, it's together isn't it'.

While family and friends are likely to be the most important providers of social support after a loved one has died, Benkel et al. (2009) also identify professionals – particularly health professionals – as playing a key role in supporting bereaved families during this time. While acknowledging that social support for bereaved parents is provided most often by family, friends and sometimes work colleagues, we have also sought to show how hospital professionals can also act as an important source of social support for families. Such support can sometimes be quite challenging for professionals, especially in cases where family members are in conflict. It is, however, often the part of their job that professionals value most (Zaider et al., 2016), with parental and professional relationships sometimes continuing for a long time after a child has died. This again highlights the centrality of social relationships to the experience of grief, something we reflect on more fully in this chapter's conclusion.

Conclusion

In this chapter we have sought to examine the impact of baby loss on social relationships, as well as exploring the ways in which social relations shape parental experiences of grief. Drawing on sociological understandings of relationality (Emirbayer, 1997; Roseneil and Ketokivi, 2016), we have explored the role of family and friends in perinatal loss, as well as wider social networks including work colleagues and health professionals. As we have highlighted, social relationships are dynamic. While the loss of a baby can bring people together, it can also lead to significant conflict and, in some cases, to a complete relationship breakdown.

Although the death of a baby can and does affect entire families, the relationship perhaps most affected by perinatal loss is that between mothers and fathers. Our data reinforces the findings of existing studies by showing how men are often forgotten mourners, highlighting the potentially gendered nature of disenfranchised grief (Doka and Martin, 2002, 2010). While most respondents in our study felt that such a traumatic experience brought them closer together as a couple, the loss of a baby could sometimes cause conflict between parents, leading in some cases to divorce (Najman et al., 1993; Cacciatore et al., 2008; Fernández-Sola et al., 2020). While the loss had a significant effect on parents' relationships with one another, it also affected the way they continued to parent their existing and subsequent children. Most parents continued to talk to their children about their sibling, placing the deceased baby within the wider family context in the process. In some cases, it appeared that children also sought to continue their relationship with their dead sibling, including them in various games and activities (Davies, 2019). These activities all serve to reinforce the relationality of death and dying, by emphasising the significance of ongoing social relationships between the living and the dead (Kellehear, 2008; Valentine, 2008).

Participants in our study often emphasised the importance of biological relatives; however, family members who were connected to them by marriage could also be a source of both conflict and support. For example, some participants discussed the ways in which step-parents (grandparents) could provide vital support; other respondents reported significant conflict between themselves and their in-laws. As sociologists have frequently argued, it is important to recognise significant diversity in family forms (Allan et al., 2011), noting the varied impact that this can have on parental grief.

As well as focusing on family, we have also sought to shed light on the impact of baby loss on other social relationships. Parents frequently felt that friends and acquaintances kept an emotional and physical distance from them, even crossing the road to avoid speaking to them after their baby had died. This relates, perhaps, to the ways in which social relationships are influenced by a broader set of norms around the sequestered and taboo nature of death and dying (Mellor and Shilling, 1993; Lawton, 1998, 2000). According to Hazen (2006), perinatal loss is often particularly hidden and silenced in society, especially in the social context of the workplace. Several of our participants talked about the impact of their loss on work relationships. While some of our respondents (especially men) found work colleagues a great source of support, others found colleagues (specifically line managers) particularly unsympathetic. This supports the findings of other studies that have shown that while the workplace can offer bereaved individuals a productive context for facilitating relational connection (Bauer and Murray, 2018), grief often remains silenced (Bento, 1994; Eyetsemitan, 1998; Thompson and Bevan, 2015). Relational connections between families and professionals were also significant in our study. As shown, these relationships might be fleeting, or they might endure over several years. Although sometimes challenging, such relationships can and do play a significant role in shaping parents' longer-term experience of grief.

Having sought to situate baby loss within the wider context of social relationships in this chapter, we now move on in the final chapter to bring together some of the key themes highlighted throughout the book and reflect on their sociological significance.

Conclusion

Life after death

In the preceding chapters of this book, we have sought to provide an in-depth sociological account of a range of pertinent themes relating to baby loss and post-mortem examination. We began our analysis in Chapter 1 by focusing on the initial trauma that parents experienced after the loss of their baby. We sought to offer an original contribution to the nascent socio-theoretical literature on trauma. The notion of choice in the context of start- and end-of-life decision-making was then problematised in Chapter 2, before we moved on in Chapter 3 to shed light on the emerging role of technology in the post-mortem process. The enduring sociological themes of emotion and care became the central focus of our analysis in Chapters 4 and 5, before we turned our attention to the role of memory-making after baby loss in Chapter 6. The centrality of social relationships as analysed through a relational lens then provided the main theme for our final substantive chapter.

In order to advance this thematic analysis, the book has drawn on literature from a range of different conceptual, methodological and substantive areas of sociology, STS and social studies of death and dying. It is based specifically, however, on primary data collected from bereaved parents and a range of different professionals who work in this sensitive area of medicine (from midwives to pathologists). The book has attempted to capture parental experiences of different types of baby loss, including SIDS and stillbirth, second trimester miscarriage, late stage fetal loss and termination of pregnancy due to fetal anomaly. Due to the sensitive and politically charged nature of debates over termination, it might seem somewhat controversial to include TOP in a book on baby loss (Pitt et al., 2016). As we argued in Chapter 2, however, women often feel strongly bonded with their baby during the second and third trimester of pregnancy, and frequently experience termination as an embodied sense of loss. As well as exploring TOP within existing feminist debates on choice and prenatal diagnosis (Press and Browner, 1997; Markens et al., 2003; Earle and Letherby, 2007; Reed, 2012), we also argued for the need to recognise these experiences as a form of loss (Pitt et al., 2016). In exploring such different types of baby loss, we are not attempting to generalise about parental experiences of any particular form of loss based on data from our small-scale study. Rather, we understand that parents experience baby loss in many ways. We have sought, therefore, only to offer a snapshot of these experiences. Similarly, this book does not claim to represent the views of particular occupational groups, but has rather aimed to explore the experiences of professionals who work to support parents at different points along their baby loss and post-mortem journey.

In this concluding chapter, we draw together some of the significant conceptual, substantive and methodological themes that have emerged throughout the book, reflecting on their wider significance for existing debates in medical sociology, science and technology studies, death and dying studies, and research methods. We begin by examining the complex relationship between life and death, analysing and reflecting on the boundaries between the two. The chapter also considers the relationship between gender and reproduction, shedding light on the implications of our research findings for wider sociological debates on gender and masculinity. Existing conceptualisations of post-mortem practice tend to focus only on the clinical aspects of the examination. We aim to use the space offered by this conclusion to lobby for the development of a more enlightened approach to post-mortem practice, one that acknowledges the centrality of care and emotion. Conducting research on such a sensitive topic can be a very challenging experience. We also reflect, therefore, on the sensory and sensitive nature of the research on which this book is based, offering suggestions on how researchers can successfully navigate emotions in research. The conclusion ends by addressing perhaps the biggest and most important theme of all – the classic sociological relationship between the individual and society. As we have argued throughout this book, while baby loss occurs to individual mothers and fathers, both parental and professional experience of this loss are profoundly shaped and mediated by the social.

The intersectionality of life and death

The ancient Greeks had two words for life: *zoe*, the fact common to all living beings (humans, animals and gods) of being alive, the principle of life in the spirit and soul; and *bios*, which indicated the form or way of living a life (Dubreuil and Eagle, 2006; Brinkmann, 2020). Braidotti offers the notion of *zoe* as a post-human yet affirmative life-force, a force that undoes any distinction between living and dying. According to Braidotti (2013: 131), while death is an unthinkable and unproductive black hole, it is also 'a creative synthesis of flows, energies and perpetual becoming', because for her *zoe* as life-force carries on even after death. Throughout this book, we have sought to highlight the ways in which the loss of a baby is as much about the continuation of (social) life as it is about (physical) death. Drawing on data from the study and arguments made throughout the book, this section focuses its reflections on the juxtaposition and intersection of life and death. We conclude by arguing, as Braidotti does, that *zoe* as life-force in this context transcends the traditional boundaries between life and death.

Our analysis of the complex juxtaposition of life and death began in Chapter 2 on decision-making. Throughout this chapter we sought to show how the decision about whether and when to restart or end life is complex. Decisions made during this time by either parents or professionals seldom resulted in the extension of physical life. We moved on in Chapter 3 to examine the potential for MRI use in post-mortem examination to challenge or extend the boundaries between life and death. As Howarth (2000) argues, by facilitating life beyond the point where it might once have been viable, medical technology can also contribute to a confusion of the boundaries between life and death. The use and value of MRI post-mortem begins during life with fetal MRI, which can be used to aid parental decision-making over termination death and assist professionals to plan for birth. It can be used both to inform and cross-check the findings of a full post-mortem examination, thus reaffirming or refuting cause of death. MRI can also be used as adjunct to full post-mortem, guiding the examination as well as forming a crucial part of MIA. This not only helps to establish cause of death, but can also be used to inform life potential by helping parents plan future pregnancies and the creation of new life. We argue that MRI use in this context appears to facilitate the endurance of *zoe* as a life-force that transcends the existing binary relationship between life and death.

The contested boundaries between life and death were further illuminated in Chapter 4, which focused on emotions. In particular, the complex relationship between life and death was highlighted by the simultaneous expressions of joy at experiencing new life through giving birth and the profound sadness that parents felt when their baby died. The social life of a baby was preserved by parents and family members long after the baby had died, as shown in Chapter 6 through the activity of memory-making. Research on baby loss has focused on exploring the role of ultrasound images, footprints, photos and gift-giving as part of the creation and maintenance of fetal personhood and memorialisation (Layne, 2000; Garattini, 2007; Woodthorpe, 2012). This work has, however, seldom explored the role of professionals in this process. Our chapter focused on three key issues: preparing for memories (highlighting the role of professionals in particular), making memories (exploring how parents spent time with their deceased baby after death) and materialising memories (an analysis of written words, photographs and memory 'spaces' such as boxes). Throughout the chapter we sought to convey how the social production of memory is both processual and dynamic, with parents and professionals actively creating (prepar*ing*, mak*ing* and materialis*ing*) memories. Ultimately, our data shows how memory-making can help to strengthen continuing bonds and social relationships between parents and their babies (Kellehear, 2008; Valentine, 2008). As shown in Chapter 7 on relationships, it can also help to continue to place the baby within the ongoing dynamic and changing structure of the family (Davies, 2019). While memory-making helped parents to create lasting memories of their baby's identity and short life, it also illustrates the persistence of *zoe*, the endurance of the spirit and soul.

Scholars of death and dying studies have often sought to distinguish between physical and social death, discussing the ways in which social 'life' can extend beyond the boundaries of physical 'death' through various practices that continue to yoke the dead to the living (Howarth, 2000; Borgstrom, 2017). Our study reinforces this argument. The social life of deceased babies is often maintained by parents and families long after their physical death (Kellehear, 2008;

Valentine, 2008). However, we want to conclude by offering a slightly nuanced argument. It is not just the social life of babies that continues after their physical death through memory-making and various other family practices (Ellis, 2013, 2018). Rather, it is the unstoppable *zoe* as life-force that perpetuates after physical death. It is the very essence of the baby's spirit and soul that persists; the baby who has died is always in the process of becoming, what Probyn (1996: 35) refers to as the restless process 'in-between being and longing'. By making the case for the endurance of *zoe* in this context, this book seeks to offer an original contribution to debates about life and death in STS, studies of death and dying and medical sociology.

Having focused on the complex relationship between life and death in this section, we move on in the following section to explore issues of gender and reproductive loss, reflecting on the book's wider sociological contribution to existing debates on gender.

Rethinking gender and reproductive loss

Although men's roles in pregnancy and childbirth have expanded considerably over the past few decades (Reed, 2012), men can often find themselves marginalised in the context of pregnancy and childbirth (Dolan and Coe, 2011). As argued throughout this book, differences in embodied knowledge also influence mothers' and fathers' experience of baby loss (Murphy, 2012). We interviewed seven men as part of our study. Two of these men were interviewed alone, the rest with their female partners. We also interviewed twenty women (five with partners, the others individually).[1] Data from our study showed that although the men were all involved fathers, there were clear differences in gender roles during and after baby loss. Men's roles often appeared to be reflective of masculinity in transition (Robinson and Hockey, 2008), because they performed different types of masculinity depending on the situation. They were active fathers and partners in some instances, while reverting to more traditional masculine roles of breadwinner and protector in others (Reed, 2012). We explore the gendered nature of baby loss in this section, reflecting on the wider sociological literature on gender.

As articulated in Chapter 1, gender often appeared to influence parents' initial experiences of trauma. For example, mothers were almost always with their baby when it died – either through giving birth, or because the baby was in their care. By contrast, men were often physically absent. As we discussed, while men were sometimes direct participants in events (for example, administering CPR), their main role was to act as an eyewitness to the unfolding trauma, providing testimonials on what had occurred. They did, however, also bear witness to unspeakable loss. While gender could influence parents' experience of initial trauma, it also seemed to influence mental health, with women more likely to talk about and be diagnosed with PTSD. This reinforces the findings of existing psychological research on baby loss and PTSD specifically (Murphy et al., 2014), but also resonates with the broader literature on gender and mental health. As studies often show, women are more likely to self-report mental health problems and suffer psychological distress (Tedstone Doherty and Kartalova-O'Doherty, 2010). Research has also tended to show that while women are more likely to experience depression, men are more likely to report alcohol problems (Kessler et al., 1994). There is, however, also gender bias and stereotyping evident in the diagnosis and treatment of mental health problems, with research showing that women are often more likely to be diagnosed with depression and prescribed medication (Stoppe et al., 1999; Simoni-Wastila, 2000). As Tedstone Doherty and Kartalova-O'Doherty (2010) argue, this can limit the interpretation of gender differences in mental health.

Sociologists have highlighted the ways in which the articulation and experience of emotion and emotion work are often gendered (McCreight, 2005; Shields et al., 2006; Simon, 2014; Hess, 2015). According to Nichols (2019), it is, however, becoming more widely acceptable to view men as emotional. There is a growing body of research that shows that men not only have an active understanding of their emotions, but in many cases practise more emotional forms of masculinity (de Boise and Hearn, 2017). As articulated in Chapter 4, data from our study shows that men are aware of their emotions and want to express them, but sometimes feel inhibited by the existing gender order. For example, while mothers in our study tended to discuss feelings of grief openly, men often felt that they could not fully express their grief as they needed to be strong for their partner. This highlights the ways in which men are often forgotten mourners, denoting the potentially gendered nature of disenfranchised grief (Doka and Martin, 2002, 2010). It also indicates the ongoing paradoxical nature of gender roles, and the ways in which men often articulate multiple forms of masculinity according to setting and context (Lorber, 1994; Reed, 2012; Robinson and Hockey, 2011).

There has been a significant amount of research exploring emotional work in a range of health and social care settings, such as nursing, healthcare assistance, paramedic work and professions associated with bereavement (Hockey, 1993; Bolton, 2000; Boyle, 2005; Lewis, 2005). Such studies have tended to concentrate their analysis on the ways in which certain professional groups – such as nurses – perform the bulk of emotional work, work that is then often viewed as marginalised, feminised and devalued (McCreight, 2005). While female professionals in our study were often more vocal about emotion work than men, contrary to arguments made in existing literature this was not just true of nurses, midwives and allied health professionals but also of senior doctors. Furthermore, while women performed a lot of emotion work, men did too (Reed and Ellis, 2020). Professional data on emotion work from our study therefore supports the notion of gender roles in transition, or what Lorber (1994) refers to as the paradox of gender. This indicates two issues: first, that the rapidly changing nature of gender and emotion in the context of reproduction needs further interrogation, and secondly, that there needs to be greater sociological awareness of the ways in which emotion work is becoming a more acceptable part of professional practice in healthcare.

Related to emotion work is our understanding of the gendered nature of care. Feminist authors researching care in various settings have consistently shown that it remains a predominantly female activity (Graham, 1983, 1991; Ungerson, 1990; Thomas, 1993). In addition, sociological research has often highlighted the ways in which care work is a type of body work (Twigg, 2000, 2004; Fine, 2005), a form of labour that is often labelled as 'dirty', unskilled and undervalued (Twigg, 2000; Twigg et al., 2011; Nettleton, 2021). Data from our study again highlighted a more complex picture. Female professionals in the study were more likely to perform intimate body work care practices, such as dressing and washing babies. Men, however, also performed care in different ways – from providing pastoral and spiritual care through to tender body work during the post-mortem examination. Furthermore, although allied health professionals – such as nurses, APTs and bereavement support workers – do provide a significant amount of intimate body work care (for example, dressing babies), so too did senior female doctors. As with emotional labour, we seek in this conclusion to make a case for sociological research to develop a more fine-grained analysis of care work as performed in healthcare, one that allows for the increasing complexity of the gender order and the changing nature of medical work.

Several decades ago, Judith Lorber (1994) argued that gender was paradoxical because, when examined closely, much of what we take for granted about gender and its causes and effects either does not hold up or can be explained differently. One of the paradoxes of gender for her related directly to reproduction. It is assumed that genetic or physiological differences between women and men lead to gender inequalities. However, she argues that females have the advantage over men in reproduction as they can give birth; thus, according to her, it is the institutions of gender that structure the unequal relations of reproduction, not the other way around (Reed, 2012). In the UK context public support for a traditional division of gender roles in the home and the workplace has declined sub-stantially over the last three decades, a change that goes hand in hand with the marked increase in the participation of women and mothers in the labour force (Scott and Clery, 2013). Gender equality in terms of who does the bulk of the chores and who is primarily responsible for looking after children has, however, made very little progress in terms of what happens in people's homes. According to Scott and Clery (2013), there is a mismatch between depictions of gender-neutral 'adult worker' families and the practical realities of the gender division of paid and unpaid labour. This mismatch, we argue, continues to underpin the gendered nature of reproduction, and frames the differential experiences and roles that men and women face after a baby has died. Whether and how this may change over time remains unclear.

Reconceptualising post-mortem work

Although there has been an increasing amount of qualitative research on post-mortem practice, much of it focuses on the profession of pathology and on certain sub-specialisms within it, for example anatomical (Horsley, 2012) or forensic pathology (Gassaway, 2007). In such work, particular attention is often lavished on forensic pathology, and on the scientific rather than emotional aspects of post-mortem examination (Timmermans, 2006; Brysiewicz, 2007). Less is known about the caring and affective nature of post-mortem practice. Throughout this book we have sought to illuminate some of the hidden emotional work and care practices that take place in the mortuary. Such practices are central to this form of work, despite being concealed from public view (Reed and Ellis, 2019, 2020). In this section, we reflect on these hidden forms of post-mortem work, making the case for a broader conceptualisation of post-mortem practice in the future.

Mortuary staff in our study, such as pathologists and APTs, tended to see their roles as twofold: first, to find out the cause of death through conducting a clinical examination, and secondly, to provide care to help support families in their grief. One of the most striking findings in our study was the way that professionals in the mortuary continued to care for babies as if they were alive, holding, talking and singing to them while performing the clinical death work that is required. As research has shown, sensory perception – sight, smell, touch – have long been seen as integral components of diagnosis during autopsy (Horsley, 2012). In our study, however, touch was not only a diagnostic tool, but was also central to care in post-mortem practice. Care is performed in this context by professionals on babies both *with* and *for* parents. Providing such care, as we have sought to show, can be a very emotive experience for the professionals involved, resulting in them employing different types of emotion-management strategies to cope (Reed and Ellis, 2020). As other research on care work has shown, the social relationships and deep emotional bonds formed between carers and the recipients of care often provide significant fulfilment in this type of work (Stacey, 2005). This was the case for many participants in our study. Despite the emotional nature of this form of work and the various constraints on care, it was a form of work that was highly valued by professionals. Such value, we argue, undoubtedly contributes to professionals in this context being able to reject the label of dirty work (Gassaway, 2007; Woodthorpe and Komaromy, 2013).

Post-mortem practice as a form of health work has been under-explored in literature on emotional and care work. Furthermore, while research has started to focus on the increasing personalisation of post-mortem examination (Schafer, 2012), ethnographies in this area continue to be centrally concerned with dissection and pathology (Ashforth and Kreiner, 1999; Timmermans, 2006; Gassaway, 2007; Horsley 2008, 2012). We emphasise the value of extending the focus of sociology of emotions and care work to include the hidden world of post-mortem practice, as well as broadening the scope of research on post-mortem examination to include the more emotive aspects of this form of work. Post-mortem examination cannot be reduced to a set of clinical processes on the body that take place in the mortuary. Rather it involves a range of practices that tend to be hidden from public view. Hospitals across the UK are beginning to offer mortuary tours, opening their doors to members of the public to demystify these hidden worlds.[2] We argue, therefore, for the development of a more enlightened approach to post-mortem work in social research, one that departs from the existing focus on dissection (Reed and Ellis, 2020).

Data from our study indicates that post-mortem practice is changing as emotional and other forms of care work become increasingly central. Such work is highly valued by both professionals and families in this context. Although perhaps less recognised publicly, emotional work also appears to be becoming a more accepted part of the organisational culture in hospital settings. These shifts combined could perhaps be indicative of a broader *affective* turn in production. Affective labour, according to Hardt (2007), engages at once with rational intelligence and with passion or feeling. Our data does appear to reinforce this shift, suggesting that 'feelings' and 'emotions' are beginning to be better accepted and integrated into various occupational practices in the sensitive area of perinatal post-mortem.

While this section has focused on exploring emotion work and care in the context of post-mortem practice, we move on in the following section to consider the role of researcher emotions in sensitive research.

Sense and sensitivity: doing research on emotive topics

In this book we have sought to use our sociological senses to try to 'make sense' of the sensitive and traumatic arena of baby loss and post-mortem practice. As with Goffman, we have attempted to use a sharp ethnographic eye for detail to lift the veil on the taboo world of post-mortem examination, to uncover a range of hidden experiences and practices (Crow, 2005). The challenging subject matter of this book has meant that we needed to engage in critical sociological listening (Back, 2007) to effectively *hear* participant stories. We also sought to use our sociological sense of *feeling* or *Gefühl* to feel our way along the baby loss and post-mortem journey. Drawing on our senses in this way, we argue, enabled us to deepen our sense of *Verstehen* (understanding) (Weber, 1968). For example, we took a mobile go-along ethnographic approach with professionals, examining the role of material objects (from baby clothes to medical implements) in the post-mortem and bereavement process. Not only did this enable us to build a strong picture of the different post-mortem routes in and out of hospital, but it also meant that we could develop a clear understanding of the various roles that professionals played throughout the process. Being able to *see* and *touch* material objects throughout fieldwork also enabled us to appreciate the emotional and physical journeys that parents might take. *Looking* through photographs and memory boxes during interviews with parents further illuminated our understanding of these parents' experiences. Using our sociological senses and taking an in-depth ethnographic approach, therefore, clearly enhanced our ability to gain high-quality data. We would strongly recommend that social researchers – particularly those researching sensitive topics – adopt such an approach in the future.

Such detailed ethnographic attention, however, does come at a cost, namely its impact on the emotional well-being of the researcher. Both Kate and Julie were deeply affected by the research. They were affected by what they saw, heard and felt during interviews and ethnographic observations. They felt emotional when listening to parents' heart-breaking stories of loss. Witnessing the passion and care that professionals often displayed as part of their jobs also made the researchers very emotional during interviews. To deal with their emotions during the research, both Julie and Kate adopted a range of reflexive self-care practices, from keeping a diary to peer debriefing (Rager, 2005; Borgstrom and Ellis, 2017). Reflexive self-care techniques such as sharing experiences with peers and keeping a diary can provide useful tools in dealing with researcher emotions

(Reed and Towers, 2021). Certain caveats, however, must be noted. For example, diary-keeping, while therapeutic, can be tiring and the usefulness of sharing experiences is often contingent on the availability of appropriate collaborators and networks (Reed and Towers, 2021). Reflexive self-care practices, therefore, as Borgstrom and Ellis (2021) note, while heightening a researcher's emotional awareness, cannot always provide an outlet for emotion. Researchers may start to internalise the sensitivities they are researching, carrying difficult emotions with them beyond the end of a project. This was certainly the case for Julie and Kate, who both continued to feel the emotional after-effects of the research long after data collection had ended. Presenting papers at academic conferences and conducting knowledge exchange and impact activities was often a very emotional experience for the research team.

Such emotional challenges suggest that researchers need, perhaps, to develop more nuanced forms of emotion management during research. Reed and Towers (2021), for example, developed what they refer to as an *almost confessional* approach to research. Such an approach, they argue, requires the researcher to tread the boundaries between the engaged and the analytic. It encourages researchers to build empathy with potential and consented participants through reflexive practice (for example, keeping a diary) before, during and after research. Full emotional disclosure by the researcher, however, to either participants or publics is neither the aim nor an expectation of this approach. Rather, the focus remains on developing a systematic account of participants' words and stories. Such an approach acknowledges the role of researcher emotions privately, while ensuring that the voice of the participants remain centre stage in public accounts.

Research on sensitive subjects, such as baby loss and post-mortem examination, can, as Jones and Murphy (2021) argue, lead to a myriad of emotions in the researcher. It can be very emotionally challenging. It can also, however, be an immensely life-affirming experience for all concerned. Although doing this research made Kate and Julie sad at times, it also moved them deeply and reminded them of the things in life and death that are important.

As well as enabling the research team to craft some high-quality academic outputs, the study has also had significant impact on bereaved parents, charities and health professionals. It has changed the way the researchers conduct social research and deeply informed the way they teach. The research has taught Julie and Kate (both sociologists) the value of collaborating with researchers and practitioners, such as Elspeth, who work in the biomedical sciences. It also reminded them of the intellectual pleasure that can be found in conducting research that is rooted in sociology but that engages disciplines across the social sciences and beyond. Most importantly, perhaps, this project emphasises the ways in which research on difficult and taboo topics can enrich people's lives (including those of the researchers) (Reed and Towers, 2021). This is something that needs to be factored more fully into methodological debates on emotions in sensitive research. Everyday social life is 'dual-edged': it can be pleasurable, but is also often fraught with experiences that are deeply traumatic and challenging. As sociologists, we need to make sure we incorporate accounts of this difficult side of life into our analyses, no matter how hard and uncomfortable that might be (Reed, 2019).

We have sought, in this section, to reflect on both the challenges and benefits of doing social research on sensitive subjects. We now want to move in the final section to focus on the relationship between individual and society, reinforcing the centrality of 'the social' to the experience of baby loss

The social relations of loss

As sociologist C. Wright Mills (2000: 14) stated, the relationship between 'personal troubles' and 'the public issues of social structure' should be central to the discipline of sociology. This fraught, complex and heterogeneous interconnection between the individual and society is at the heart of the discipline of sociology, and, as we have sought to show in this book, is also fundamental to experiences of baby loss. We end, therefore, by reflecting on the relationship between the individual and society as articulated through the experience of baby loss. As shown throughout several chapters, while baby loss is experienced by individual parents, it is collectively felt – and mediated and made sense of by meaningful social relationships with others. We argue, therefore, that the relationship between the individual and society in this context is dialectical. While individual experience might be in tension or at odds with collective experience at times, at other times the two are mutually constitutive (Reed, 2003).

We began, in Chapter 1, by exploring the ways in which the trauma associated with baby loss is experienced by parents on an individual level, but is also collectively felt by family members, friends, professionals, work colleagues, neighbours and so on. While sociologists have often focused on individual and collective experiences of trauma as distinct analytical categories, Erikson argues that the trauma that sets an individual apart from society can also form the basis for new forms of communality. This often involves a common language, a kinship among those who have come to see themselves as different (Erikson, 1991: 461). In Chapter 1 we sought to show how trauma can inflict a huge blow to parents' individual sense of self, posing a threat to their identity and feelings of ontological security (Thompson and Walsh, 2010). Our main aim in the chapter, however, was to highlight the ways in which the trauma of baby loss is framed and mediated by the social (for example, social context, gender roles, social relations etc.) (Alexander, 2012). This indicates the value of taking a dialectical approach to individual and collective experiences of trauma. While parents experienced trauma on an individual basis, they often grieved collectively, thus reinforcing the deeply social experience of trauma in this context (Erikson, 1991).

In Chapter 2 we explored the issue of choice in life and death decision-making. We focused our discussion on four specific issues: TOP, resuscitation, and end-of-life and post-mortem decision-making. As argued in the chapter, the notion of choice is fundamentally tied to the shift in contemporary society towards individualisation (Beck, 1992; Giddens, 1994). Choice is viewed as a fundamental and distinguishing feature of contemporary social life. It is supposedly at the heart of neoliberal health and welfare policies which focus on the importance of informed individual choice and which proffer patient-centred/shared decision-making in healthcare (Nettleton, 2021). As sociologists have often sought to show, however, choices are rarely made freely, but are rather mediated by social norms and values as well as social and cultural structures that frame and mediate people's lives (Brannen and Nilsen, 2005; Nettleton, 2021). This chapter also emphasised the presence of a dialectical relationship between the individual and society. While choice in start- and end-of-life decision-making might be framed as individual choice, it is socially and culturally mediated and informed by the medical setting in which it takes place (Earle and Letherby, 2007; Nettleton, 2021).

The importance of 'the social' in mediating both parental and professional experience of baby loss is highlighted throughout this book. For example, Chapter 3 on technology emphasised the centrality of the social by highlighting the ways in which the emerging use of MRI post-mortem is mediated by the social and cultural context in which it operates (Timmermans and Berg, 2003). However, the final substantive chapter placed the social at the heart of its analysis by focusing on relationships. Sociologists have increasingly sought to explore family and intimate relationships through a relational lens (Roseneil and Ketokivi, 2016). Scholars of death and dying have also frequently shown how cultural forces are involved in the shaping of dying as a social and relational process (Seale, 1998; Howarth, 2007; Kellehear, 2008; Borgstrom et al., 2019). Although the loss of a baby occurs to individual mothers and fathers, we sought to show the effects of such individual losses on wider social relationships. We have also highlighted the ways in which social relationships can in turn shape parental experiences of grief. This again indicates a dialectical relationship between the individual and the collective.

As we have highlighted, social relationships are dynamic. While the loss of a baby can bring people together, it can also create significant conflict, leading in some cases to relationship breakdown and experiences of loneliness and social isolation. Ultimately, however, the loss of a baby and the all-consuming grief that parents experience afterwards are profoundly and infinitely shaped, constrained and mediated by the social.

Notes

1 While we recognise the importance of considering the impact of baby loss on same-sex parents (Peel, 2010), due to the nature of our sample we have only been able to comment on parents in heterosexual relationships.

2 There are several examples of this practice in hospitals across the UK; see https://www.bbc.co.uk/news/uk-england-tees-43767071 (accessed March 2022).

References

Abrams, P. (1989). *Neighbourhood Care and Social Policy*. London: HMSO.

Addison, S., Arthurs, O. J., and Thayyil, S. (2014). Post-mortem MRI as an alternative to non-forensic autopsy in foetuses and children: from research into clinical practice. *The British Journal of Radiology*, 87(1036). https://doi.org/10.1259/bjr.20130621.

Alexander, G. (2012). *Trauma: A Social Theory*, Cambridge: Polity.

Allan, G., Crow, G., and Hawkins, S. (2011). *Stepfamiles*. London: Palgrave Macmillan.

Allen, D. (ed.) (2019 [2013]). *The Sociology of Care Work*. The Francis Reports Virtual Special Issue Series: Care Standards, Regulation and Accountability. *Sociology of Health and Illness*. https://onlinelibrary.wiley.com/doi/toc/10.1111/(ISSN)1467-9566.the_sociology_of_care.

Almack, K. (2022). A death in the family: experiences of dying and death in which everyday family practices are embedded and enacted. *Families, Relationships and Societies*, 11(2): 227–41.

APA (American Psychiatric Association) (1994). *Diagnostic and Statistical Manual of Mental Disorders*. 4th edn. Washington, DC: American Psychiatric Publishing.

Arber, S., and Gilbert, N. (1989). Men: the forgotten carers. *Sociology*, 23(1): 111–18.

Armstrong, D. S. (2004). Impact of prior perinatal loss on subsequent pregnancies. *Journal of Obstetric and Gynecologic Neonatal Nursing*, 33(6): 765–73. https://doi.org/10.1177/0884217504270714.

Armstrong D., and Hutti, M. (1998). Pregnancy after perinatal loss: the relationship between anxiety and prenatal attachment. *Journal of Obstetric and Gynecologic Neonatal Nursing*, 27(2): 183–9. https://doi.org/10.1111/j.1552–6909.1998.tb02609.x.

Ashforth, B., and Kreiner, G. (1999). 'How can you do it?': dirty work and the challenge of constructing a positive identity. *The Academy of Management Review*, 24(3): 413–34.

Back, D., and Rooke, V. (1994). The presence of relatives in the resuscitation room. *Nursing Times*, 90: 34–5.

Back, L. (2007). *The Art of Listening*. London: Bloomsbury Academic.

Back, L. (2015). Why everyday life matters: class, community and making life livable. *Sociology*, 49(5): 820–36.

Badenhorst, W., Riches, S., Turton, P., and Hughes, P. (2006). The psychological effects of stillbirth and neonatal death on fathers: systematic review. *Journal of Psychosomatic Obstetrics & Gynecology*, 27(4): 245–56. https://doi.org/10.1080/01674320600870327.

Bailey, T. (2010). When commerce meets care: emotion management in UK funeral directing. *Mortality*, 15(3): 205–22. https://doi.org/10.108 0/13576275.2010.496613.

Barbalet, J. (1998). *Emotion, Social Theory, and Social Structure: A Macrosociological Approach*. Cambridge: Cambridge University Press.

Bauer, J. C., and Murray, M. A. (2018). 'Leave your emotions at home': bereavement, organizational space, and professional identity. *Women's Studies in Communication*, 41(1): 60–81. https://doi.org/10.1080/07491409. 2018.1424061.

Bauman, Z. (2007). *Consuming Life*. Cambridge: Polity.

Beck, U. (1992). *Risk Society: Towards a New Modernity*. London: Sage.

Beck, U., and Beck-Gernsheim, E. (1995). *The Normal Chaos of Love*. Cambridge: Polity.

Beck, U., and Beck-Gernsheim, E. (2002). *Individualization*. London: Sage.

Bedard-Gilligan, M., and Zoellner, L. A. (2008). The utility of the A1 and A2 criteria in the diagnosis of PTSD. *Behaviour Research and Therapy*, 46(9): 1062–9.

Ben-Sasi, K., Chitty, L. S., Franck, L. S., Thayyil, S., Judge-Kronis, L., Taylor, A. M., and Sebire, N. J. (2013). Acceptability of a minimally invasive perinatal/paediatric autopsy: healthcare professionals' views and implications for practice. *Prenatal Diagnosis*, 33(4): 307–12.

Benkel, I., Wijk, H., and Molander, U. (2009). Family and friends provide most social support for the bereaved. *Palliative Medicine* 23(2): 141–9.

Bennett, S., Litz, B., Maguen, S., and Ehrenreich, J. (2008). An exploratory study of the psychological impact and clinical care of perinatal loss. *Journal of Loss & Trauma*, 13: 485–510.

Bento, R. F. (1994). When the show must go on: disenfranchised grief in organizations. *Journal of Managerial Psychology*, 9(6): 35–44.

Benzer, M., and Reed, K. (2019). *Social Life: Contemporary Social Theory*. London: Sage.

Berg, M., and Mol, A. M. (eds) (1998). *Differences in Medicine: Unravelling Techniques, Practices and Bodies*. Durham, NC: Duke University Press.

Bericat, E. (2016). The sociology of emotions: four decades of progress. *Current Sociology*, 64(3): 491–513. https://doi.org/10.1177/0011392115588355.

Berry, S. N., Severtsen, B., Davis, A., Nelson, L., Hutti, M. H., and Oneal, G. (2022). The impact of anencephaly on parents: a mixed-methods study. *Death Studies*, 46(9): 2198–207.

Bjerregaard, K., Haslam, S., Mewse, A., and Morton, T. (2017). The shared experience of caring: a study of care-workers' motivations and identifications at work. *Ageing and Society*, 37(1): 113–38.

Blaxter, M. (2009). The case of the vanishing patient? Image and experience. *Sociology of Health & Illness*, 31: 762–78. https://doi.org/10.111 1/j.1467-9566.2009.01178.x.

Blood, C., and Cacciatore, J. (2014). Parental grief and memento mori photography: narrative, meaning, culture, and context. *Death Studies*, 38(4): 224–33.

Bolton, S. C. (2000). Who cares? Offering emotion work as a 'gift' in the nursing labour process. *Journal of Advanced Nursing*, 32: 580–6.

Bolton, S. C. (2001). Changing faces: nurses as emotional jugglers. *Sociology of Health and Illness*, 23(1): 85–100.

Bolton, S., and Boyd, C. (2003). Trolley dolly or skilled emotion manager? Moving on from Hochschild's *Managed Heart*. *Work, Employment and Society*, 17(2): 289–308.

Borgstrom, E. (2017). Social death. *QJM: An International Journal of Medicine*, 110(1): 5–7. https://doi.org/10.1093/qjmed/hcw183.

Borgstrom, E., and Ellis, J. (2017). Introduction: researching death, dying and bereavement. *Mortality*, 22(2): 93–104.

Borgstrom, E., and Ellis, J. (2021). Internalising 'sensitivity': vulnerability, reflexivity and death research(ers). *International Journal of Social Research Methodology*, 24(5): 589–602. https://doi.org/10.108 0/13645579.2020.1857972.

Borgstrom, E., Ellis, J., and Woodthorpe, K. (2019). 'We don't want to go and be idle ducks': family practices at the end of life. *Sociology*, 53(6): 1127–42.

Bornemisza, A. Y., Javor, R., and Erdos, M. B. (2021). Sibling grief over perinatal loss—a retrospective qualitative study. *Journal of Loss and Trauma*, 27(6), 530–46.

Bourdieu, P. (1999). *The Weight of the World: Social Suffering in Contemporary Society*. Cambridge: Polity.

Boyle, M. (2005). 'You wait until you get home': emotional regions, emotional process work, and the role of onstage and offstage support. In Charmine E. J. Härtel., Wilfred J. Zerbe and Neal M. Ashkanasy (eds), *Emotions in Organizational Behavior*. Abingdon: Routledge, 45–65.

Braidotti, R. (2013). *The Posthuman*. Cambridge: Polity.

Brannen, J., and Nilsen, A. (2005). Individualisation, choice and structure: a discussion of current trends in sociological analysis. *The Sociological Review*, 53(3): 412–28. https://doi.org/10.1111/j.1467–954X.2005.00559.x.

Braun, V., and Clarke, V. (2006). Using thematic analysis in psychology. *Qualitative Research in Psychology*, 3(2): 77–101.

Breen, L. J., and O'Connor, M. (2011). Family and social networks after bereavement: experiences of support, change and isolation. *Journal of Family Therapy*, 33(1): 98–120.

Breeze, A., Statham, H., Hackett, G., Jessop, F., and Lees, C. (2012). Perinatal postmortems: what is important to parents and how do they decide? *Birth*, 39: 57–64.

Breheny, M., Stephens, C., and Spilsbury, L. (2013). Involvement without interference: how grandparents negotiate intergenerational expectations in relationships with grandchildren, *Journal of Family Studies*, 19(2): 174–84. https://doi.org/10.5172/jfs.2013.19.2.174.

Brenneis, D. (2005). Afterword: sense, sentiment and sociality. *Etnofoor*, 18(1): 142–9.

Brierley-Jones, L., Crawley, R., Lomax, S., and Ayers, S. (2015). Stillbirth and stigma: the spoiling and repair of multiple social identities. *OMEGA – Journal of Death and Dying*, 70(2): 143–68.

Brinkmann, S. (2020). Psychology as a science of life. *Theory & Psychology*, 30(1): 3–17.

Brody, L. R. (1999). *Gender, Emotion, and the Family*. Cambridge, MA: Harvard University Press.

Brookes, J., and Hagmann, C. (2006). MRI in fetal necropsy. *Journal of Magnetic Resonance Imaging*, 24(6): 1221–8.

Brookes, J. A. S., Hall-Crages, M. A., Sams, V. R., and Lees, W. R. (1996). Non-invasive necropsy by magnetic resonance imaging. *Lancet*, 348(9035): 1139–41.

Broom, A., and Kirby, E. (2013). The end of life and the family: hospice patients' views on dying as relational. *Sociology of Health and Illness*, 35(4): 499–513.

Brown, N., and Webster, A. (2004). *New Medical Technologies and Society: Reordering Life*. Cambridge: Polity.

Brownlie, J. (2011). 'Being there': multidimensionality, reflexivity and the study of emotional lives. *British Journal of Sociology*, 62(3): 462–81.

Brysiewicz, P. (2007). The lived experience of working in a mortuary. *Accident and Emergency Nursing*, 15: 88–93.

Burden, C., Bradley, S., Storey, C., Ellis, A., Heazell, A. E. P., Doone, S., Cacciatore, J., and Siassakos, D. (2016). From grief, guilt, pain and stigma to hope and pride – a systematic review and meta-analysis of mixed-method research of the psychosocial impact of stillbirth. *BMC Pregnancy Childbirth*, 16(9). https://doi.org/10.1186/s12884-016-0800-8.

Burkitt, I. (2012). Emotional reflexivity: feeling, emotion and imagination in reflexive dialogues. *Sociology*, 46(3): 458–72.

Burton, J. L., and Underwood, J. (2007). Clinical, educational, and epidemiological value of autopsy. *Lancet*, 369(9571): 1471–80.

Buse, C., Martin, D., and Nettleton, S. (2018). Conceptualising 'materialities of care': making visible mundane material culture in health and social care contexts. *Sociology of Health and Illness*, 40(20): 243–55.

Cacciatore, J., DeFrain, J., and Jones, K. L. C. (2008). When a baby dies: ambiguity and stillbirth. *Marriage & Family Review*, 44(4): 439–54.

Cacciatore, J., and Flint, M. (2012). Mediating grief: postmortem ritualization after child death. *Journal of Loss and Trauma*, 17(2): 158–72.

Cadge, W., Fox, N., and Lin, Q. (2016). 'Watch over us sweet angels': how loved ones remember babies in a hospital memory book. *OMEGA – Journal of Death and Dying*, 73(4): 287–307.

Cann, C. K. (2014). *Virtual Afterlives: Grieving the Dead in the Twenty-First Century*. Lexington: University Press of Kentucky.

Cardoen, L., De Catte, L., Demaerel, P., Devlieger, R., Lewi, L., Deprest, J., and Claus, F. (2011). The role of magnetic resonance imaging in the diagnostic work-up of fetal ventriculomegaly. *Facts, Views & Vision in ObGyn*, 3(3): 159–63.

Casper, M. (1998). *The Making of the Unborn Patient: Social Anatomy of Fetal Surgery*. New Brunswick, NJ: Rutgers University Press.

CDC (Centers for Disease Control and Prevention) (2020). What is stillbirth? https://www.cdc.gov/ncbddd/stillbirth/facts.html (accessed 2022)

Cecil, R. (1994). 'I wouldn't have minded a wee one running about': miscarriage and the family. *Social Science & Medicine*, 38(10): 1415–22.

Clarke, M. C., Tanskanen, A., Huttunen, M. O., and Cannon, M. (2013). Sudden death of father or sibling in early childhood increases risk for psychotic disorder. *Schizophrenia Research*, 143(2–3): 363–6.

Cohen, M. C., Paley, M. N., Griffiths, P. D., and Whitby, E. H. (2008). Less invasive autopsy: benefits and limitations of the use of magnetic resonance imaging in the perinatal postmortem. *Pediatric and Developmental Pathology*, 11(1): 1–9.

Collier, A., and Broom, A. (2021). Unsettling place(s) at the end of life. *Social Science and Medicine*, 288. https://doi.org/10.1016/j.socscimed.2020.113536.

Committee on Bioethics and Committee on Hospital Care (2000). Palliative care for children. *Pediatrics*, 106(2): 351–7.

Conklin, B., and Morgan, L. (1996). Babies, bodies, and the production of personhood in North America and a native Amazonian society. *Ethos*, 24(4): 657–94.

Conrad, P. (1979). Types of medical social control, *Sociology of Health and Illness*, 1(1): 1–11.

Connolly, A. J., Finkbeiner, W. E., Ursell, P. C., and Davis, R. L. (2016). Legal, social, and ethical issues. In A. J. Connolly, W. E. Finkbeiner, P. C. Ursell and R. L. Davis, *Autopsy Pathology: A Manual and Atlas*. Philadelphia: Elsevier, 15–23.

Coombs, R. H., Chopra, S., Schenx, D. R., and Yutan, E. (1993). Medical slang and its functions. *Social Science & Medicine*, 36(8): 987–98.

Corea, C. (1985). *The Mother Machine: Reproductive Technologies from Artificial Insemination to the Artificial Womb*. New York: Harper and Row.

Corrigan, O. (2003). Empty ethics: the problem with informed consent. *Sociology of Health & Illness*, 25(7): 768–92.

Cortezzo, D. M. E., and Meyer, M. (2020). Neonatal end-of-life symptom management. *Frontiers in Pediatrics*, 8, https://www.frontiersin.org/article/10.3389/fped.2020.574121.

Côté-Arsenault, D., and Morrison-Beedy, D. (2001). Women's voices reflecting changed expectations for pregnancy after perinatal loss. *Journal of Nursing Scholarship*, 33: 239–44.

Crossley, N. (2011). *Towards Relational Sociology*. Abingdon: Routledge.

Crow, G. (2005). *The Art of Sociological Argument*. Basingstoke: Palgrave Macmillan.

Cunningham, C. J. L., Panda, M., Lambert, J., Daniel, G., and DeMars, K. (2017) Perceptions of chaplains' value and impact within hospital care teams. *Journal of Religion and Health*, 56(4): 1231–47.

Daly, M., and Lewis, J. (2000). The concept of social care and the analysis of contemporary welfare states. *British Journal of Sociology*, 51(2): 281–98.

D'Andrea, W., Sharma, R., Zelechoski, A. D., and Spinazzola, J. (2011). Physical health problems after single trauma exposure: when stress takes root in the body. *Journal of the American Psychiatric Nurses Association*, 17(6): 378–92.

Das, V. (2000). The act of witnessing: violence, poisonous knowledge, and subjectivity. In V. Das, A. Klenman, M. Ramphele and P. Reynolds (eds), *Violence and Subjectivity*. Berkeley: University of California Press, 205–25.

Das, V. (2001). Introduction. In V. Das, A. Klenman, M. Ramphele, M. Lock and P. Reynolds (eds), *Remaking a World: Violence, Social Suffering and Recovery*. Berkeley: University of California Press, 1–30.

Davidson, D., and Letherby, G. (2019). Use of the internet and griefwork in perinatal loss: motivations, methodologies and meaning making. *Women's Studies International Forum*, 74: 52–8.

Davidsson Bremborg, A. (2012). The memorialization of stillbirth in the internet age. In S. Earle, C. Komaromy and L. Layne (eds), *Understanding Reproductive Loss: Perspectives on Life, Death and Fertility*. Abingdon: Routledge, 155–65.

Davies, H. (2019). Embodied and sensory encounters: death, bereavement and remembering in children's family and personal lives. *Children's Geographies*, 17(5): 552–64.

Davies, K. (2011). Knocking on doors: recruitment and enrichment in a qualitative interview-based study. *International Journal of Social Research Methodology*, 14(4): 289–300.

Davies, K. (2015). Siblings, stories and the self: the sociological significance of young people's sibling relationships. *Sociology*, 49(4): 679–95.

Daykin, N., and Clarke, B. (2000). 'They'll still get the bodily care'. Discourses of care and relationships between nurses and health care assistants in the NHS. *Sociology of Health & Illness*, 22: 349–63.

de Boise, S., and Hearn, J. (2017). Are men getting more emotional? Critical sociological perspectives on men, masculinities and emotions. *The Sociological Review*, 65(4): 779–96.

Denzin, N. K. (2009 [1984]). *On Understanding Emotion*. New Brunswick, NJ: Transaction Publishers.

Dickson-Swift, V., James, E., Kippen, S., and Liamputtong, P. (2009). Researching sensitive topics: qualitative research as emotion work. *Qualitative Research*, 9(1): 61–79.

Dingeman, R. S., Mitchell, E. A., Meyer, E. C., and Curley, M. A. (2007). Parental presence during complex invasive procedures and cardiopulmonary resuscitation: a systematic review of the literature. *Pediatrics*, 120: 842–54.

Doka, K. (ed.) (1989). *Disenfranchised Grief: Recognizing Hidden Sorrow*. Lexington, KY: Lexington Books.

Doka, K., and Martin, T. L. (2002). How we grieve: culture, class, and gender. In K. Doka (ed.), *Disenfranchised Grief: New Directions, Challenges, and Strategies for Practice*. Champaign, IL: Research Press, 337–47.

Doka, K. J., and Martin, T. L. (2010). *Grieving Beyond Gender: Understanding the Ways Men and Women Mourn*. Rev. edn. Abingdon: Routledge.

Dolan, A., and Coe, C. (2011). Men, masculine identities and childbirth. *Sociology of Health & Illness*, 33: 1019–34.

Donati, P. (2011). *Relational Sociology: A New Paradigm for the Social Sciences*. Abingdon: Routledge.

Downe, S., Kingdon, C., Kennedy, R., Norwell, H., and McLaughlin, M. J. (2012). Post-mortem examination after stillbirth: views of UK-based practitioners. *European Journal of Obstetrics, Gynecology, and Reproductive Biology*, 162: 33–7.

Draper, J. (2002). 'It was a real good show': the ultrasound scan, fathers and the power of visual knowledge. *Sociology of Health & Illness*, 24(6): 771–95.

Driessen, A., Borgstrom, E., and Co.n, S. (2021). Placing death and dying: making place at the end of life. *Social Science & Medicine*, 291: 113974.

Dubreuil, L., and Eagle, C. C. (2006). Leaving politics: *bios, zōē*, life. *Diacritics*, 36(2): 83–98.

Duncan, C., and Cacciatore, J. (2015). A systematic review of the peer-reviewed literature on self-blame, guilt, and shame. *OMEGA–Journal of Death and Dying*, 71(4): 312–42.

Dyer, E., Bell, R., Graham, R., and Rankin, J. (2019). Pregnancy decisions after fetal or perinatal death: systematic review of qualitative research. *BMJ open*, 9(12): e029950.

Dyer, K., Mitu, M., and Vindrola-Padros, C. (2012). The social shaping of fertility loss due to cancer treatment: a comparative perspective. In S. Earle, C. Komaromy and L. Layne (eds), *Understanding Reproductive Loss: Perspectives on Life, Death and Fertility*. Abingdon: Routledge, 37–50.

Earle, S., Komaromy, C. and Layne, L. (eds) (2012). *Understanding Reproductive Loss: Perspectives on Life, Death and Fertility*. Abingdon: Routledge.

Earle, S., and Letherby, G. (2007). Conceiving time? Women who do or do not conceive. *Sociology of Health & Illness*, 29: 233–50.

Edwards, E. (1999). Photographs as objects of memory. In M. Kwint, C. Breward and J. Aynsley (eds), *Material Memories: Design and Evocation*. Oxford: Berg, 221–36.

Elias, N. (1985). *The Loneliness of the Dying*. Hoboken, NJ: Wiley-Blackwell.

Ellis, J. (2013). Thinking beyond rupture: continuity and relationality in everyday illness and dying experience, *Mortality*, 18(3): 251–69.

Ellis, J. (2018). Family food practices: relationships, materiality and the everyday at the end of life. *Sociology of Health and Illness*, 40(2), 353–65.

Emerald, E., and Carpenter, L. (2015). Vulnerability and emotions in research: risks, dilemmas and doubts. *Qualitative Inquiry*, 21(8): 741–50.

Emirbayer, M. (1997). Manifesto for a relational sociology. *American Journal of Sociology*, 103(2): 281–317.

Erikson, K. T. (1976). *Everything in its Path*. New York: Simon and Schuster.

Erikson, K. (1991). Notes on trauma and community. *American Imago*, 48(4): 455–72.

Eyetsemitan, F. (1998). Stifled grief in the workplace. *Death Studies*, 22(5): 469–79.

Faria, C., and Mollett, S. (2016). Critical feminist reflexivity and the politics of whiteness in the 'field'. *Gender, Place & Culture*, 23(1): 79–93.

Faro, L. (2021). Monuments for stillborn children and disenfranchised grief in the Netherlands: recognition, protest and solace. *Mortality*, 26(3): 264–83.

Fernández-Sola, C., Camacho-Ávila, M., Hernández-Padilla, J. M., Fernández-Medina, I. M., Jiménez-López, F. R., Hernández-Sánchez, E., Conesa-Ferrer, M. B., and Granero-Molina, J. (2020). Impact of perinatal death on the social and family context of the parents. *International Journal of Environmental Research and Public Health*, 17(10): 3421.

Finch, J. (2007). Displaying families. *Sociology*, 41(1): 65–81.

Finch, J. (2008). Naming names: kinship, individuality and personal names. *Sociology*, 42(4): 709–25.

Finch, J., and Mason, J. (1993). *Negotiating Family Responsibilities*. London: Routledge.

Fine, M. (2005). Individualization, risk and the body: sociology and care. *Journal of Sociology*, 41(3): 247–66.

Finlay, L. (2002). 'Outing' the researcher: the provenance, process, and practice of reflexivity. *Qualitative Health Research*, 12(4): 531–45.

Firestone, S. (2003 [1970]). *The Dialectic of Sex: The Case for Feminist Revolution*. New York: Farrar, Straus, and Giroux.

Fisher, J., and Lafarge, C. (2015). Women's experience of care when undergoing termination of pregnancy for fetal anomaly in England. *Journal of Reproductive and Infant Psychology*, 33(1): 69–87.

Fligner, C., and Dighe, M. (2011). Fetal and perinatal death investigation: redefining the autopsy and the role of radiologic imaging. *Ultrasound Clinics*, 6(1): 105–17.

Foucault, M. (1975). *Birth of the Clinic*. London: Vintage.

Francis, B., and Humphreys, J. (1999). Enrolled nurses and the professionalisation of nursing: a comparison of nurse education and skill-mix in Australia and the UK. *International Journal of Nursing Studies*, 36(2): 127–35.

Freidson, E. (1970). *Profession of Medicine: A Study of the Sociology of Applied Knowledge*. New York: Dodd Mead.

Frost, J., Bradley, H., Levitas, R., Smith, L., and Garcia, J. (2007). The loss of possibility: scientisation of death and the special case of early miscarriage. *Sociology of Health and Illness*, 29(7): 1003–22.

Fuller, D., and Kuberska, K. (2020). Outside the (memory) box: how unpredictable objects disrupt the discourse of bereavement in narratives if pregnancy loss. *Mortality*, 22(1): 1–17.

Funk, A., Jenkins, S., Astroth, K., Braswell, G., and Kerber, C. (2017). A narrative analysis of sibling grief. *Journal of Loss and Trauma*, 23: 1–14.

Gabbert, L. (2020). Suffering in medical contexts: laughter, humor, and the medical carnivalesque. *The Journal of American Folklore*, 133(527): 3–26.

Galea, S., Vlahov, D., Resnick, H., Ahern, J., Susser, E., Gold, J., Bucuvalas, M., and Kilpatrick D. (2003). Trends of probable post-traumatic stress disorder in New York City after the September 11 terrorist attacks. *American Journal of Epidemiology*, 158: 514–24.

Garattini, C. (2007). Creating memories: material culture and infantile death in contemporary Ireland. *Mortality*, 12(2): 193–206.

Gassaway, B. (2007). The death doctors. In S. K. Drew, M. B. Mills and B. M. Gassaway (eds), *Dirty Work*. Waco, TX: Baylor University Press, 195–214.

Gibson, M. (2008). *Objects of the Dead: Mourning and Memory in Everyday Life*. Melbourne: Melbourne University Press.

Giddens, A. (1991). *Modernity and Self-Identity: Self and Society in the Late Modern Age*. Cambridge: Polity.

Giddens, A. (1992). *The Transformation of Intimacy: Sexuality, Love and Eroticism in Modern Societies*. Cambridge: Polity.

Giddens, A. (1994). Risk, trust, reflexivity. In U. Beck, A. Giddens and S. Lash, *Reflexive Modernization*. Cambridge: Polity, 184–97.

Gilbert, K., and Gilbert, R. (2017). Sibling grief and its effect on the family system. In B. Marshall and H. Winokuer (eds), *Sibling Loss Across the Lifespan*. New York: Routledge, 159–66.

Gilrane-McGarry, U., and O'Grady, T. (2011). Forgotten grievers: an exploration of the grief experiences of bereaved grandparents. *International Journal of Palliative Nursing*, 17(4): 170–6.

Glenister, D. (2012). Creative spaces in palliative care facilities: tradition, culture, and experience. *American Journal of Hospice and Palliative Medicine*, 29(2): 89–92.

Godel, M. (2007). Images of stillbirth: memory, mourning and memorial. *Visual Studies*, 22(3): 253–69.

Goffman, I. (1959). *The Presentation of Self in Everyday Life*. New York: Doubleday.

Gold, K. J., Sen, A., and Leon, I. (2018). Whose fault is it anyway? Guilt, blame, and death attribution by mothers after stillbirth or infant death. *Illness, Crisis & Loss*, 26(1): 40–57.

Graham, H. (1983). Caring, a labour of love. In J. Finch and D. Groves (eds), *A Labour of Love: Women, Work and Caring*. London: Routledge and Kegan Paul, 13–30.

Graham, H. (1991). The concept of caring in feminist research: the case of domestic service. *Sociology*, 25(1): 61–78.

Graham, R. H., Robson, S. C. and Rankin, J. M. (2008). Understanding feticide: an analytic review. *Social Science & Medicine*, 66(2): 289–300.

Granter, E., McCann, L., and Boyle, M. (2015). Extreme work/normal work: intensification, storytelling and hypermediation in the (re)construction of 'the new normal'. *Organization*, 22(4): 443–56.

Green, J. W. (2008). *Beyond the Good Death: The Anthropology of Modern Dying*. Philadelphia: University of Pennsylvania Press.

Gregory, D., and Urry, J. (1985). Introduction. In D. Gregory and J. Urry (eds), *Social Relations and Spatial Structures*. Basingstoke: Macmillan, 1–8.

Griffin, A., and Yancey, V. (2009). Spiritual dimensions of perioperative experience. *AORN Journal*, 89(5): 877.

Griffiths, P. D., Paley, M. N., and Whitby, E. H. (2005). Post-mortem MRI as an adjunct to fetal or neonatal autopsy. *Lancet*, 365(9466): 1271–3.

Hadders, H. (2009). Enacting death in the intensive care unit: medical technology and the multiple ontologies of death. *Health*, 13(6): 571–87.

Hale, B. (2007). Culpability and blame after pregnancy loss. *Journal of Medical Ethics*, 33(1): 24–7.

Hallam, E., and Hockey, J. (2001). *Death, Memory and Material Culture*. Oxford: Berg.

Hallam, E., Hockey, J., and Howarth, G. (1999). *Beyond the Body: Death and Social Identity*. London: Routledge.

Hardt, M. (2007). Foreword: what affects are good for. In P. T. Clough with J. Halley (eds), *The Affective Turn*. Durham, NC: Duke University Press.

Hazen, M. A. (2006). Silences, perinatal loss, and polyphony: a post-modern perspective. *Journal of Organizational Change Management*, 19(2): 237–49.

Heazell, A. E. P., Siassakos, D., Blencowe, H., Burden, C., Bhutta, Z. A., Cacciatore, J., Dang, N., Das, J., Flenady, V., Gold, K. J., Mensah, O. K., Millum, J., Nuzum, D., O'Donoghue, K., Redshaw, M., Rizvi, A., Roberts, T., Toyin Saraki, H. E., Storey, C., Wojcieszek, A. M., and Downe, S. (2016). *Lancet* ending preventable stillbirths investigator group. Stillbirths: economic and psychosocial consequences. *Lancet*, 387(10018): 604–16.

Heazell, A. E. P., McLaughlin M. J., Schmidt E. B., Cox. P., Flenady, V., Khong T. Y., and Downe S. (2012). A difficult conversation? The views and experiences of parents and professionals on the consent process for perinatal postmortem after stillbirth. *BJOG: An International Journal of Obstetrics & Gynaecology*, 119(8): 987–97.

Heineman, E. (2014). *Ghost Belly: A Memoir*. New York: Feminist Press.

Henderson, J., and Redshaw, M. (2017). Parents' experience of perinatal post-mortem following stillbirth: a mixed methods study. *PLoS One*, 12(6): e0178475.

Hess, U. (2015). Introduction: gender and emotion. *Emotion Review*, 7(1): 4.

Highmore, B. (2002). *Everyday Life and Cultural Theory: An Introduction*. London: Routledge.

Hirschberger, G. (2018). Collective trauma and the social construction of meaning. *Frontiers in Psychology*, 9: 1441. https://doi.org/10.3389/fpsyg.2018.01441.

Hochberg, T. (2011). The art of medicine: moments held—photographing perinatal loss. *The Lancet*, 377(9774): 1310–11.

Hochschild, A. R. (1983). *The Managed Heart: Commercialisation of Human Feeling*. Berkeley: University of California Press.

Hochschild, A. R. (2009). Invited commentary: can emotional labour be fun? *International Journal of Work Organisation and Emotion*, 3(2): 112–19.

Hockey, J. (1993). The acceptable face of human grieving? The clergy's role in managing emotional expression during funerals. In D. Clark (ed.), *The Sociology of Death*. Oxford: Blackwell, 129–48.

Hockey, J., Komaromy, C., and Woodthorpe, K. (eds) (2010a). *The Matter of Death: Space, Place and Materiality*. Basingstoke: Palgrave Macmillan.

Hockey, J., Komaromy, C., and Woodthorpe, K. (2010b). Materialising absence. In J. Hockey, C. Komaromy and K. Woodthorpe (eds), *The Matter of Death: Space, Place and Materiality*. Basingstoke: Palgrave Macmillan, 1–18.

Hockey, J., Penhale, B., and Sibley, D. (2005). Environments of memory: home space, later life and grief. In J. Davidson, L. Bondi and M. Smith (eds), *Emotional Geographies*. Aldershot: Ashgate, 135–46.

Holland, J. (2009). Emotions and research: some general and personal thoughts. In S. Weller and C. Caballero (eds), *Up Close and Personal: Relationships and Emotions Within and Through Research*. Families & Social Capital Research Group. London South Bank University, Working Paper No. 25, 11–23.

Holloway, M., Bailey, L., Dikomitis, L., Evans, N. J., Goodhead, A., Hukelova, M., Inall, Y., Lillie, M., and Nicol, L. (2019). *Remember Me: The Changing Face of Memorialisation: Final Report*. https:// remembermeproject.files.wordpress.com/2020/04/remember-me-overarching-report-e-version-final.pdf (accessed 2 July 2022).

Holste, C., Pilo, C., Pettersson, K., Rådestad, I., and Papagogiannakis, N. (2011). Mothers' attitudes towards perinatal autopsy after stillbirth. *Acta Obstetricia et Gynecologica Scandinavica*, 90: 1287–90.

Horsley, P. A. (2008). Death dwells in spaces: bodies in the hospital mortuary. *Anthropology & Medicine*, 15(2): 133–46.

Horsley, P. A. (2012). 'How dead the dead are': sensing the science of death. *Qualitative Research*, 12(5): 540–53.

Horton, J., and Kraftl, P. (2012). Clearing out a cupboard: memory, materiality and transitions. In C. Jones and J. Garde-Hansen (eds), *Geography and Memory*. London: Palgrave Macmillan, 25–44.

Howarth, G. (1996). *Last Rites: The Work of the Modern Funeral Director*. London: Routledge.

Howarth, G. (2000). Dismantling the boundaries between life and death. *Mortality*, 5(2): 127–38. https://doi.org/10.1080/713685998.

Howarth, G. (2007). *Death and Dying*. Cambridge: Polity.

Howell, S. (2007). *The Kinning of Foreigners: Transnational Adoption in a Global Perspective*. New York: Berghahn Books.

Hubbard, R. (1997). Abortion and disability: who should and who should not inhabit the world? In L. Davis (ed.), *The Disability Reader*. New York: Routledge, 74–86.

Hughes, C. (2010). *Key Concepts in Feminist Theory and Research*. London: Sage.

Hughes, P., Turton, P., Hopper, E., and Evans, C. D. H. (2002). Assessment of guidelines for good practice in psychosocial care of mothers after stillbirth: a cohort study. *Lancet*, 360(9327): 114–18.

Hyde, G., Rummery, R., Whitby, E. H., Bloor, J., Raghavan, A., and Cohen M. C. (2020). Benefits and limitations of the minimally invasive postmortem: a review of an innovative service development. *Pediatric and Developmental Pathology*, 23(6): 431–7.

James, N. (1992). Care = organisation + physical labour + emotional labour. *Sociology of Health & Illness*, 14: 488–509.

Janoff-Bulman, R. (1992). *Shattered Assumptions: Towards a New Psychology of Trauma*. New York: Free Press.

Jokhi, R. P., and Whitby, E. H. (2010). Magnetic resonance imaging of the fetus. *Developmental Medicine and Child Neurology*, 53(1): 18–28.

Jones, K., and Murphy, S. (2021). Researching perinatal death: managing the myriad of emotions in the field. *International Journal of Social Research Methodology*, 24(5): 603–15.

Joyce, K. (2006). From numbers to pictures: the development of magnetic resonance imaging and the visual turn in medicine. *Science as Culture*, 15(1): 1–22.

Kang, X., Cos, T., Guizani, M., Cannie, M. M., Segers, V., and Jani, J. C. (2014). Parental acceptance of minimally invasive fetal and neonatal autopsy compared with conventional autopsy. *Prenatal Diagnosis*, 34: 1106–10.

Kazak, A. E., Rourke, M. T., Alderfer, M. A., Pai, A., Reilly, A. F., and Meadows, A. T. (2007). Evidence-based assessment, intervention and psychosocial care in pediatric oncology: a blueprint for comprehensive services across treatment. *Journal of Pediatric Psychology*, 32: 1099–110.

Keane, H. (2009). Foetal personhood and representations of the absent child in pregnancy loss memorialization. *Feminist Theory*, 10(2): 153–71.

Kellehear, A. (2008). Dying as a social relationship: a sociological review of debates on the determination of death. *Social Science & Medicine*, 66(7): 1533–44.

Kemper, T. D. (1991). Predicting emotions from social relations. *Social Psychology Quarterly*, 54: 330–42.

Kerr, A. (2004). *Genetics and Society: A Sociology of Disease*. London: Routledge.

Kessler, R. C., McGonagle, K. A., and Zhao, S. (1994). Lifetime and 12 month prevalence of DSM-111-R psychiatric disorders in the United States. *Archives of General Psychiatry*, 51: 8–19.

Kilshaw, S. (2020). Introduction: ambiguities and navigations. In S. Kilshaw and K. Borg (eds), *Navigating Miscarriage: Social, Medical and Conceptual Perspectives*. Oxford: Berghahn Books, 1–32.

Kimmel, M., and Holler, J. S. (2011). *The Gendered Society*. Oxford: Oxford University Press.

Kingdon, C., Givens, J. L., O'Donnell, E., and Turner, M. (2015). Seeing and holding baby: systematic review of clinical management and parental outcomes after stillbirth. *Birth*, 42(3): 206–18.

Klass, D., Silverman, P. R., and Nickman, S. L. (eds) (1996). *Continuing Bonds. New Understandings of Grief*. London: Routledge.

Kleinman, S., and Copp, M. A. (1993). *Emotions and Fieldwork*. Newbury Park, CA: Sage.

Kleinman, A., Das, V., and Lock, M. (eds) (1997). *Social Suffering*. Berkeley: University of California Press.

Knowles, S., Combs, R., Kirk, S., Griffiths, M., Patel, N., and Sanders, C. (2016). Hidden caring, hidden carers? Exploring the experience of carers for people with long-term conditions. *Health & Social Care in the Community*, 24(2): 203–13.

Komaromy, C. (2012). Managing emotions at the time of stillbirth and neonatal death. In S. Earle, C. Komaromy and L. Layne (eds), *Understanding Reproductive Loss: Perspectives on Life, Death and Fertility*. Abingdon: Routledge, 193–203.

Krause, F., and Boldt, J. (2018). Understanding care: introductory remarks. In F. Krause and J. Boldt (eds), *Care in Healthcare: Reflections on Practice*. Basingstoke: Palgrave Macmillan, 1–9.

Kuberska, K., and Turner, S. (2019). The presence of absence: tensions and frictions of pregnancy losses – an introduction. *Women's Studies International Forum*, 74: 91–3.

Laing, I. (2004). Clinical aspects of neonatal death and autopsy. *Seminars in Neonatology*, 9(4): 247–54.

Larson, E. B., and Yao X. (2005). Clinical empathy as emotional labor in the patient–physician relationship. *Journal of American Medical Association*, 293(9): 1100–6.

Latimer, J. (2013). *The Gene, the Clinic and the Family: Diagnosing Dysmorphology, Reviving Medical Dominance*. Abingdon: Routledge.

Law, A. (2015). *Social Theory for Today: Making Sense of Social Worlds*. London: Sage.

Lawton, J. (1998), Contemporary hospice care: the sequestration of the unbounded body and 'dirty dying'. *Sociology of Health & Illness*, 20: 121–43.

Lawton, J. (2000). *The Dying Process: Patients' Experiences of Palliative Care*. London: Routledge.

Layne, L. L. (1997). Breaking the silence: an agenda for a feminist discourse of pregnancy loss. *Feminist Studies*, 23(2): 289–315.

Layne L. L. (2000). 'He was a real baby with baby things': a material culture analysis of personhood, parenthood and pregnancy loss. *Journal of Material Culture*, 5(3): 321–45.

Layne, L. L. (2003). *Motherhood Lost: A Feminist Account of Pregnancy Loss in America*. London: Routledge.

Layne, L. L. (2012). Troubling the normal: 'angel babies' and the canny/uncanny nexus. In S. Earle, C. Komaromy and L. Layne (eds), *Understanding Reproductive Loss: Perspectives on Life, Death and Fertility*. Abingdon: Routledge, 129–41.

Letherby, G. (2012). 'Infertility' and 'involuntary childlessness': losses, ambivalences and resolutions. In S. Earle, C. Komaromy and L. Layne (eds), *Understanding Reproductive Loss: Perspectives on Life, Death and Fertility*. Abingdon: Routledge, 9–21.

Lewis, C., Hill, M., Arthurs, O., Hutchinson, J., Chitty, L., and Sebire, N. (2017). Factors affecting uptake of postmortem examination in the prenatal, perinatal and paediatric setting: a systematic review, *BJOG: An International Journal of Obstetrics & Gynaecology*, 125(10): 172–81.

Lewis, C., Hill, M., Arthurs, O. J., Hutchinson, J. C., Chitty, L. S., and Sebire, N. (2018). Health professionals' and coroners' views on less invasive perinatal and paediatric autopsy: a qualitative study. *Archives of Disease in Childhood*, 103(6): 572–8.

Lewis, C., Riddington, M., Hill, M., Bevan, C., Fisher, J., Lyas, L., Chalmers, A., Arthurs, O., Hutchinson, J., Chitty, L., and Sebire, N. (2019). 'The communication and support from the health professional is incredibly important': a qualitative study exploring the processes and practices that support parental decision-making about postmortem examination. *Prenatal Diagnosis*, 39(13): 1242–53.

Lewis, P. (2005). Suppression or expression: an exploration of emotion management in a special care baby unit. *Work, Employment and Society*, 19(3): 565–81.

Lockton, J., Oxlad, M., and Due, C. (2021). Grandfathers' experiences of grief and support following pregnancy loss or neonatal death of a grandchild. *Qualitative Health Research*, 31(14): 2715–29.

Lorber, J. (1994). *Paradoxes of Gender*. New Haven, CT: Yale University Press.

Lovell, A. (1983). Some questions of identity: late miscarriage, stillbirth and perinatal loss. *Social Science & Medicine*, 17(11): 755–61.

Lullaby Trust (2022). What is Sudden Infant Death Syndrome (SIDS)? https://www.lullabytrust.org.uk/safer-sleep-advice/what-is-sids/ (accessed 2022).

Maddrell, A. (2015). Mapping grief: A conceptual framework for understanding the spatial dimensions of bereavement, mourning and remembrance. *Social and Cultural Geography*, 17(2): 166–88.

Mahase, E. (2019). Consider active management for premature babies born at 22 weeks, says new guidance. *BMJ* 367: 16151

Manalo, M. F. (2013). End-of-life decisions about withholding or withdrawing therapy: medical, ethical, and religio-cultural considerations. *Palliative Care*, 10(7): 1–5.

Markens, S., Browner, C. H. and Preloran, H. M. (2003). 'I'm not the one they're sticking the needle into': Latino couples, fetal diagnosis, and the discourse of reproductive rights. *Gender and Society*, 17(3): 462–81.

Martin, A. (2019). 'Who do I look like?': kinning and resemblance in the experience of French donor conceived adults. *Anthropologia*, 6(2): 46–62.

Mason, J. (2004). Personal narratives, relational selves: residential histories in the living and telling. *Sociological Review*, 52(2). 162–79.

Mason, J. (2018). *Affinities: Potent Connections in Personal Life*. Cambridge: Polity.

Maxton, F. J. (2008). Parental presence during resuscitation in the PICU: the parents' experience. Sharing and surviving the resuscitation: a phenomenological study. *Journal of Clinical Nursing*, 17(23): 3168–76.

May, V. (2011). Introducing a sociology of personal life. In V. May (ed.), *Sociology of Personal Life*. Basingstoke: Palgrave Macmillan, 1–10.

McCarroll, J. E., Ursano, R. J., Wright, K. M., and Fullerton, C. S. (1993). Handling bodies after violent death: strategies for coping. *American Journal of Orthopsychiatry*, 63: 209–14.

McCarthy, J. R., Hooper, C.-A., and Gillies, V. (2013). Troubling normalities and normal family troubles: diversities, experiences and tensions. In J. R. McCarthy, C.-A. Hooper and V. Gillies (eds), *Family Troubles?* Bristol: Policy Press, 1–22.

McCreight, B. S. (2004). A grief ignored: narratives of pregnancy loss from a male perspective. *Sociology of Health & Illness*, 26: 326–50.

McCreight, B. S. (2005). Perinatal grief and emotional labour: a study of nurses' experiences in gynae wards. *International Journal of Nursing Studies*, 42(4): 439–48.

McGahey-Oakland, P. R., Lieder, H. S., Young, A., and Jefferson, L. S. (2007). Family experiences during resuscitation at a children's hospital emergency department. *Journal of Pediatric Health Care*, 21: 217–25.

McHaffie, H. E., Cuttini, M., Brölz-Voit, G., Randag, L., Mousty, R., Duguet, A. M., Wennergren, B., and Benciolini, P. (1999). Withholding/withdrawing treatment from neonates: legislation and official guidelines across Europe. *Journal of Medical Ethics*, 25(6): 440–6.

McIntosh, P. (2008). Poetics and space: developing a reflective landscape through imagery and human geography. *Reflective Practice*, 9(1): 69–78.

McLeod, D. L, Tapp, D. M., Moules, N. J., and Campbell, M. E. (2010). Knowing the family: interpretations of family nursing in oncology and palliative care. *European Journal of Oncology Nursing*, 14: 93–100.

Meerabeau, L. (1991). Husbands' participation in fertility treatment. They also serve who stand and wait. *Sociology of Health and Illness*, 13: 396–410.

Mellor, P. A., and Shilling, C. (1993). Modernity, self-identity and the sequestration of death. *Sociology*, 27(3): 411–31.

Meštrović, S. G. (1985). A sociological conceptualization of trauma. *Social Science & Medicine*, 21(8): 835–48.

Miller, D. (2008). *The Comfort of Things*. Cambridge: Polity.

Miller, D. (2010). *Stuff*. Cambridge: Polity.

Miller, D., and Parrott, F. (2007). Death, ritual and material culture in South London. In B. Brooks-Gorden, F. Ebtehaj, J. Herring, M. H. Johnson and M. Richards (eds), *Death Rites and Rights*. Oxford: Hart Publishing, 147–62.

Milligan, C., and Wiles, J. (2010). Landscapes of care. *Progress in Human Geography*, 34(6): 736–54.

Mitchell, L. M. (2016). 'Time with babe': seeing fetal remains after pregnancy termination for impairment. *Medical Anthropology Quarterly*, 30(2): 168–85.

Moore, J. B., and Kordick, M. F. (2006). Sources of conflict between families and health care professionals. *Journal of Pediatric Oncology Nursing*, 23(2): 82–91.

Morgan, D. (1996). *Family Connections: An Introduction to Family Studies*. Cambridge: Polity.

Morgan, D. (2011). *Rethinking Family Practices*. London: Palgrave Macmillan.

Moules, N. J., Laing, C. M., McCaffrey, G., Tapp, D. M., and Strother, D. (2012). Grandparents' experiences of childhood cancer, part 1: doubled and silenced. *Journal of Pediatric Oncology Nursing*, 29(3): 119–32. https://doi.org/10.1177/1043454212439626.

Murphy, S. (2012). Bereaved parents: a contradiction in terms? In S. Earle, C. Komaromy and L. Layne (eds), *Understanding Reproductive Loss: Perspectives on Life, Death and Fertility*. Abingdon: Routledge, 117–27.

Murphy, S., Shevlin, M., and Elklit, A. (2014). Psychological consequences of pregnancy loss and infant death in a sample of bereaved parents. *Journal of Loss and Trauma*, 19(1): 56–69.

Murphy, S., and Thomas, H. (2013). Stillbirth and loss: family practices and display. *Sociological Research Online*, 18(1): 27–37.

Najman, J. M., Vance, J. C., Boyle, F., Embleton, G., Foster, B., and Thearle, J. (1993). The impact of a child death on marital adjustment. *Social Science & Medicine* 37: 1005–10.

Nehari, M., Grebler, D., and Toren, A. (2007). A voice unheard: grandparents' grief over children who died of cancer. *Mortality*, 12(1): 66–78.

Nettleton, S. (2021). *The Sociology of Health and Illness*. 4th edn, Cambridge: Polity.

Nettleton, S., Burrows, R., and Watt, I. (2008). How do you feel doctor? An analysis of emotional aspects of routine professional medical work. *Social Theory and Health*. 6: 18–36.

Nguyen, V., Temple-Smith, M., and Bilardi, J. (2019). Men's lived experiences of perinatal loss: a review of the literature. *The Australian & New Zealand Journal of Obstetrics & Gynaecology*, 59(6): 757–66.

NHS (2012). *Can Cross-Sectional Imaging as an Adjunct and/or Alternative to the Invasive Autopsy be Implemented within the NHS?* http://www.aaptuk.org/downloads/Cross-Sectional-Imaging-October-2012.pdf (accessed May 2023).

Nichols, K. (2019). Learning from Love Island? Diversification of the hegemonic man. *Frontiers in Sociology*, 4. https://www.frontiersin.org/article/10.3389/fsoc.2019.00072 (accessed 22 May 2023).

Nordqvist, P. (2017). Genetic thinking and everyday living: on family practices and family imaginaries. *The Sociological Review*, 65(4): 865–81.

Northouse, L. L. (2012). Helping patients and their family caregivers cope with cancer. *Oncology Nursing Forum*, 39: 500–6.

Norwood, T. (2021). Something good enough. *Lancet*, 398(10318): 2305–6.

Nuzum, D., Meaney, S., and O'Donoghue, K. (2018). The impact of stillbirth on bereaved parents: a qualitative study. *PLoS One*, 13(1): e0191635. https://doi.org/10.1371/journal.pone.0191635

Oakley, A. (1974). *Housewife*. Harmondsworth: Penguin.

Obst, K. L., and Due, C. (2019). Australian men's experiences of support following pregnancy loss: a qualitative study. *Midwifery*, 70: 1–6.

O'Donnell, C., and Woodford, N. (2008). Post-mortem radiology – a new sub-speciality? *Clinical Radiology*, 63(11): 1189–94. https://doi.org/10.1016/j.crad.2008.05.008.

Okah, F. A. (2002). The autopsy: experience of a regional neonatal intensive care unit. *Paediatric and Perinatal Epidemiology*, 16(4): 350–4.

O'Leary, J., Warland, J., and Parker, L. (2011). Bereaved parents' perception of the grandparents' reactions to perinatal loss and the pregnancy that follows. *Journal of Family Nursing*, 17: 330–56.

Oliver, K. (2015). Witnessing, recognition, and response ethics. *Philosophy & Rhetoric*, 48(4): 473–93.

Packman, W., Horsley, H., Davies, B., and Kramer, R. (2006). Sibling bereavement and continuing bonds. *Death Studies*, 30(9): 817–41.

Pahl, J. (2007). Power, ideology and resources within families: a theoretical context for empirical research on sleep. *Sociological Research Online*, 12(5). https://doi.org/10.5153/sro.162.

Parker, R. (1981). Tending and social policy. In E. M. Goldberg and S. Hatch (eds), *A New Look at the Personal Social Services*. Discussion Paper 4. London: Policy Studies.

Parsons, G. N., Kinsman, S. B., Bosk, C. L., Sankar, P., and Ubel, P. A. (2001). Between two worlds: medical student perceptions of humor and slang in the hospital setting. *Journal of General Internal Medicine*, 16(8): 544–9.

Pawłowska, B. (2020). Emotions in research and everyday life. From feeling to acting. *Qualitative Sociology Review*, 16(1): 6–10.

Peel, E. (2010). Pregnancy loss in lesbian and bisexual women: an online survey of experiences. *Human Reproduction*, 25(3): 721–7.

Peel, E., and Cain, R. (2012). 'Silent' miscarriage and deafening heteronormativity: a British experimental and critical feminist account. In S. Earle, C. Komaromy and L. Layne (eds), *Understanding Reproductive Loss: Perspectives on Life, Death and Fertility*. Abingdon: Routledge, 79–91.

Petchesky, R. (1984). *Abortion and Woman's Choice: The State, Sexuality and Reproductive Freedom*. Boston, MA: Northeastern University Press.

Pilnick, A. (2002). *Genetics and Society: An Introduction*. Buckingham: Open University Press.

Pink, S. (2008). An urban tour: the sensory sociality of ethnographic place-making. *Ethnography*, 9(2): 175–96.

Pitimson, N. (2021). Work after death: an examination of the relationship between grief, emotional labour, and the lived experience of returning to work after a bereavement. *Sociological Research Online*, 26(3): 469–84.

Pitt, P., McClaren, B. J., and Hodgson, J. (2016). Embodied experiences of prenatal diagnosis of fetal abnormality and pregnancy termination. *Reproductive Health Matters*, 24(47): 168–77.

Pollack, C. E. (2003). Burial at Srebrenica: linking place and trauma. *Social Science & Medicine*, 56(4): 793–801.

Prasad, A. (2005). Making images/making bodies: visualising and disciplining through magnetic resonance imaging (MRI). *Science, Technology and Human Values*, 30(2): 291–316.

Prendergast, D., Hockey, J., and Kelleher, L. (2006). Blowing in the wind? Identity, materiality, and the destinations of human ashes. *The Journal of the Royal Anthropological Institute*, 12(4): 881–98.

Press, N., and Browner, C. H. (1997). Why women say yes to prenatal diagnosis. *Social Science and Medicine*, 45(7): 979–89.

Prior, L. (1987). Policing the dead: a sociology of the mortuary. *Sociology*, 21(3): 355–76.

Probyn, E. (1996). *Outside Belongings*. London: Routledge.

Purcell, C., Cameron, S., Lawton, J., Glasier, A., and Harden, J. (2017). The changing body work of abortion: a qualitative study of the experiences of health professionals. *Sociology of Health and Illness*, 39: 78–94.

Radstake, M. (2007). *Visions of Illness: An Endography of Real-time Medical Imaging*. Utrecht: Maastricht University.

Rager, K. (2005). Self-care and the qualitative researcher: when collecting data can break your heart. *Educational Researcher*, 34: 23–7.

Rankin, J., Wright, C., and Lind, T. (2002). Cross sectional survey of parents' experience and views of the postmortem examination. *BMJ* 324(7341): 816–18.

Rapp, R. (2000). *Testing Women, Testing the Fetus*. London: Routledge.

RCOG (The Royal College of Obstetricians and Gynaecologists) (2010). *Termination of Pregnancy for Fetal Abnormality in England, Wales and Scotland*. Working Party Report. London: RCOG.

RCP (The Royal College of Pathologists) (2016). *Sudden Unexpected Death in Infancy and Childhood. Multi-agency Guidelines for Care and Investigation. The Report of a Working Group Convened by The Royal College of Pathologists and Endorsed by The Royal College of Paediatrics and Child Health*. https://www.rcpath.org/discover-pathology/news/new-guidelines-for-the-investigation-of-sudden-unexpected-death-in-infancy-launched.html (accessed 22 May 2023).

Reed, K. (2003). *Worlds of Health*. Westport, CT: Praeger.

Reed, K. (2012). *Gender and Genetics: Sociology of the Prenatal*. Abingdon: Routledge.

Reed, K. (2013). *Constructing the Fetal Patient*. Research report, British Academy, 1–7.

Reed, K. (2019). Too sensitive for sociology? Researching the taboo subject of baby loss and post-mortem. British Sociological Association, Everyday Society, 10 October. http://es.britsoc.co.uk/too-sensitive-for-sociology-researching-the-taboo-subject-of-baby-loss-and-post-mortem (accessed May 2023).

Reed, K., and Ellis, J. (2019). Movement, materiality, and the mortuary: adopting go-along ethnography in research on fetal and neonatal post-mortem. *Journal of Contemporary Ethnography*, 48(2): 209–35.

Reed, K., and Ellis, J. (2020). Uncovering hidden emotional work: professional practice in paediatric post-mortem. *Sociology*, 54(2): 312–28.

Reed, K., Ferazzoli, M. T., and Whitby, E. (2020). Miscarriage, SUDI and neonatal death: paramedic experience and practice. *Journal of Paramedic Practice*, 12(12): 472–7.

Reed, K., Ferazzoli, M. T., and Whitby, E. (2021). 'Why didn't we do it?' Reproductive loss and the problem of post-mortem consent. *Social Science & Medicine*, 276. https://doi.org/10.1016/j.socscimed.2021. 113835.

Reed, K., Kochetkova, I., and Molyneux-Hodgson, S. (2016). 'You're looking for different parts in a jigsaw': fetal MRI (magnetic resonance imaging) as an emerging technology in professional practice. *Sociology of Health and Illness*, 38(5): 736–52.

Reed, K., and Towers, L. (2021). Almost confessional: managing emotions when research breaks your heart. *Sociological Research Online*, 28(1). https://doi.org/10.1177/13607804211036719.

Reed, M. L. (2000). *Grandparents Cry Twice: Help for Bereaved Grandparents*. New York: Baywood.

Rhys-Taylor, A. (2013). The essences of multiculture: a sensory exploration of an inner-city street market. *Identities*, 20(4): 393–406.

Richardson, T. (2014). Spousal bereavement in later life: a material culture perspective. *Mortality*, 19(1): 61–79.

Riches, G., and Dawson, P. (1998). Lost children, living memories: the role of photographs in processes of grief and adjustment among bereaved parents. *Death Studies*, 22(2): 121–40.

Robinson, V. (2008). *Everyday Masculinities and Extreme Sport: Male Identity and Rock Climbing*. London: Bloomsbury Publishing.

Robinson, V. (2015). Reconceptualising the mundane and the extraordinary: a lens through which to explore transformation within women's everyday footwear practices. *Sociology*, 49(5): 903–18.

Robinson, V., and Hockey, J. (2011). *Masculinities in Transition*. Basingstoke: Palgrave Macmillan.

Rose, C., Evans, M., and Tooley, J. (2006). Falling rates of perinatal post-mortem examination: are we to blame? *Archives of Disease in Childhood. Fetal and Neonatal Edition*, 91(6): F465.

Rose, N. (2001). The politics of life itself. *Theory, Culture and Society*, 18(6): 1–30.

Rosenberg, J. P. (2012). 'You can name her': ritualised grieving by an Australian woman for her stillborn twin. *Health Sociology Review*, 21(4): 406–12.

Roseneil, S., and Ketokivi, K. (2016). Relational persons and relational processes: developing the notion of relationality for the sociology of personal life. *Sociology*, 50(1): 143–59.

Rostila, M., Berg, L., Saarela, J., Kawachi, I., and Hjern, A. (2017). Experience of sibling death in childhood and risk of death in adulthood: a national cohort study from Sweden. *American Journal of Epidemiology*, 185(12): 1247–54.

Rothman, B. K. (1986). *The Tentative Pregnancy: How Amniocentesis Changes the Experience of Motherhood*. New York: W. W. Norton.

Ruby, J. (1995). *Secure the Shadow: Death and Photography in America*. Cambridge MA: MIT Press.

Ryninks, K., Roberts-Collins, C., McKenzie-McHarg, K., and Horsch, A. (2014). Mothers' experience of their contact with their stillborn infant: an interpretative phenomenological analysis. *BMC Pregnancy and Childbirth*, 14(203). https://doi.org/10.1186/1471-2393-14-203.

Sandelowski, M. (1994). Separate but less unequal: fetal ultrasonography and the transformation of expectant mother/fatherhood. *Gender and Society*, 8: 230–45.

Sands (2017). The Sands perinatal post mortem consent package. Human Tissue Authority. https://www.hta.gov.uk/guidance-professionals/regulated-sectors/post-mortem/post-mortem-model-consent-forms/sands (accessed 22 May 2023).

Schafer, C. (2012). Corpses, conflict and insignificance? A critical analysis of post-mortem practices. *Mortality*, 17(4): 305–21.

Schwarz, O. (2018). Cultures of choice: towards a sociology of choice as a cultural phenomenon. *British Journal of Sociology*, 69: 845–64.

Scott, J., and Clery, L. (2013). Gender roles: an incomplete revolution? In A. Park, C. Bryson, R. Clery, J. Curtice and M. Phillips (eds), *British Social Attitudes: The 30th Report*. London: National Centre for Social Research. https://www.bsa.natcen.ac.uk/media/39248/bsa35_gender.pdf (accessed May 2023).

Seale, C. (1998). *Constructing Death: The Sociology of Dying and Bereavement*. Cambridge: Cambridge University Press.

Sebire, N., and Taylor, A. (2012). Less invasive perinatal autopsies and the future of postmortem science. *Ultrasound in Obstetrics & Gynecology*, 39(6): 609–11.

Shakespeare, T. (1999). Losing the plot? Medical and activist discourses of contemporary genetics and disability. *Sociology of Health and Illness*, 21(5): 669–88.

Shaw, A. (2014). Rituals of infant death: defining life and Islamic personhood. *Bioethics*, 28: 84–95.

Sheach Leith, V. (2007). Consent and nothing but consent? The organ retention scandal. *Sociology of Health & Illness*, 29(7): 1023–42.

Shedge, R., Krishan, K., Warrier, V., and Kanchan, T. (2020). Postmortem changes. *StatPearls*. https://www.ncbi.nlm.nih.gov/books/NBK539741/ (accessed January 2022)

Shields, L., and King, S. (2001). Qualitative analysis of the care of children in hospital in four countries—Part 2. *Journal of Pediatric Nursing*, 16(3): 206–13.

Shields, S. A., Garner, D. N., Di Leone, B., and Hadley, A. M. (2006). Gender and emotion. In J. E. Stets and J. H. Turner (eds), *Handbook of the Sociology of Emotions*. Boston, MA: Springer, 63–83.

Shilling, C. (2003). *The Body and Social Theory*, London: Sage.

Simon, R. W. (2014). Sociological scholarship on gender differences in emotion and emotional wellbeing in the United States: a snapshot of the field. *Emotion Review*, 6(3): 196–201.

Simoni-Wastila, L. (2000). The use of abusable prescription drugs: the role of gender. *Journal of Women's Health and Gender Based Medicine*, 9: 289–97.

Smart, C. (2007). *Personal Life: New Directions in Sociological Thinking*. Cambridge: Polity.

Smelser, N. J. (2004). Psychological trauma and cultural trauma. In J. C. Alexander, R. Eyerman, B. Giesen, N. J. Smelser and P. Sztompka, *Cultural Trauma and Collective Identity*. Berkeley: University of California Press, 31–59.

Smith, L. K., Dickens, J., Bender Atik, R., Bevan, C., Fisher, J., and Hinton, L. (2020). Parents' experiences of care following the loss of a baby at the margins between miscarriage, stillbirth and neonatal death: a UK qualitative study. *BJOG: An International Journal of Obstetrics & Gynaecology* 127: 868–74.

Soltani Gerdfaramarzi, M., and Bazmi, S. (2020). Neonatal end-of-life decisions and ethical perspectives. *Journal of Medical Ethics and History of Medicine*, 13(19). https://doi.org/10.18502/jmehm.v13i19.4827.

Stacey, C. L. (2005). Finding dignity in dirty work: the constraints and rewards of low-wage home care labour. *Sociology of Health & Illness*, 27: 831–54.

Stephens, E. (2011). *Anatomy as Spectacle: Public Exhibitions of the Body from 1700 to the Present*. Liverpool: Liverpool University Press.

Stock, S., Goldsmith, L., Evans, M., and Laing, I. (2010). Interventions to improve rates of post-mortem examination after stillbirth. *European Journal of Obstetrics, Gynecology, and Reproductive Biology*, 153: 148–50.

Stolman, C. J., Castello, F., Yorio, M., and Mautone, S. (1994). Attitudes of pediatricians and pediatric residents toward obtaining permission for autopsy. *Archives of Pediatrics & Adolescent Medicine*, 148(8): 843–47.

Stoppe, G., Sandholzer, H., and Huppertz, C. (1999). Gender differences in the recognition of depression in old age. *Maturitas*, 32: 205–12.

Svendsen, E., and Hill, R. B. (1987). Autopsy legislation and practice in various countries. *Archives of Pathology and Laboratory Medicine*, 111: 846–50.

Sweet, L. (2008). Expressed breast milk as 'connection' and its influence on the construction of 'motherhood' for mothers of preterm infants: a qualitative study. *International Breastfeeding Journal*, 3(30), https://doi.org/10.1186/1746-4358-3-30.

Tedstone Doherty, D., and Kartalova-O'Doherty, Y. (2010). Gender and self-reported mental health problems: predictors of help seeking from a general practitioner. *British Journal of Health Psychology*, 15(1): 213–28.

Telle, K. G. (2002). The smell of death: theft, disgust and ritual practice in central Lombok, Indonesia. In B. Kapferer (ed.), *Beyond Rationalism: Rethinking Magic, Witchcraft, and Sorcery*. New York: Berghahn Books, 105–32.

Thayyil, S., Sebire, N. J., Chitty, L. S., Wade, A., Chong, W. K., Olsen, O., Gunny, R. S., Offiah, A. C., Owens, C. M., Saunders, D. E., Scott, R. J., Jones, R., Norman, W., Addison, S., Bainbridge, A., Cady, E. B., De Vita, E., Robertson, N. J., and Taylor, A. M. (2013). Post-mortem MRI versus conventional autopsy in fetuses and children: a prospective validation study. *Lancet*, 382(9888): 223–33.

Thayyil, S., Sebire, N. J., Chitty, L. S., Wade, A., Olsen, O., Gunny, R. S., Offiah, A., Saunders, D. E., Owens, C. M., Chong, W. K., Robertson, N. J., and Taylor, A. M. (2011). Post mortem magnetic resonance imaging in the fetus, infant and child: a comparative study with conventional autopsy (MaRIAS Protocol). *BMC Pediatrics*, 11. https://doi.org/10.1186/1471-2431-11-120.

Thomas, C. (1993). De-constructing concepts of care. *Sociology*, 27(4): 649–69.

Thompson, N., and Bevan, D. (2015). Death and the workplace. *Illness, Crisis & Loss*, 23(3): 211–25.

Thompson, N., and Walsh, M. (2010). The existential basis of trauma. *Journal of Social Work Practice*, 24(4): 377–89.

Tilley, L., Walmsley, J., Earle, S., and Atkinson, D. (2012). International perspectives on the sterilization of women with intellectual disabilities. In S. Earle, C. Komaromy and L. Layne (eds), *Understanding Reproductive Loss: Perspectives on Life, Death and Fertility*. Abingdon: Routledge, 23–36.

Timmermans, S. (1998). Resuscitation technology in the emergency department: towards a dignified death. *Sociology of Health & Illness*, 20(2): 144–67.

Timmermans, S. (2006). *Postmortem: How Medical Examiners Explain Suspicious Deaths*. Chicago: University of Chicago Press.

Timmermans, S., and Berg, M. (2003). The practice of medical technology. *Sociology of Health and Illness*, 25: 97–114.

Toerien, M., Reuber, M., Shaw, R., and Duncan, R. (2018). Generating the perception of choice: the remarkable malleability of option-listing. *Sociology of Health and Illness*, 40(7): 1250–67.

Tomlinson, P. S., Peden-McAlpine, C., and Sherman, S. (2012). A family systems nursing intervention model for paediatric health crisis. *Journal of Advanced Nursing*, 68: 705–14.

Towers, L. (2019). *Experiences of Sibling Bereavement Over the Life Course.* PhD thesis, University of Sheffield. https://etheses.whiterose.ac.uk/26802/ (accessed January 2022).

Turco, C. J., and Zuckerman, E. W. (2017). Verstehen for sociology: comment on Watts. *American Journal of Sociology*, 122(4): 1272–91.

Turkle, S. (2011). Introduction: the things that matter. In S. Turkle (ed.), *Evocative Objects: Things We Think With.* Cambridge, MA: MIT Press, 3–10.

Turley, D., and O'Donohoe, S. (2012). The sadness of lives and the comfort of things: goods as evocative objects in bereavement. *Journal of Marketing Management*, 28(11–12): 1331–53.

Turner, J. H. (2009). The sociology of emotions: basic theoretical arguments. *Emotion Review*, 1(4): 340–54.

Twigg, J. (1999). The spatial ordering of care: public and private in bathing support at home. *Sociology of Health & Illness*, 21: 381–400. https://doi.org/10.1111/1467-9566.00163.

Twigg, J. (2000). Carework as a form of bodywork. *Ageing and Society*, 20(4): 389–411.

Twigg, J. (2004). The body, gender, and age: feminist insights in social gerontology. *Journal of Aging Studies*, 18(1): 59–73.

Twigg, J., Wolkowitz, C., Cohen, R. L., and Nettleton, S. (2011). Conceptualising body work in health and social care. *Sociology of Health & Illness*, 33(2): 171–88.

Ungerson, C. (ed.) (1990). *Gender and Caring: Work and Welfare in Britain and Scandinavia.* Hemel Hempstead: Harvester Wheatsheaf.

Üstündağ-Budak, A. M., Larkin, M., Harris, G., and Blissett, J. (2015). Mothers' accounts of their stillbirth experiences and of their subsequent relationships with their living infant: an interpretative phenomenological analysis. *BMC Pregnancy and Childbirth*, 15: 263.

Valentine, C. (2007). Methodological reflections: attending and tending to the role of the researcher in the construction of bereavement narratives. *Qualitative Social Work*, 6(2): 159–76.

Valentine, C. (2008). *Bereavement Narratives: Continuing Bonds in the Twenty-first Century.* Abingdon: Routledge.

Van den Tweel, J. G., and Taylor, C. R. (2013). The rise and fall of the autopsy. *Virchows Archive: European Journal of Pathology*, 462: 371–80.

Van Gennep, A. (1960 [1909]). *The Rites of Passage*. Chicago: University of Chicago Press.

Van Keer, R. L., Deschepper, R., Francke, A. L., Huyghens, L., and Bilsen, J. (2015). Conflicts between healthcare professionals and families of a multi-ethnic patient population during critical care: an ethnographic study. *Critical Care*, 19: 441. https://doi.org/10.1186/s13054-015-1158-4.

Vannini, P., Waskul, D., and Gottschalk, S. (2012). *The Senses in Self, Society, and Culture: A Sociology of the Senses*. Abingdon: Routledge.

Visser, R. (2017). 'Doing death': reflecting on the researcher's subjectivity and emotions. *Death Studies*, 41(1): 6–13.

Waerness, K. (1987). On the rationality of caring. In A. S. Sassoon (ed.), *Women and the State*. London: Hutchinson, 207–34.

Walford, G. (2009). The practice of writing ethnographic fieldnotes. *Ethnography and Education*, 4(2): 117–30.

Walter, T. (1996). A new model of grief: bereavement and biography. *Mortality*, 1(19): 7–25.

Watts, G. (2010). Imaging the dead. *BMJ* 341: c6600.

Way, J., Back, A. L., and Curtis, J. R. (2002). Withdrawing life support and resolution of conflict with families. *BMJ*, 325(7376): 1342–5.

Weaver-Hightower, M. B. (2012). Waltzing Matilda: an autoethnography of a father's stillbirth. *Journal of Contemporary Ethnography*, 41(4): 462–91.

Weber, M. (1968). *Economy and Society: An Outline of Interpretive Sociology*. New York: Bedminster Press.

Whitby, E. (2009). Minimally invasive autopsy. *Lancet*, 374(9688): 432–3.

Whitby, E., Paley, M. N. K. and Griffiths, P. D. (2006). Post-mortem foetal MRI: what do we learn from it? *European Journal of Radiology*, 57(2): 250–5.

Whitby, E., and Wright, P. (2015). Non-central nervous system fetal magnetic resonance imaging. *Seminars in Fetal Neonatal Medicine*, 20(3): 130–7.

WHO (World Health Organization) (2006). *Neonatal and Perinatal Mortality: Country, Regional and Global Estimates*. Geneva: World Health Organization.

Wilkinson, I. (2004). The problem of 'social suffering': the challenge to social science. *Health Sociology Review*, 13(2): 113–21.

Wilkinson, I. (2005). *Suffering: A Sociological Introduction*. Cambridge: Polity.

Wood, L. A. (2016). Con-forming bodies: the interplay of machines and bodies and the implications of agency in medical imaging. *Sociology of Health and Illness*, 38: 768–81.

Woodthorpe, K. (2010). Private grief in public spaces: interpreting memorialisation in the contemporary cemetery. In J. Hockey, C. Komaromy and K. Woodthorpe (eds), *The Matter of Death: Space, Place and Materiality.* Basingstoke: Palgrave Macmillan, 117–32.

Woodthorpe, K. (2012). Baby gardens: a privilege or predicament? In S. Earle, C. Komaromy and L. Layne (eds), *Understanding Reproductive Loss: Perspectives on Life, Death and Fertility.* Abingdon: Routledge, 143–54.

Woodthorpe, K., and Komaromy, C. (2013). A missing link? The role of mortuary staff in hospital-based bereavement care services. *Bereavement Care*, 32(3): 124–30.

Wouters, C. (1989). The sociology of emotions and flight attendants: Hochschild's managed heart. *Theory, Culture and Society*, 6(1): 95–123.

Wright Mills, C. (2000 [1959]). *The Sociological Imagination.* Oxford: Oxford University Press.

Zaider, T. I., Banerjee, S. C., Manna, R., Coyle, N., Pehrson, C., Hammonds, S., Krueger, C. A., and Bylund, C. L. (2016). Responding to challenging interactions with families: a training module for inpatient oncology nurses. *Families, Systems & Health: The Journal of Collaborative Family Healthcare*, 34(3), 204–12. https://doi.org/10.1037/fsh0000159.

Zechmeister, I. (2001). Foetal images: the power of visual technology in antenatal care and the implications for women's reproductive freedom. *Health Care Analysis*, 9(4): 387–400.

Index

EU authorised representative for GPSR:
Easy Access System Europe, Mustamäe tee 50,
10621 Tallinn, Estonia
gpsr.requests@easproject.com

www.ingramcontent.com/pod-product-compliance
Lightning Source LLC
Chambersburg PA
CBHW052001270326
41929CB00015B/2741